Sellers, Charles
Andrew Jackson

ANDREW JACKSON

Also by Charles Sellers

James K. Polk, Jacksonian, 1795–1843

James K. Polk, Continentalist, 1843–1846

The Southerner as American (editor and co-author)

Andrew Jackson
A PROFILE

EDITED BY

CHARLES SELLERS

AMERICAN PROFILES

General Editor: Aïda DiPace Donald

HILL AND WANG : NEW YORK

Contents

Introduction

The Age of Jackson seems curiously inaccessible to us. It is at once too familiar and too exotic. An earnestly ambitious Amos Kendall and a meanly avaricious Colonel Beriah Sellers are as readily recognizable as our grandfathers and the used-car dealer across town. But the pioneering heroics of a Davy Crockett or the homeric military style of an Andrew Jackson are so remote from our experience that they elude our imaginative grasp. How can we understand a generation that combines the commonplaceness of Warren Harding with the historical distance of John Winthrop?

It is especially difficult for us to understand why Jackson's contemporaries invested such emotion in the political battles that raged around his person and policies. We readily see more distant historical figures—the framers and opponents of the Constitution, for example, or Jefferson's Republicans and Hamilton's Federalists—as protagonists in debates that still matter to us. But as Arthur M. Schlesinger, Jr., learned from the critical reception of his *The Age of Jackson,* we have more difficulty seeing this kind of contemporary relevance in the battles between Jackson's Democrats and their Whig opponents.

In the generations immediately succeeding Jackson, his own historical reputation was shaped in terms of the continuing vitality of the most conspicuous Jacksonian issue. During the last half of the nineteenth century patrician critics damned the Tennessee General for the strident political egalitarianism that had enabled demagogues, bosses, and spoilsmen to drive gentlemen from public life. When the voice of the people was finally sanctified by the academic elites during the Progressive era, Jackson was elevated to the conventional patriotic pantheon alongside Franklin, Washington, Jefferson, and Lincoln.

Today the Jacksonian democratic dogma commands such universal lip service that we can only wonder why the Jacksonians got so exercised over it, or how they managed to rest so comfortably in their assumption that it applied to white men only. We perceive, too, that something else was bothering them, but we are hard put to explain what it was that could have caused Jackson to be as passionately idolized or hated in his time as Franklin Roosevelt has been more recently.

Our difficulties in relating to the Jacksonians may grow out of peculiar demands that we Americans make on our past. English historians, for example, occasionally express bemusement at our American tendency to interpret every aspect of our past in the categories of the present, to consider our entire historical experience as a unilinear development along essentially unchanging lines, and to make all our historical figures protagonists in trends or conflicts that have unvaryingly structured our historical experience from Jamestown to the present. Englishmen, by contrast, seem to manage a fondly proprietary interest in both Charles I and the regicides, neither taking sides between them nor lapsing into an antiquarianism that sees no vital relation of past to present.

Doubtless our rather different attitude toward the American historical experience is justified in part by its comparative brevity and homogeneity. Certainly Americans have been preoccupied through much of their history with the developing institutions and styles of a formally democratic polity. Certainly this aspect of the Jacksonian past continued to be vitally "present" for many succeeding Americans into the early twentieth century.

But even in America parts of the past eventually become really "past" and no longer vitally "present." The central preoccupations of some generations eventually cease to be absorbing or even readily intelligible to subsequent generations. Perhaps Andrew Jackson, who lived in his own day on the celebrated moving frontier of the westering pioneer, lives for us on a more elusive moving historiographical frontier, the frontier between the past that is still "present" and the past that has become for us really "past."

As the pace of change accelerates in the present, this historiographical frontier advances ever more rapidly across more and more of our past. As more and more of our history becomes really "past," our relation to it is being profoundly altered. If our past is to be usable, we increasingly see, we must first strive to comprehend it in its own terms. Before we can ask what is relevant for us in the experience of our forebears, we must first seek to determine what was most important for them in that experience.

With the publication of Arthur M. Schlesinger, Jr.'s *The Age of Jackson* in 1945, Jackson and his age became a major focus for this largely unconscious reorientation toward our American past. The selection from Schlesinger and many of the other writings reprinted in the present volume reflect this reorientation. The three writings earlier than Schlesinger's, those by John Spencer Bassett, Thomas Perkins Abernethy, and Richard R. Stenberg, represent the last gasps of historical partisanship over the merits of democracy and the democratic politician.

John Spencer Bassett's discussion of Jackson's personal characteristics was published in 1911 as part of a distinguished two-volume biography. A leader of the first generation of professionally trained academic historians, Bassett echoed Frederick Jackson Turner's apotheosis of American democracy and saw Jackson as one of its most heroic protagonists. This ideological affinity helped him to make Jackson a believable human being, while Bassett's thoroughness and honesty enabled him to see Jackson's shortcomings as well as his strengths. Bassett's biography remains the most satisfyingly balanced of the extended treatments of Old Hickory.

Thomas Perkins Abernethy, writing in 1927, represents the other side of the protracted historical argument over democracy. Abernethy has devoted most of a fruitful scholarly career to an extended critique of Turner's proposition that the frontier bred democracy. His books and articles array a mass of evidence indicating that the southwestern frontier was dominated by a group of land-speculating nabobs, among them Andrew Jackson. Portraying

the pre-Presidential Jackson in Tennessee as a demagogic opportunist, he calls into question the whole pro-democratic tradition in
American historiography.

Jackson's most inveterate scholarly foe has been Richard R.
Stenberg. Stenberg never published the "extensive critique of Jackson's career and character" that he intended to call *The Insidious
Andrew Jackson*. But he did publish between 1932 and 1939 a
series of carefully researched though frequently tendentious articles on the more dubious episodes in Jackson's long career. The
article reprinted here is one of the more convincing of these and
indicates the difficulty of making simple judgments about Jackson's complex character.

By the time Abernethy and Stenberg wrote, however, the historical argument over democracy had worn so threadbare that
interest in the Jacksonian era was waning among scholars and the
public alike. It was this waning interest that Arthur M. Schlesinger,
Jr., so brilliantly revived by making the Jacksonians once again so
vividly present, this time in new terms, as to focus attention
sharply on our whole presentist orientation toward our past.

Writing amid the dying embers of the political passion that
burned around Franklin Roosevelt's New Deal, Schlesinger found
the meaning of the Jacksonians not in their democracy but in what
they tried to do with their democracy. With a greater explicitness
than any previous historian, he affirmed the essential unity and
unfailing presentness of the American historical experience. "The
tradition of Jefferson and Jackson," he wrote, ". . . was bound to
endure in America as long as liberal capitalist society endured." It
was bound to endure because "the struggle among competing
groups for the control of the state" was inevitable and desirable in
such a society. "The business community has been ordinarily the
most powerful of these groups," Schesinger argued, "and liberalism in America has been ordinarily the movement on the part of
the other sections of society to restrain the power of the business
community." Jackson—like Jefferson before him, and as the
reader readily perceives, like Roosevelt after him—led a great
coalition of "the other sections of society to restrain the power of
the business community."

What made *The Age of Jackson* so arresting was not just

Schlesinger's point of view but the depth of his research and the felicity and intellectual sophistication with which he argued his interpretation. No other scholar since Bassett had worked so carefully through the relevant sources, and the sources themselves revealed some aspects of the Jacksonian past that had been forgotten in the long preoccupation with the merits of democracy. Most importantly, he discovered the deep opposition of Jackson and many of his followers not just to the National Bank but to all banks, and the growing importance of the hard-money doctrine as Jacksonian policy unfolded.

No piece of American historical writing has provoked a more decided critical reaction. In a notable review Bray Hammond criticized Schlesinger's partisanship for the Jacksonians in their destruction of a great and valuable financial institution, the Second Bank of the United States. This scholarly official of the Federal Reserve System was especially impressed with the central banking functions that Bank president Nicholas Biddle had been exercising so precociously and beneficially. But Hammond's critique, as he elaborated it in subsequent articles and in his book *Banks and Politics in America* (1957), went far beyond partisanship for Biddle against Jackson. In place of Schlesinger's conflict between the business community and other sections of society, he proposed an alternative interpretation of the Bank war as a conflict between two sections of the business community. Jackson, he granted, may have sincerely though ignorantly held the quaint hard-money views he professed, but he was actually used by men having opposite ends in view. Hammond argued that the real Jacksonian impulse was furnished by a host of aggressive new entrepreneurs spawned by the intoxicating growth of the American economy. Centering their get-rich-quick ambitions on credit from the state banks, especially in New York, these entrepreneurial Democrats sought to destroy the curbs imposed on credit expansion by the National Bank, representing long-established and conservative businessmen.

Hammond's interpretation of the Bank war was simultaneously being elaborated into a more general interpretation of much of American history by Professor Richard Hofstadter. In an essay on Jackson published the year after Schlesinger's book, Hofstadter argued that the central reality of the period was the spread of entrepreneurial ambition through all ranks of society. In Hofstadter's view, Jackson himself was an authentic representative of this impulse of entrepreneurial democracy, and the movement he led was "a phase in the expansion of liberated capitalism."

In some respects Hammond and Hofstadter seem to be proposing merely another presentist interpretation, identifying a central tendency in the American historical experience about which they have value preferences in the present. Instead of seeing American history as revolving around an inexorable advance of political democracy, or a persisting struggle against the power of the business community, they may be read as positing a continuing impulse of entrepreneurial democracy having consequences they care about in their own world. Indeed, their interpretations echo something of the old patrician disdain for democracy, except that the democracy is now more economic than political. Hammond makes no secret of his distaste for the entrepreneurial Jacksonians whom he portrays so unflatteringly, and both authors draw heavily on Abernethy's view of Jackson.

Yet the predominant mood of their writings is detached and ironic rather than partisan. Confessing his aesthetic preference for the hard-money dogma, Hammond nevertheless pronounces it anachronistic, and destructively so, given the economic and social realities of the nineteenth-century United States. Though Hofstadter's rhetoric betrays no sense of identification with the "host of 'rural capitalists and village entrepreneurs' " he describes, he can nevertheless speak respectfully of their "fight against economic privilege" and their belief "in expanding opportunity through equal rights."

That these two writers represent a new stance toward the American past is most evident when Hofstadter addresses himself most explicitly to Schlesinger's interpretation. Acknowledging that "the Jacksonian movement and the New Deal were both struggles of large sections of the community against a business elite and its allies," he nevertheless sees this resemblance as superficial. It is superficial because the New Deal operated on the premise that "economic opportunities were disappearing" while the Jacksonian movement "grew out of expanding opportunities and a common desire to enlarge these opportunities still further." Therefore the New Deal sought to establish "governmental ascendancy over the affairs of business," while the Jacksonian movement moved in the opposite direction "to divorce government and business."

Thus, for Hofstadter and Hammond, the Jacksonian past is really past. In their view, the Jacksonian victory of entrepreneurial democracy is relevant for us, not because we face today essentially the same Jacksonian choices, but because the contrast helps us understand how different our situation is.

Yet there are some unresolved ambiguities in their accounts. Where did the hard-money idea come from, why did it win such a following, and how did it interact with the opposed entrepreneurial idea? These questions are brought to a focus in the related question of the personal role of Jackson. Was the indomitable Old Hickory a hard-money ideologue, as Hammond thinks, but at the same time a tool or a fool in the hands of meaner men whose purposes were antithetical to his? Or was he, as Hofstadter implies, caught indecisively or opportunistically between the hard-money and the entrepreneurial impulses?

My doubts on these points were first raised by my investigations of the area that Abernethy had studied. I found in Tennessee in the 1820's, as reported in the two articles that are combined in this volume, ample evidence of the entrepreneurial mood. But I found also, quite as strong or stronger, a hard-money mood that reacted not just against the National Bank but against banks in general and the entrepreneurial mood that they had come to represent. Furthermore, and contrary to Abernethy, I found Jackson articulating during these pre-Presidential years both the hard-money mood and the political stance that Schlesinger attributes to him after he occupied the White House.

These findings suggested that both Old Hickory and the hard-money mood played a more positive role in the Jacksonian years than Hammond and Hofstadter had perceived. Perhaps a lingering presentism had caused them to exaggerate the strength of an entrepreneurial mood that still echoes in our present experience, at the expense of a hard-money mood so anachronistic that we can hardly imagine it. While they had penetrated far enough beyond presentism to identify an important and previously neglected aspect of the Jacksonian past, perhaps they had not yet penetrated Jacksonian reality wholly in its own terms.

Meanwhile two other historians, George Dangerfield and Robert

V. Remini, were writing about Jackson in terms derived directly form the sources and revealing no presentist bias. Dangerfield's English origin doubtless contributed to the detachment with which he discussed Jackson's role against the diplomatic and political backdrop of *The Era of Good Feelings*. Included here is his thorough and dispassionate analysis of Jackson's shocking invasion of Spanish Florida. Remini, while at work on a massive biography of Martin Van Buren, has found time for three short books in which Jackson is a central figure. The selection included here from his study of the election of 1828 portrays Jackson as playing a central and forceful role rather than yielding to manipulation by his advisers.

But it was left for a student of Professor Hofstadter's, employing an unusual historiographical technique, to break most completely out of the presentist framework. Professor Marvin Meyers' starting point was the insufficiency of previous interpretations to account for the emotions invested in the Jacksonian political battles. In the article on "The Jacksonian Persuasion" reprinted here, which Meyers later expanded into an absorbing book of the same title, he examined the political rhetoric that issued from Jackson and his more articulate supporters. Through careful content analysis he sought to identify "the half-formulated moral perspective involving an emotional commitment," "the persuasion," to which the electorate so fervently responded. What he found was "no vision of a fresh creation at the Western edge of civilization, certainly no dream of enterprise unbound," but instead an appeal to rescue and restore the moral values of an Old Republican way of life. Jacksonian rhetoric denounced the "Monster Bank," Meyers argues, primarily because it was corrupting the morals of a simple agrarian society in which men enjoyed the modest fruits of their useful labors rather than pursuing sudden riches through exploiting their neighbors. Hard money—gold and silver coin—thus took on for Jackson and his public a profound moral significance, representing palpable value based on honest labor as opposed to the exploitative and unstable meretriciousness of bank paper.

Meyers' problem was to reconcile this surprising finding with the entrepreneurial mood that Hofstadter and Hammond had found so prominent in Jacksonian America. At one point he describes Jackson's Whig opponents as straightforward champions of enterprise. But he is less clear about Jackson's Democratic supporters, partly because he refers to "the Jacksonians" without indicating whether he means Jackson's political partisans or Jackson's generation as a whole. These Jacksonians he sees as ambivalent, as "venturous conservatives" caught uncomfortably between their entrepreneurial appetites and their Old Republican morality. Meyers even suggests that they brought off one of history's most brilliant feats of moral legerdemain—satisfying their Old Republican consciences by destroying the National Bank, while by the same act they were loosing the reins on state bank credit and entrepreneurial ambition. "With one courageous amputation," he writes, "society could save its character—and safely seek the goods it hungered for."

Meyers' approach was brilliantly successful in delineating the attitudes—entrepreneurial, hard-money, and ambivalent—that were central to the experience of the Jacksonian generation. But his speculations about how these attitudes were distributed among Whigs and Democrats must be checked against the positions that various groups took in the long and complicated debates over banking policy in Washington and the states. As I read the research that has been done in this area, some of it still unpublished, Jackson's party was much less ambivalent than Meyers supposes.

Jackson himself seems to me to have been primarily responsible for pressing the Bank war on the country. As the issues sharpened, he increasingly bent the Democratic politicians to the hard-money stance that he uncompromisingly articulated and to which the electorate increasingly responded. To be sure, during the initial phase of the struggle, when the primary target was the National Bank, Jackson drew support from the element of entrepreneurial democracy. But this element proved to be a distinct minority of the Democrats when Jackson's opposition to state-bank as well as national-bank paper became apparent. Joined with a united Whig opposition, this small minority of entrepreneurial Democrats provided just enough votes to defeat again and again the serious efforts of the main body of the party to implement a hard-money policy.

The ambivalence described by Meyers helps to explain this out-

come, but this ambivalence became most pronounced in the later
stages of the struggle. While thoroughgoing hard-money policies
were repeatedly defeated, the struggle did produce enough reform
to eliminate the worst excesses of unrestrained banking, and meanwhile the continued spectacular expansion of the economy was
making enterprise seductive to more and more people. In all these
ways the Jacksonian hard-money impulse was vitiated, until by the
1840's most of the country was willing to accept a policy of
moderately controlled credit and business expansion through regu-
lated state banking. The American people had finally made their
psychological and moral adjustment to the new world of democratic enterprise.

If this was the central experience of the Jacksonians, they have
moved across the historiographical boundary into the real past.
But this Jacksonian past takes on a new kind of relevance. It can
help us understand the moral and psychological strains that are
created when economic change alters the life styles and moral
perspective of a people. If we understand how such strains accompanied the advent of an era of democratic enterprise and competitive striving, we who live at the end of that era may better
understand and deal with the comparable strains we experience as
we enter an era as yet only dimly glimpsed.

This view of the Jacksonian past gives an added significance to
the personal role of Old Hickory. With a self-trust and political
courage that no other President has matched, he singlehandedly
brought his generation's anxieties to a tangible focus in the symbolic drama of the Bank war. Finding a particular solution to the
monetary problem was less important for Jackson's contemporaries than legitimizing their egalitarian impulses and accommodat-
ing their agrarian morality to the unprecedented entrepreneurial
opportunities that were opening up. Jackson's leadership, particularly through its moral and psychological symbolism, eased the
painful transition to an age of egalitarian enterprise.

Only in this light can we understand Jackson's enormous impact
on the imagination of his generation. John William Ward has given
us some measure of this impact in the selections from his *Andrew
Jackson, Symbol for an Age* with which this volume concludes.
Using Meyers' technique of extracting the value content from the

rhetoric of the age, he examines what people said about Jackson instead of what people responded to in Jackson's rhetoric. Jackson's contemporaries not only embraced the "persuasion" he offered them, but they also perceived and fashioned him in a way that made his figure the carrier of their deepest and most general values. "The age was not his," Ward concludes. "He was the age's."

Thus the Jacksonian past gives us some notion of the symbolic possibilities of democratic leadership in a time of transition and strain like our own. But the emergence of such leadership may depend on historical accident. The "military-industrial complex" —merely the most portentous aspect of our increasingly complex and decreasingly responsive bureaucracies of business, labor, and government—seems a sufficiently eligible "Monster" to focus our discontents. But is there among the Richard Nixons and Hubert Humphreys a Jackson who can bring our anxieties and tensions to bear on our Monster, and thus lead us toward resolving them?

Andrew Jackson, 1767–1845

Andrew Jackson was born March 13, 1767, in the Waxhaws settlement on the northern boundary of interior South Carolina. During the Revolution the adolescent Jackson suffered indignities from invading British soldiers and was orphaned as an indirect result of the war. After the war he read law with an attorney in Salisbury, North Carolina, and in 1788 rode west to begin practicing at Nashville in the pioneer area that soon became Tennessee. Three years after his arrival he married the divorced Mrs. Rachel Donelson Robards. The childless couple enjoyed an especially close relationship until Mrs. Jackson's death in 1828.

Young Jackson quickly won the confidence of Tennessee's leading magnates. He was elected in 1796 to the national House of Representatives, then served as a Senator by appointment in the session of 1797–1798, and for six years thereafter sat on the state supreme court. Meanwhile he was pursuing wealth through land speculation and mercantile ventures, developing a plantation called the Hermitage near Nashville, and rising to a Major Generalship in the Tennessee militia.

The War of 1812 brought Jackson his opportunity for a brilliant military career. In a devastating campaign against the Creeks he permanently broke the power of the Southwestern Indians. Commissioned a Major General in the regular Army, he seized Spanish Pensacola without authorization and then moved on to New Orleans to defeat an invading British army in the most spectacular American victory of the war.

Three years after peace returned, General Jackson was ordered to pacify the marauding Indians along the Florida boundary. Again without authorization he invaded Spanish territory, hanged two British citizens, and occupied the provincial capital. This diplomatically indefensible venture probably hastened Spain's cession of Florida to the United States in 1821, and Jackson served briefly as the American territorial Governor.

In the Presidential election of 1824 the Hero of New Orleans astonished the politicians by receiving the largest popular and electoral vote in a field of four. But no candidate had a majority, and the House of Representatives decided for the runner-up, John Quincy Adams. Jackson became the rallying point for all the anti-Adams forces and defeated Adams in the Presidential election of 1828.

President Jackson began his administration by removing political opponents from the federal offices to make way for his friends. His veto of the Maysville Road bill in 1830 checked the movement for a federally developed transportation system.

The most exciting issue of Jackson's administration was raised in 1832 when the President vetoed a bill to extend the charter of the Second Bank of the United States. In the Presidential election shortly afterward he decisively defeated Henry Clay. Fearing that the Bank could still use its economic power to force through a recharter bill over his veto, Jackson sought to cripple it by transferring the large federal deposits to selected state-chartered banks. This encouraged an extravagant expansion of credit by the state banks, which Jackson sought to check in 1836 by issuing a Specie Circular requiring public lands to be paid for in gold or silver coin rather than bank notes. His enemies blamed his policies for the Panic of 1837, which broke shortly after he left office.

The other great issue of Jackson's administration was nullification. Immediately after his re-election a South Carolina convention declared the federal tariff laws unconstitutional and forbade their enforcement in the state. Jackson demonstrated his determination to enforce the laws at all costs, but at the same time advocated tariff reform. When Congress enacted the Compromise Tariff of 1833, South Carolina withdrew its declaration nullifying the tariff laws.

At the end of his second term Jackson secured the election of his handpicked successor, Martin Van Buren. In retirement at the Hermitage the former President became the most influential proponent of the annexation of Texas. In the spring of 1845 he had the satisfaction of seeing annexation accomplished and his protégé James K. Polk inaugurated as President. His death came several months later, on June 8.

ANDREW JACKSON

✪

The General

The most interesting feature in the military career of Andrew
Jackson was its brevity; the next most interesting feature was the
indomitable spirit of Andrew Jackson. Good fortune would appear
to have been the third: The rest were insignificant. Brevity, intensity, good fortune—what more was needed to fix the General
securely in the American firmament? The meteor and its fiery track
stayed in mid-heaven; the rocket burst into a fountain of stars, but
never faded or fell. In 1818, when one spoke of the Military Hero,
one did not mean General Jacob Brown or General Winfield Scott
or, still less, General William Henry Harrison: Andrew Jackson
was the man. He stood poised in the imagination of his country-
men above the mud rampart of the Rodrigues Canal, a position
from which no amount of honest alarm or ingenious calumny
could ever dislodge him. Here, in fact, on January 8, 1815, he had
presided over the defeat of the British, who were kind enough not
to attack him where he was most vulnerable but wasted their
superb valor on an impossible frontal assault. Yet would the
assault have been impossible if Jackson had not been there? His
good fortune was obvious: The Battle of New Orleans conspicuously demonstrates that mixture of courage and incapacity which
the British generals of that era reserved, to do them justice, only
for their American campaigns. No less obvious was Jackson's
fierce, intractable spirit. He seemed to hold the battle together, and

to draw the British to their doom, not by superior ability, but by sheer will. His energy was the energy of a magnet, which defies gravity.

Behind the Battle of New Orleans lay the storming of Pensacola; behind the storming of Pensacola lay the victories of Talladega, Emuckfaw, Enotachopco, and Horseshoe Bend; and sandwiched between Horseshoe Bend and Pensacola were twenty-three million acres ravished from the vanquished Creeks at the Treaty of Fort Jackson. Such were the military achievements of Andrew Jackson, and they had been crowded into the space of fourteen months.

In 1818, Andrew Jackson was, as it were, a military silhouette, an outline and nothing more. Few people outside the state of Tennessee knew the details of his civilian career—an odd jumble that only upon close inspection resolved itself into the typical progression of a frontier *arriviste*. Horse-coper, lawyer, politician, judge, enterpriser—by these rungs the General had ascended to the position of slaveholder and country gentleman. There was little to set him apart from the rest, except a passionate idiosyncrasy, a conviction that he was always right, which, enforced by an imaginative temperament and a fierce will, transformed him into the most generous of friends and the most remorseless of enemies. His marriage to Rachel Donelson (one can say it without risk of sentimentality) is one of the great love stories in American history. His feelings toward his enemies, in speech or writing or action, commonly expressed themselves in terms of caning, slitting throats, or shooting. He was all tenderness on the one hand, and all savagery on the other; and the events of his daily life, subjected to the impulsive tribunal of his singular conscience, from which there was no appeal, might as easily call forth the one as the other. At the root of his social being lay the simple ethic he had once expounded for the instruction of a refractory Spanish official: "An eye for an Eye, Toothe for Toothe, and Scalp for Scalp."[1] It was the dominant motif of a long and great career.

Feral in his enmities, conservative in his politics, absorbed in the

1. Jackson to Don Matteo Gonzalez y Manrique, August 24, 1814, J. S. Bassett, ed., *The Correspondence of Andrew Jackson* (Washington, 1926–1933), II, 29.

pursuit of wealth,[2] Andrew Jackson might have crouched forever among the lights and shadows of Middle Tennessee, perfectly camouflaged against the aim of history. But Andrew Jackson had military ambitions; he would rather be a Major General of militia than anything else; and it was as a Major General of militia, more responsive to the imperialism than to the democracy of the frontier, that he was caught up in the whirl of high events and placed at last upon the mud rampart of the Rodrigues Canal. By then he was already transformed into a Major General in the regular Army, and thereafter he was a national figure. The figure was enigmatic: no one could say which path, politically, the General would take, or if he would take any. Only in these days may one assert that he was not an opportunist, willing to head any cause that would sweep him into power. He was shrewd and calculating, as his environment required him to be; one could not otherwise survive on the frontier, or just behind it. But he was essentially an imaginative man, slow to make up his mind on great issues, and responding at length to the depth of his feelings and not to the dictates of his reason. As a rational man, he was a temperate conservative; as a feeling man, he was an intemperate rebel. The imperatives of debtor democracy, grand and confusing as they were, were bound to carry more appeal to such a man than the cold enticements of industrialists, investors, and manipulators of credit. But all that was in the future. In 1818, General Jackson was a rare metal, not indeed free of some natural alloy, waiting for the nineteenth century to stamp upon it an enduring image.

I

That the Virginia Dynasty should have given Jackson the opportunity to increase his military reputation was a little ironical: it was not too fond of military heroes. In 1815, nonetheless, when Jackson rode to Washington, Thomas Jefferson came down from his inventive mountain to meet him on the way; and at the capital he carried all before him.[3] He had now begun to resemble the

2. Marquis James, *Andrew Jackson: The Border Captain* (Indianapolis, 1933), p. 94.
3. James Parton, *Life of Andrew Jackson,* 3 vols. (New York, 1859–1860), II, 333–336.

Jackson of history. The long, narrow face, lined with pain and passion, the small blue eyes, the surmounting brush of stiff gray hair; the high bony nose, firm chin, and generous mouth; the emaciated body: this was the apparition which startled and delighted Washington. The General's fine manners, when he chose to use them, were decidedly prepossessing. He used them to good effect; President Madison and his Cabinet were all impressed; and with Secretary Monroe his discussions verged upon the confidential.[4] When Monroe became President, however, the relationship thus established was seriously threatened. In an agitated correspondence with the Assistant Secretary of War, the President, and Mr. Secretary Calhoun, General Jackson insisted that he was the sole channel through which the commands of the War Department might be transmitted to his subordinates in the Southern Division.[5] The difficulty was eventually smoothed out; but the commander-in-chief must have realized, if he did not know it before, that whatever the military virtues of the Southern Major General may have been, a nice respect for authority was not among them.

Was it wise to entrust to such a man the conduct of a campaign that involved the chastisement of the Seminole Indians who lived across the border in Spanish Florida? Was it wise, that is to say, if the government wished to remain upon good terms with Spain? Florida politics were rarely easy to understand; and they were never less intelligible than on December 26, 1817, when orders were sent to General Jackson requiring him to assume direction of the Seminole campaign.[6] If anything was ascertainable in the General's composition, besides his magnificent courage and his evident disregard for higher authority, it was his extreme nationalism—the nationalism of the frontier, with its ingrown hatred of Indians and Spaniards. Was it because of this nationalism, or in spite of it, that the General was sent into Florida? The mystery has never been

   4. James, pp. 275, 282, 304.
   5. *Correspondence of Andrew Jackson,* II, 273–275, 277–282, 291–292, 319, 320–321, 329–332, 343; Emory Upton, *The Military Policy of the United States* (Washington, 1917), pp. 145–147; *Niles' Weekly Register,* XIII, 342; Charles M. Wiltse, *John C. Calhoun: Nationalist, 1782–1828* (Indianapolis, 1944, pp. 150–151; James, pp. 302, 306.
   6. *American State Papers, Military Affairs,* I, 690.

cleared up. Whatever the reason, the results were spectacular: within a few weeks of assuming command on the Georgia border, the General had planted the American flag on two Spanish fortresses, and court-martialed and executed two British citizens.

II

The Seminole Indians were, as to their nucleus, the members of a tribe called the Oconee, affiliated with the Creeks, but always on the outer edge of the Creek confederacy. This tribe may have come to Florida in 1750. It was increased by runaways from the Creek nation—the word "Seminole" was applied by the Creeks to people who removed from populous districts and went to live by themselves—and after the Creek war of 1813–1814, and the invasion of sacred grounds at the Battle of Horseshoe Bend, more Creeks fled across the border and transformed themselves into Seminoles. They lived in villages of log and palmetto huts, surrounded by cleared fields of from two to twenty acres of land; and from their custom, which was distinctively Creek, of circulating red war-clubs among these villages as a preliminary to going to war, they were sometimes known as Red-Sticks.[7]

These "Seminoles" were usually at odds with the runaway slaves, who formed another group—perhaps eight hundred in all— in the northern parts of Florida. In the year 1816, most of these Negroes lived in or near a fort that overlooked the narrow, crooked Apalachicola River. The fort was a relic of British adventures in Spanish Florida during the War of 1812, and the British had left it well stocked with arms—10 or 12 pieces of cannon, 2,500 muskets, 500 carbines, 500 steel-scabbarded swords, 400 pistols, 300 quarter-casks of rifle powder, and 763 barrels of common powder.[8] It was a formidable and mischievous legacy. The Negroes who fell heirs to it considered themselves unas-

7. John R. Swanton, "Early History of the Creek Indians and their Neighbors," Bureau of American Ethnology, Bulletin 73 (Washington, 1922), pp. 398 ff; Jedediah Morse, *A Report to the Secretary of War, on Indian Affairs, Comprising a Narrative of a Tour Performed in the Summer of 1820* (New Haven, 1822), p. 311; John T. Sprague, *The Origin, Progress, and Conclusion of the Florida War* (New York, 1848), p. 19.

8. Parton, II, 399.

sailable; and, being always mindful of the inhuman circumstances that had driven them into Florida, not unnaturally behaved in a hateful way. At length they made the mistake of attacking an American convoy ascending the Apalachicola toward Fort Scott, the last outpost of the United States upon the Georgia-Florida boundary. One American sailor was captured, tarred, and burned alive; four others were shot down. On July 26, 1816, the convoy struck back. A cannonball made red-hot in the galley of one of its gunboats was fired into the fort and penetrated its larger magazine. There was a fearful explosion; a shower of blood, flesh, and debris descended upon the shallow river and the stunned Americans; and from the ruins of the fort, which had housed 344 men, women, and children, only three wretches crept out alive. They were handed over to the Seminoles for execution; and to the Seminoles, also, were given whatever weapons had been uninjured by the explosion.[9]

This somber event, which casts a shadow upon the name Apalachicola, made a deep impression upon the Seminoles. But the impression was more deep than lasting. Fortified by their new store of weapons, the Indians began to ask themselves whether they had not been cheated of certain lands across the border at the confluence of the Chattahoochee and the Flint. Early in 1817, trouble broke out between the Americans and the Seminoles of lower Georgia, trouble which, as was usually the case upon the frontier, might as easily have been attributed to one side as to the other. The frontiersman, who was adept in all the arts of savage intercourse, such as lifting scalps and cattle, probably gave as much provocation as he received, and may have given more.[10] The Seminoles observed the *lex talionis,* and, according to their reckoning in September, 1817, the Americans had slain ten warriors and owed them three: in other words, they admitted to seven murders

9. *Ibid.,* pp. 402–407.

10. General D. Mitchell, when Governor of Georgia in 1817, said that the first outrage committed after the Treaty of Fort Jackson was by white banditti—"a set of lawless and abandoned characters." Parton, II, 409. So also Mitchell to the Secretary of War, February 24, 1817—"some worthless white men who reside on the frontiers of East Florida, and who live by plunder." *American State Papers, Indian Affairs,* I, 156.

as against the Americans' ten.[11] Their bookkeeping in this respect was usually accurate. In November, Brevet Major General Edmund P. Gaines, who commanded in Georgia, dispatched a force of 250 men, under Major Twiggs, to the Seminole village of Fowltown, some fourteen miles from Fort Scott, with orders to bring back the chiefs and warriors for a conference. Major Twiggs's invitation was refused; the village was burned and two warriors and a woman were slain; and the Seminoles in reprisal ambushed an American hospital boat as it crawled up the Apalachicola, killing thirty-four ill soldiers and seven women. The commander, Lieutenant R. W. Scott, was generally believed to have been tortured to death.[12] This was on November 30. On December 16, General Gaines was authorized to cross the border if necessary and attack the Seminoles *"unless they should shelter under a Spanish post."*[13] On December 26, it was decided that General Gaines's presence was needed in Amelia Island, another fragment of the Spanish Empire, which had fallen into the hands of pirates, and offered, among other things, serious competition to the vested smuggling interests of the Atlantic Coast. On December 26, General Jackson was requested to proceed to Fort Scott and assume command, his orders being the same as those given to General Gaines.[14] He had anticipated these orders to this extent —that on January 6, 1818, before they reached him in Nashville, he had already written to the President, suggesting the advisability of a forcible seizure of Spanish East Florida. This could be done without implicating the government. "Let it be signified to me through any channel (say Mr. J. Rhea), that the possession of the Floridas would be desirable to the United States, and in sixty days it will be accomplished."[15] No one could say that the administration had not been warned.

11. Major General E. P. Gaines to Secretary of War, October 1, 1817, *ibid.,* p. 159.

12. *American State Papers, Military Affairs,* I, 687.

13. Secretary Calhoun to Gaines, December 16, 1817, *ibid.,* I, 689. The italics are inserted.

14. *Ibid.,* I, 690.

15. Jackson to Monroe, January 6, 1818, *Correspondence of Andrew Jackson,* II, 345.

III

The confusion of local interests upon those distant, those almost fabled borders is beyond the wit of man to disentangle. The great land cession wrested from the Creeks at Fort Jackson was presumably at the bottom of it all; and since one land cession commonly suggested another, General Jackson's "Rhea letter" may have been a simple application of frontier logic to nationalist premises. Then again, the slaveholders of Georgia and South Carolina saw in East Florida a mere invitation to their slaves to run away; while certain gentlemen in Tennessee had invested heavily in Florida lands. Land speculation is woven into the texture of American history. General Jackson was not himself interested in Florida real estate; his feelings were as altruistic as they could well be under the circumstances; but the speculations of his relatives and neighbors may have added some yeast to the general ferment.[16] As for the Seminoles, their belief that they had been cheated of their rights at Fort Jackson was not diminished by the promises British officers had made them before the end of the War of 1812. Indeed, a certain Colonel Nicholls, after the war was over, had actually made an offensive and defensive alliance between the Seminoles and Great Britain. This alliance was explicitly disavowed by Lords Bathurst and Castlereagh; but the Seminole prophet Francis, whom Nicholls took with him to London, was invested with the scarlet coat of a Brigadier General, presented with a ceremonial tomahawk, and received in audience by the Prince Regent, who said some very kind things and gave him a snuffbox.[17] Colonel Nicholls' parting advice to the Seminoles was hardly pacific. "I ordered them," he wrote, "to stand on the defensive, and have sent them a large supply of arms and ammunition, and told them to put to death without mercy, any one molesting them."[18] It is not to be wondered at that the prophet Francis,

16. Parton, II, 408.
17. Samuel Flagg Bemis, *John Quincy Adams and the Foundations of American Foreign Policy* (New York, 1949), p. 303; Parton, II, 307; *American State Papers, Foreign Relations,* IV, 50.
18. Nicholls to Benjamin Hawkins, May 12, 1815, *American State Papers, Foreign Relations,* IV, 34.

returning to Florida with his scarlet uniform, his tomahawk, and his snuffbox, believed that he had the backing of the British Empire in any undertaking against the Americans.

The Spanish in Florida were a handful of men too weak to govern and too proud to confess it. Their King was a brute, and his government, with the exception of the honest Pizarro and the ingenious De Garay, was a preposterous archaism. In Washington, the Spanish Minister, Don Luis de Onís y Gonzalez, was engaged in a rueful negotiation with Secretary Adams, respecting the eventual transfer of the Floridas to the United States.

IV

The Floridas, like Canada, had long provoked the appetite of American imperialists; but, unlike Canada, their position justified the appetite. People used to say that whoever possessed the Floridas held a pistol at the heart of the Republic, and the Floridas conveniently shaped themselves to this concept, East Florida representing the butt of the pistol and West Florida the barrel. James Madison had gone so far—too far, perhaps, for a President—as to encourage in 1810 the revolutionary sentiments of the inhabitants of West Florida, with the result that the United States felt obliged to occupy that province as far east as the Pearl River. This was in October, 1810.[19] In April, 1812, an act of Congress incorporated this area in the state of Louisiana; while an act of May 14, 1812, added to the Territory of Mississippi a further slice of Spanish West Florida, extending as far east as the Perdido River.[20] The pistol now had a distinctly snub-nosed look; but it was nonetheless dangerous for that. The immediate sanction for these two acts was yet another act of January 15, 1811, which empowered the President to take custody both of West and of East Florida if they

19. Proclamation of October 27, 1810, James D. Richardson, *A Compilation of Messages and Papers of the Presidents,* 10 vols. (Washington, 1907), I, 480–481.

20. *Statutes at Large of the United States,* II, 708, 734. In 1804, Congress passed two acts: one, of February 4, for laying and collecting duties in these disputed areas; the other, of March 6, erecting Louisiana into two territories, the Territory of Orleans to contain the disputed areas. *Ibid.,* II, 251, 285.

were in danger of occupation by some foreign power other than Spain, and which was based in turn upon a justly famous resolution.[21] The war passed; the danger of a British occupation of Florida vanished; the United States remained upon the east bank of the Perdido River. It was now clear that Spain would have to cede the Floridas: the question was, upon what terms would she do so? There were claims and counterclaims. The United States contended that Spain had not lived up to the terms of Pinkney's Treaty of 1795, not least in failing to control her Seminole Indians; the Spaniards complained that the United States violated neutrality by openly befriending the rebellious Spanish colonies of South America. . . .

The Spanish Minister at Washington was supposed to prevent the United States from recognizing the rebelling Spanish colonies. He was also, in a way, the guardian of those portions of the empire which—like the Floridas, Texas, and New Mexico—lay upon the southern and western borders of the Republic. A discussion involving one would involve all: the cession of one implied the cession of the rest. To postpone the inevitable by obstinacy, opaqueness, procrastination, and all the arts of sticking in the mud—this was the duty of the Spanish Minister; and there was much in the temperament and training of Don Luis de Onís which fitted him for this difficult task. . . .

The cession of the Floridas was, of course, not the only bargaining point at the disposal of Don Luis in his attempt to prevent the United States from recognizing or even befriending the Spanish revolutionaries in South America. He was also ready to discuss the boundaries of the Louisiana Purchase in their relation to the em-

---

21. The No-Transfer Resolution, which declared that the United States, "taking into view the peculiar situation of Spain and her American provinces; and considering the influence which the destiny of the territory adjoining the southern border of the United States may have upon their security, tranquillity, and commerce . . . cannot without serious inquietude see any part of the said territory pass into the hands of any foreign power." *Annals of Congress,* 2nd Congress, 3rd Session, pp. 374–376. The resolution declared that any occupation of territory should be temporary. And President Madison's Proclamation of October 27, 1810, while it asserted that West Florida as far as the Perdido was part of the Louisiana Purchase, also said that the occupation of West Florida would not cease "to be a subject of fair and friendly negotiation and adjustment."

pire of Spain. As regards the southwestern aspect of this immense and vital problem, he derived his knowledge from a manuscript prepared by two priests—the learned Father Melchior de Talamantes, whose labors had been unfortunately cut short by his arrest for complicity in a revolutionary plot, and the even more learned Father José Antonio Pichardo. It was called *A Treatise on the Limits of Louisiana and Texas,* and it had attained a peculiar sanctity in the eyes of Don Luis and his superiors because it was perhaps a million words in length.[22] It must be evident that only a new and forthright energy—General Jackson's perhaps?—could relieve the Spanish mind of this formidable weight of literature.

Don Luis de Onís began his conversations with Secretary of State James Monroe by asserting that the Louisiana Purchase was, in effect, a gigantic fraud. His government would cede the Floridas, he said, if the Americans would agree to accept the Mississippi River as their western boundary. When John Quincy Adams took up the negotiation in December, 1817, Onís was prepared to modify this fantastic proposition, but only to the extent of admitting that a line drawn between the Mermentau and Calcasieu rivers, in the very midst of the state of Louisiana, might be considered the southwesternmost limit of the United States. Mr. Adams, like Mr. Monroe before him, offered the Colorado River of Texas as a possible boundary in the southwest.[23] . . . When General Jackson burst into Florida, the positions of Mr. Adams and Don Luis had not changed. Mr. Adams still stood upon the Colorado River of Texas; Don Luis was firmly planted between the rivers Mermentau and Calcasieu. Between them lay half the state of Louisiana and half the province of Texas. Their movements in either direction, it seemed, were becoming more and more dependent upon those of General Jackson.

V

Eleven days after he had received his orders from Washington, General Jackson set out for Fort Scott with an advance guard of

22. The University of Texas published this treatise in four volumes between the years 1931 and 1947. The editor and translator is Charles W. Hackett.

23. *American State Papers, Foreign Relations,* IV, 450 ff.

two mounted companies. In the absence of the Governor of Tennessee, he had upon his own responsibility ordered the Tennessee mounted volunteers (two regiments of mounted gunmen, or about one thousand men in all) to meet at Fayetteville on or before the first of February.[24] The population of Nashville turned out to cheer as Old Hickory, at the head of his advance guard, rode out into the future.[25]

On February 14, when he met General Gaines, he discovered that the commissariat, as was commonly the case in remote campaigns, had broken down. General Gaines, by the unusual exertions of his own quartermaster, had kept his troops from starving; but on February 19, the two Generals learned that the officer in charge of Fort Scott proposed to abandon that important stronghold if food did not reach him. General Gaines, with twelve men, disappeared down the swollen Flint in a small boat, hoping to arrive at Fort Scott in time to prevent this movement.[26] General Jackson, with his mounted troops, Gaines's nine hundred Georgia volunteers, and a body of Indians, moved on to Fort Early, where he found himself on February 26 without a barrel of flour or a bushel of corn. But he had "pork on foot," and he proposed to continue his march toward Fort Scott. He reached the fort on March 9, with starvation at his heels and ahead of him a dismal prospect of swollen rivers and swampy grounds.[27] He was now in command of two thousand hungry men.[28] And so the campaign began.

The General did not hesitate on the border, but hurried across toward the ruins of the Negro fort on the Apalachicola, which he rebuilt and renamed Fort Gadsden. For nine days he lingered in this ominous spot, waiting for supplies. The remainder of his Tennessee volunteers were still in Georgia, held back by rumors of starvation further ahead. The pangs of his troops were slightly assuaged by a single shipment of flour up the Apalachicola. Gen-

24. Jackson to Calhoun, January 20, 1818, *American State Papers, Military Affairs,* I, 696.
25. Parton, II, 441.
26. Jackson to Calhoun, February 26, 1818, *American State Papers, Military Affairs,* I, 698.
27. *Ibid.*
28. Parton, II, 443.

eral Gaines, who had vanished from sight during the previous
month, reappeared on March 24 dressed only in a pair of panta-
loons: his boat had capsized, he had lost all his baggage and three
of his men, and he had been wandering half-naked in the woods
for four and a half days. Washington was as distant as if it had
been upon another planet. Half-starved in this wet wilderness, in
this imperial solitude, the General was preoccupied with visions of
the Spanish garrison of St. Marks.

"The Spanish Government," he wrote, "is bound by treaty to keep the
Indians at peace with us. They have acknowledged their incompetency
to do this, and are consequently bound, by the laws of nations, to
yield us the facilities to reduce them. Under this consideration, should
I be able, I shall take possession of the garrison as a depot for my
supplies, should it be found in the hands of the Spaniards, they having
supplied the Indians; but if in the hands of the Indians, I will possess
it, for the benefit of the United States, as a necessary position for me
to hold, to give peace and security to this frontier."[29]

With these words, the campaign began to lose its character of an
Indian war, and to merge into an intrigue to seize the Floridas—an
extension of that Jeffersonian-Madisonian intrigue which had so
perturbed the conscience of Mr. Gallatin at Ghent.

The arrival of Captain McKeever on the evening of the 25th,
with provisions and gunboats, assured the General of support on
his right flank as he advanced toward St. Marks.[30] He was now
working out a military theme with a typically Jacksonian tempo,
the solution of which was to be made manifest in the council
chambers of Washington, London, and Madrid.

VI

The General left Fort Gadsden on March 26. On April 1, he was
reinforced by a party of friendly Creeks under the half-breed Mc-

29. Jackson to Calhoun, March 25, 1818, *American State Papers, Military
Affairs,* I, 698.
30. *Ibid.,* I, 698.

Intosh, and by a detachment of Tennessee volunteers under Colonel Elliott.[31] A skirmish on April 1, and a pursuit on April 2, were sufficient to disperse the neighboring Seminoles and to destroy their settlements. "In the centre of the public square, the old Red Stick's standard, a red pole, was erected crowned with scalps, recognized by the hair, as torn from the heads of the unfortunate companions of Scott."[32] About one thousand cattle, and more than three thousand bushels of corn, fell into the hands of the hungry invaders.[33] On April 6, the army halted in sight of the Spanish fort of St. Marks.

The Spanish commandant was helpless before the evident purpose of General Jackson to seize and garrison his fort. On April 7 the protesting official and his garrison were furnished with transport to Pensacola; the Spanish flag was lowered; the Stars and Stripes floated in its place. The Americans discovered, anxiously lingering in the commandant's quarters, an elderly gentleman with long white hair and a reserved but benevolent countenance. "My love," wrote the General to his wife, "I entered the Town of St. marks on yesterday . . . I found in St. marks the noted Scotch villain Arbuthnot . . . I hold him for trial."[34]

At the same time Captain McKeever of the United States Navy, by the ingenious device of flying the British colors as he brought his gunboat into St. Marks Bay, lured into his clutches no less a personage than Francis, the Seminole prophet, the *ci-devant* Brigadier General, who had not lost his faith in the British Empire. With him was another chief, "A savage-looking man . . . taciturn and morose," whose name was Homollimico, and who was believed responsible for the torture and death of Lieutenant Scott.

All now depended, the General thought, "upon the rapidity of my movements." He began by hanging Francis and Homollimico on April 8. On April 9, taking with him eight days' rations, he set out for Boleck's Town, the home of a great chief who was not unkind to refugee Negroes. It was 107 miles away, on the banks of the mysterious Suwanee. To reach it one had to cross a dim,

31. *Ibid.*, I, 699.
32. *Ibid.*, I, 700.
33. Parton, II, 450.
34. James, p. 311; *American State Papers, Military Affairs,* I, 700.

uncharted forest, dismally rooted in swamps and quagmires. The infantry sank to their waists in the morass; the horses "gave out daily in great numbers"; but the determined General completed his march in eight days. At sunset on April 18 the desperate army rushed upon the town; but the town was empty. Warned in advance, the great chief Boleck (or Bowlegs as he was generally called), his warriors, his women, and the ex-slaves who had sought his protection and entered his service, had vanished across the broad river. Only a few stern souls remained to engage the Americans. Of these, nine Negroes and two Indians were slain.[35] On the next day, General Gaines crossed the river in pursuit, but returned empty-handed. That night, as the army lay encamped on the level banks of the Suwanee, in a silence broken only by "the measured tread of the sentinels and the murmur of the long-leafed pines," there stumbled into the arms of one of its pickets a certain Lieutenant Robert C. Ambrister, late of the British Royal Colonial Marines, his servant Peter B. Cook, and two Negro attendants.[36]

On April 21, Jackson turned back toward St. Marks. He had with him Lieutenant Ambrister and certain documentary evidence —found upon one of Ambrister's attendants—which implicated Arbuthnot in the warning of Boleck. He believed that the Indians were now "divided and scattered, and cut off from all communication with those unprincipled agents of foreign nations who had deluded them to their ruin.[37] He made the return march in five days.

He had always contended that foreign agents were at the bottom of the Seminole disturbances. The capture of Arbuthnot and Ambrister, and the further discovery of suspicious documents on Arbuthnot's schooner when it was captured by Captain Gadsden at the mouth of the Suwanee, convinced him that he had these agents in his power.[38] On April 26, a special court, composed of fourteen officers, was convened at St. Marks to try the two prisoners.

35. *Ibid.*, I, 701.
36. Parton, II, 462. Parton quotes from the Ms. journal of J. B. Rodgers, of the Tennessee volunteers.
37. *American State Papers, Military Affairs,* I, 701.
38. *Ibid.*, I, 702.

VII

The trial of two British subjects before an American court in a fortress legally the property of Spain was a circumstance too complex for anyone ever to make any sense out of it. Putting aside the legal aspects of the case, one may venture to assert that Alexander Arbuthnot deserved more sympathy than recrimination. He was a merchant of New Providence (Nassau) in the Bahamas, who came to Florida in 1817 in order to trade with the Indians. Hitherto this trade had largely been conducted by the Scottish firm of Forbes & Company, which had never been known to temper its injustice with mercy. Mr. Arbuthnot made his profits, too, but they were relatively fair ones. So the Indians brought him more and more of their skins and beeswax; and the agents of Forbes & Company, gnashing their teeth in rage, noised it abroad that Mr. Arbuthnot was nothing more than a paid agitator. Certainly the Indians brought to Arbuthnot something else than skins and beeswax. Over the council fires they poured into his ears their manifold complaints. He came to be their father, their spokesman; and many were the letters he addressed to American, British, and Spanish officials, declaring that the United States had violated the Treaty of Ghent by not restoring to the Indians the lands ceded by them at the Treaty of Fort Jackson.[39] The kindly old man had unquestionably conceived a deep affection for his Indian children; but it is equally beyond question that he had written to warn chief Boleck of Jackson's advance toward the Suwanee.[40] He was arraigned upon three charges: inciting the Creek Indians to war, acting as a spy, and exciting the Indians to attack, with intent to murder, two agents of Forbes & Company, William Hambly and Edmund Doyle. The third charge was manifestly absurd, and was not pressed; of the second charge he was no doubt technically guilty.

Robert Christy Ambrister was arraigned on a charge of aiding and comforting the enemy, and levying war against the United

39. For the gist of Arbuthnot's correspondence see *American State Papers, Military Affairs,* I, 682, 723–726, 729.
40. Arbuthnot to J. Arbuthnot, April 2, 1818, *ibid.,* I, 722.

States. He was a young man of an engaging appearance, charming manners, and an adventurous background. He had fought in Florida under Colonel Nicholls, and subsequently at Waterloo; he had been one of Napoleon's guard at St. Helena; and he had gone to Nassau to stay with his uncle, the Governor, because he had been suspended from all military duties for dueling with a brother officer in the East Indies.[41] In Nassau he had yielded to the persuasions of George Woodbine, a professional agitator with some obscure interests in Florida real estate, and had gone adventuring among the Seminoles. To the charges against him he pleaded, "guilty, with justification."[42]

Mr. Arbuthnot did not think himself guilty; and, indeed, his worst crimes had been fair trading and friendship for the Indians. The case against him was completed on March 27. He spent the night studying the Rules of Evidence to such good effect that he was able to prove, to our satisfaction though not to the court's, that the chief evidence against him was inadmissible, because it was based on hearsay. On April 28 he was condemned to be hanged; while the verdict of death by shooting, passed the same day upon Lieutenant Ambrister, was reconsidered and changed to one of fifty lashes and confinement for a year.[43] On April 29 Jackson approved the sentence of Arbuthnot and the finding and first sentence of Ambrister, and disapproved the reconsideration.[44] The sentences were carried out that same morning.[45]

The two men took their deaths very patiently. No one who ventured into the weird limbo of Florida in those days did so with much thought for the morrow. When the sound of the drum and fife was heard, parading the platoon for his execution, "There," exclaimed Ambrister, "I suppose that admonishes me to be ready;

41. James, p. 313.

42. *American State Papers, Military Affairs,* I, 731. For the belief that he was plotting with Gregor McGregor, the Venezuelan patriot who had once occupied Amelia Island, to make an invasion of Tampa Bay, see Philip C. Brooks, *Diplomacy and the Borderlands: the Adams-Otis Treaty of 1819,* University of California, *Publications in History* (Berkeley, 1939), XXIV, 94, citing Davis T. Frederick, "McGregor's Invasion of Florida," *Florida Historical Society Quarterly,* VII, 4–5.

43. For the trial, see *American State Papers, Military Affairs,* I, 721–734.

44. *Ibid.*

45. *Ibid.*

a sound I have heard in every quarter of the globe, and now heard by me for the last time."[46] He had made himself very popular with his captors, and all but one of his judges followed his body to its grave.

Twenty minutes after Ambrister's death, the body of the aged Arbuthnot, decently clad in black, swung from the yardarm of his own schooner, the *Chance*. "It is fair to say," reflected Lieutenant Rodgers of the Tennessee volunteers, "that in person he would remind the observer of Aaron Burr."[47]

VIII

General Jackson conscientiously believed that his two victims deserved to die; for if he was a relentless judge, he was also an upright one.[48] The fact that he had now seriously wounded the susceptibilities of two empires bothered him not at all; he was already meditating an even more audacious move. Across the border from Fort Gadsden, in the exiguous Spanish province of West Florida, lay the little town of Pensacola, whose wooden houses and ruined gardens bore witness to the decay of Spain. Jackson was beginning to convince himself that the Governor of this dismal capital, Don José Masot, had connived with the Indians in certain murders and depredations committed in the Territory of Alabama. (This was not the case: Masot's commerce was chiefly with pirates and slave traders.) Jackson had already taken Pensacola by assault in the War of 1812, and he was by no means unwilling to take it again. He hoped, he told the Secretary of War in an extraordinary letter written on May 5, that such a measure— "adopted in pursuance of your instructions"—would meet with the approbation of the President.[49] The lights of international law had grown exceedingly dim for the nationalist General in his steamy wilderness.

46. Parton, II, 477.
47. Parton, II, 480.
48. So Benjamin F. Butler in his eulogy of Jackson delivered at New York after Jackson's death. *Ibid.,* II, 485.
49. Jackson to Calhoun, May 5, 1818, *American State Papers, Military Affairs,* I, 702.

It would appear from the correspondence Jackson wrote at Boleck's Town that he did not then propose to capture Pensacola; a reconnaissance and a skirmish were all that he had in mind.[50] The idea may have come to him at St. Marks, but not until after the executions of Arbuthnot and Ambrister. On the morning of their trials, he was still talking of an immediate return to Nashville.[51] At Fort Gadsden, however, where he arrived on May 2 and rested for a few days, he seems finally to have decided that an invasion of West Florida was a necessity; and he had crossed the border with what remained of his army, and was already beyond the Escambia River, when a message was received from Governor Masot, requesting him to retire. "Otherwise," said the Governor, "I shall repel force with force."[52] Masot had already had some unfriendly correspondence with the General concerning the navigation of the Apalachicola and Escambia rivers; and this challenge, which it was no more than Masot's duty to make, was construed by the General into an expression of inveterate hostility.[53] It was all that he needed. On May 24 he had occupied St. Michael's fort, overlooking Pensacola, and the Governor had fled the town and was immured in the fortress of Barancas, commanding the entrance to the harbor, six miles away. From the letters that passed between the two forts it would seem that Jackson's evidence against Masot—accusing him of supplying the In-

50. Jackson to Rachel Jackson, April 20, 1818. "I am advised that there are a few red sticks west of the appelachecola, should this be true, I will have to disperse them, this done, I shall commence my Journey home." *Correspondence of Andrew Jackson*, II, 360. Jackson to Calhoun, April 20, 1818. "I shall order, or take myself, a reconnaissance west of the Appelachicola at Pensacola Point, where I am informed there are a few sticks assembled." However, he adds a little ominously that the Seminoles "are fed and supplied by the Governor of Pensacola." *Ibid.*, II, 362.

51. Parton, II, 489.

52. Masot to Jackson, May 23, 1818, *American State Papers, Military Affairs*, I, 712.

53. Jackson to Masot, March 25, 1818, *American State Papers, Foreign Relations*, IV, 562; Masot to Jackson, April 16, 1818, *American State Papers, Military Affairs*, I, 706 (also in *American State Papers, Foreign Affairs*, IV, 506, with some verbal alterations and dated April 15, 1818); also May 18, 1818, denying that he has encouraged Indian hostilities; Jackson to Masot, April 27, 1814, attempting to implicate the Governor in the murder of Lieutenant Scott in 1817, *ibid.*, I, 709.

dians with arms and ammunition—was just about as slender as were Masot's chances of defending his stronghold against Jackson.[54] Masot replied, nonetheless, that he proposed to defend Barancas "to the last extremity."[55] On May 28 Jackson approached the fort with one nine-pound piece and eight five-inch howitzers; there was a spirited exchange of fire; and then, honor being satisfied, Masot hoisted the white flag.[56] On May 29 Jackson seized the royal archives, appointed Colonel King of the Fourth Infantry to the post of military and civil Governor of Pensacola, and declared that the revenue laws of the United States were now in force in West Florida.[57] After this proconsular act, there was nothing left to do but to return to Tennessee; and on May 30, accordingly, he did so.

IX

The enthusiasm that greeted the General upon his return home was unbounded. He had conducted his campaign with great speed and incomparable *élan*. The fact that he had mortally offended two foreign governments, or the chance that he had chastised some innocent Seminoles along with the guilty ones—these considerations did not present themselves very forcibly to most of his fellow-citizens. The politicians might summon some high arguments

54. *American State Papers, Military Affairs,* I, 716–717.

55. Masot to Jackson, May 24, 1818. Jackson replied, May 25, 1818, applauding the Governor's feelings as a soldier, but assuring him that the sacrifice of a few brave men would be "an act of wantonness." *American State Papers, Military Affairs,* I, 712–713.

56. *Ibid.*, pp. 719–720.

57. *Correspondence of Andrew Jackson,* II, 374; Proclamation of May 29. The army with Jackson when he attacked Barancas was as follows: 4th Battalion United States Artillery—52 officers and men; Fourth Infantry Regiment—137 officers and men; 1st and 2nd Regiment of Tennessee volunteers—837 officers and men; Kentucky and Tennesse Lifeguards, 55 officers and men; staff officers—11. Total: 1,092. *American State Papers, Military Affairs,* I, 718. Jackson told Monroe that the men were "literanny barefoot" from continued wading of water. Jackson to Monroe, June 2, 1818, *Correspondence of Andrew Jackson,* II, 378. Captain Isaac McKeever of the U.S. Navy also landed two guns and was prepared to bring his vessel before the water battery in the event it was deemed necessary to storm the upper works. Parton, II, 503.

against him—Mr. Ritchie of the *Richmond Examiner* might sharpen his Virginian pen; the judicious Mr. Niles of Baltimore might remark that "General Jackson . . . does not sufficiently reflect how intimately the character of the country is connected with his own, now that he is an officer"—but the country as a whole seemed proud of the intimacy of the connection.[58] "As to polecy," said old James Tallmadge, Sr., of Poughkeepsie, "I think it is on the generals side as it will strike a terrow on the Indians and Negros and all the unprincipled scampering traders that harbour about in them regons."[59] Some of the General's supporters were more eloquent; but nobody, really, went very much further than that.

58. *Niles' Weekly Register,* XIV, 399.
59. James Tallmadge, Sr., to James Tallmadge, Jr., January 7, 1819, Tallmadge Mss., New York Historical Society.

★

A Dishonest and Insidious Intriguer

In a private letter to President James Monroe of January 6, 1818, General Andrew Jackson complained that his instructions to prosecute the Seminole War—authorizing him to cross the Florida border but forbidding molestation of the Spanish posts—were too narrow, and added: "Let it be signified to me through any channel, (say Mr. J. Rhea) that the possession of the Floridas would be desirable to the United States, and in sixty days it will be accomplished," and this "without implicating the government."[1] Ill at the time Jackson's letter arrived, the President did not read it until some months after the Florida invasion. Monroe wrote Calhoun:

I never read that letter until after the affair was concluded; nor did I ever think of it until you recalled it to my recollection by an intimation of its contents and a suggestion that it had also been read by Crawford, who had mentioned it to some person who might be disposed to turn it to some account. . . . I asked Mr. Rhea, in a general conversation, whether he had ever intimated to Genl. Jackson his opinion that the Administration had no objection to his making an attack on Pensacola; and he declared that he never had. I did not

1. Jackson to James Monroe, January 6, 1818, with Monroe's important endorsement, J. S. Bassett, ed., *The Correspondence of Andrew Jackson*, 6 vols. (Washington, 1926–1933), II, 345–346.

From *The Journal of Southern History*, Vol. II (November 1936), pp. 480–496. Copyright 1936 by the Southern Historical Association. Reprinted by permission of the Managing Editor. Originally published under the title "Jackson's 'Rhea Letter' Hoax."

know, if the General had written him to the same effect as he had to
me, as I had not read my letter, but that he might have led me inno-
cently into a conversation in which, wishing to obtain Florida, I might
have expressed a sentiment from which he might have drawn that
inference. But he assured me that no such conversation ever passed
between us. I did not apprize him of the letter which I had received
from the General on the subject, being able to ascertain my object
without doing so.[2]

Thus in conversation with Monroe, which probably took place in
the winter of 1818–1819 (and certainly before 1823, when John
Rhea left Congress), Rhea readily admitted that he had neither
written Jackson about Florida nor been authorized to do so by
Monroe. Jackson's activities in Florida shocked the administration
by whom they were deemed utterly unauthorized and censurable.[3]
The later plea by Jackson's apologists that from Monroe's failure
to answer his January letter the General may have inferred sanction of his proposal was as unsound as it was improper.[4] Jackson
asked for an express authorization and hence should have inferred
rebuke rather than sanction from the President's silence. The General's private letter of January 6, 1818, read in the light of his
subsequent actions, shows that he intended to *force upon the ad-*

2. Monroe to John C. Calhoun, December 28, 1827, S. M. Hamilton, ed.,
The Writings of James Monroe (New York, 1898–1903), VII, 139. Monroe
stated the same facts in the endorsement cited in n. 1.

3. C. F. Adams, ed., *The Memoirs of John Quincy Adams* (Philadelphia,
1874–1877), IV, 102–108 (June 18–July 15, 1818). Monroe, in fact, even
disfavored Senator John Forsyth's proposed motion in Congress to authorize
the President to occupy East Florida. "He said Forsyth's project would be
war, and if such a bill should be presented to him by Congress, he would
not sign it." *Ibid.,* pp. 66–67 (March 23, 1818).

4. This plea was first made by Jackson's close friend and "wire-puller"
William B. Lewis, in a letter over the signature "B. B." written at Nashville
and published in the *Philadelphia Aurora,* December 15, 1818. The admis-
sion that Jackson had received no reply to his January letter decisively
refutes Jackson's later version. Lewis' "Narrative" in James Parton, *Life of
Andrew Jackson* (New York, 1860–1861), III, 313. Lewis' letter, noticed
with some apprehension by Monroe and his Cabinet, perhaps partly caused
Monroe to seek the above-mentioned interview with John Rhea. See
Memoirs of John Quincy Adams, IV, 193–194 (December 17, 1818);
William H. Crawford to Calhoun, October 2, 1830, in J. E. D. Shipp, *Giant
Days: The Life and Times of William H. Crawford* (Americus, Ga., 1909),
p. 246.

ministration the annexation of Florida; and he openly confessed later, in his "Exposition against Calhoun" (1831), that he had intended to seize and occupy Florida when he entered it. His policy appeared plainly enough in his private letter to Monroe of June 2, 1818, in which he urged upon the President

the importance of the Possession of Fts. St Marks, Gadsden and Barancas . . . to the peace and security of our Southern frontier and to the growing greatness of our nation . . . and [I] hope the government will never yield it, should my acts meet your approbation it will be a source of great consolation to me, should it be disapproved, I have this consolation, that I exercised my best exertions and Judgt. and that sound national policy will dictate holding Possession as long as we are a republick.[5]

In 1831 Jackson made public a highly original and startling version of the matter—one so completely at variance with the facts, and so circumstantially narrated, that it cannot possibly be attributed to "bad memory." He declared at that time (through the mouth of the aged Rhea, whom he had brought to Washington from Tennessee for the purpose) that in 1818 the Congressman had actually written him a letter conveying Monroe's authorization to seize Florida, in reply to his January letter to Monroe; that he had received this "Rhea letter" late in February on his march toward Florida; that, when at Washington in the spring of 1819 (where he went to defend himself against the Congressional investigation of his Florida escapade and to overawe his critics), he was told by Rhea that Monroe and Secretary of War Calhoun wanted him to destroy the "Rhea letter"; and that upon returning to the Hermitage in Tennessee he accordingly burned the alleged letter, writing at the same time in his letter book (of copies) the following note on the margin of the copy of his letter to Monroe of January 6, 1818: "Mr. J. Rhea's letter in answer is burnt this 12th April 1819." As a matter of fact, so far from knowing of any

5. Jackson to Monroe, June 2, 1818, *Correspondence of Andrew Jackson*, II, 376–378. Jackson urged annexation even more strongly in a letter of August 10, 1818, to Secretary Calhoun. See also Jackson to R. K. Call, August 5, 1818, in C. M. Brevard, *A History of Florida* (Deland, Fla., 1934), I, 257–258.

authorization for Jackson's seizure of Florida, Rhea had written Jackson on December 18, 1818, after reading such documents on the Seminole War as were published: "I will for one support your conduct, believing as far as I have read that you have acted for [the] public good."[6]

Jackson's original tale, which at his request Rhea obediently set forth in his famous letter to Monroe of June 3, 1831, was pure, deliberate fiction, as James Schouler demonstrated years ago. And when the collection of Jackson's private papers became accessible Schouler was able to announce that they verified beyond cavil or doubt his previous conviction of Jackson's sole authorship of that attempt to distort history by a fabrication.[7] The Jackson Papers, many of which have now been published, show that up to the very eve of his letter to Monroe of June 3, 1831, Rhea confessedly knew nothing of the detailed story which he stated therein— avowedly from memory, but really at Jackson's instigation—and that he merely repeated the whole tale as given to him by Jackson himself in letters written to Rhea earlier in 1831. Jackson knew that his fabricated story would gain greater credit if published through Rhea's mouth, particularly as Rhea was naturally his chief witness. Rhea's letters to Jackson seem clearly to show that he wittingly perjured himself in giving the testimony Jackson asked of him. But the giving of desired *ex parte* testimony was a somewhat common form of friendly service in that day, when Judge Hugh L. White observed sagely, "He is a mean politician who can get no man to lye upon him." In a letter to Jackson of January 4, 1831, Rhea confessed that he knew nothing about the story of a "Rhea letter" which Jackson had broached to him, but asked Jackson to send him the necessary documents so that he could "refresh" his mind and give Jackson a helpful "recollection." Rhea added: "As you are on the defensive I will help you all I can. I desire nothing to be known of me in the business, untill I speak out as fully

6. *Correspondence of Andrew Jackson,* II, 403–404.

7. James Schouler, "Monroe and the Rhea Letter," *Magazine of American History* (New York), XII (1884), 308–322, reprinted in Schouler, *Historical Briefs* (New York, 1896), pp. 97–120; Schouler, *History of the United States under the Constitution* (New York, 1894–1899), III, 68–78; IV, 37–38; *ibid.* (ed. 1913), III, 505; IV, 566; Schouler, "The Jackson and Van Buren Papers," *Atlantic Monthly,* XCV (1905), 217–225.

myself as I can and therefore this letter so far CONFIDENTIAL CONFIDENTIAL."[8] In writing to Jackson on March 30, Rhea was still calling for information! Finally Jackson brought Rhea to Washington, and gave him again, in a final letter of instruction, dated June 2, 1831, the story which Rhea simply repeated in his letter to Monroe the next day. Jackson told Rhea in his letter of June 2:

On the 6 of Jany 1818 I wrote a confidential letter to Mr. Monroe a copy of which marked A I here inclose you, in which you will find the following expressions. "Let it be signified to me thro any channel, (say, J. Rhea) that the possession of the Floridas will be desirable to the U States and in 60 days it will be accomplished." About the 20 or 22d of February on my way to Fort Scott I recvd your letter informing me, that Mr. Monroe had shown you my confidential letter to him of the 6 of Jany 1818 and approved thereof; and further, that ample instructions had been, or would be given on that head. In substance going to show, that the course pointed out in my confidential letter to him was approved. I quote from memory—your letter was burned.

Towards the rise of Congress, after the debate on the Seminole question in 1819 had closed, you came to me at Strathers Hotel, and enquired if I had recvd such a letter from you, I replied that I had. You then requested me as an old friend, for gods sake to burn it as soon as I got home. I promised that I would, and did so. This was done on the 12 of April 1819, and is so endorsed on the margin of my letter Book, opposite where the confidential letter is recorded.

The object of this communication is to request you to say, whether the fact as stated, to wit, your request to me to burn the letter is not correct, and whether that request proceeded from any intimation or suggestion, of Mr. Monroe and Mr. Calhoun, or either of them.[9]

Rhea was at Washington with Jackson when this letter was written, a letter which was obviously one of instruction, its last paragraph only reflecting the Old Hero's desire to implicate Calhoun and also his characteristic respect for good appearances. The next day, June 3, Rhea proceeded to write Monroe. After citing

---

8. Rhea to Jackson, January 4, 1831, *Correspondence of Andrew Jackson,* IV, 221–222. Cf. Rhea to Jackson, March 30, 1831, *ibid.,* pp. 254–255.

9. Jackson to Rhea, June 2, 1831, *ibid.,* pp. 288–289.

Jackson's private letter of January 6, 1818, Rhea categorically told Monroe:

> I had many confidential conversations with you respecting General Jackson at that period. You communicated to me that confidential letter, or its substance, approved the opinion of Jackson therein expressed, and did authorize me to write to him. I did accordingly write to him. He says he received my letter on his way to Fort Scott, and acted accordingly. After that war a question was raised in your cabinet as to General Jackson's authority, and that question was got over. I know that General Jackson was in Washington in January, 1819, and my confidential letter was probably in his possession. You requested me to request General Jackson to burn that letter, in consequence of which I asked General Jackson, and he promised to do so. He has since informed me that April 12, 1819, he did burn it.

Rhea concluded by requesting a reply.[10] His letter, sent to Monroe in the form just quoted, had undergone considerable revision in the interest of conciseness, literacy, and intelligibility, a revision undoubtedly made either by Jackson himself or indirectly by him through one of his intimate friends.[11] Jackson similarly procured a weak corroborative statement, dated June 2, 1831, from his old friend John Overton to the effect that Jackson had shown him the "Rhea letter" in 1818—a testimony which Overton (who, like Rhea, plainly knew nothing of the matter until imposed on by Jackson) gave reluctantly.[12]

Jackson purveyed the "Rhea letter" tale in letters to a number of private friends in 1831–1832, coupled with malignant denunciations of Calhoun's "villainy" and "treachery" toward him—a groundless charge which his tale of the "Rhea letter" was intended to prove. He was not altogether consistent in his tale, saying in

10. Quoted by Schouler, "Monroe and the Rhea Letter," p. 319.

11. The long and rambling first draft of Rhea's letter to Monroe, June 3, 1831, was quoted in *Correspondence of Andrew Jackson*, IV, 288–289. It does not materially differ in substance from the revised letter sent to Monroe. This original draft shows plainly Rhea's dotage.

12. John Overton to Jackson, June 16, 1830, February 3 and June 2, 1831, *ibid.*, pp. 151, 236, 287. In his letter of June 16, 1830, giving his own recollection of the Seminole War, Overton, significantly, made no mention of any "Rhea letter." Jackson's letters to Overton are not extant.

some of his narratives that he had burned the alleged Rhea letter "in Overton's presence," while stating about Overton in other narratives, "I told him I had burned it." In the fall of 1831 or spring of 1832 Jackson wrote up his tale at great length (with some new details added, evincing a remarkable growth in his peculiar memory), intending to publish it under his own signature accompanied by Rhea's and Overton's affidavits. There are two drafts of this "Exposition against Calhoun."[13] Jackson was only restrained from publishing this manuscript by the advice of well-wishing friends and his own fearful, better judgment, he having been informed that Monroe had been so ungracious as to set down in writing a complete denial of the "Rhea letter" story before he died in July, 1831.[14] The Old Hero's action was thus for once "sicklied o'er with the pale cast of thought." Jackson insinuated, indeed, through his organ or mouthpiece, Blair's *Washington Globe,* in the fall of 1831, that he had been fully authorized in his proceedings in Florida in 1818; but when Monroe's literary executor, Samuel L. Gouverneur, wrote Blair that he held private papers of Monroe's bearing on the matter and challenged the editor to say whether Jackson himself authorized the "Rhea letter" story (as put forth in Rhea's letter of June 3, 1831, to Monroe), Blair refused to commit the President, declaring that it was an issue of veracity between Monroe and Rhea, not between Monroe and Jackson! The battle between Gouverneur and Blair waged hotly, at first privately and then in the newspapers, as late as October,

13. The final draft of Jackson's "Exposition" was published, from Jackson's Papers, by Thomas H. Benton in his *Thirty Years' View* (New York, 1852–1854), I, 169–180. A preliminary draft was published in *Correspondence of Andrew Jackson,* IV, 228–236 (incorrectly dated "Feb., 1831," by Bassett). See Jackson's letters to friends, from March 1831 to February 1832 on the alleged Rhea letter, *ibid.,* pp. 246, 304, 310, 411; VI, 505; S. G. Heiskell, *Andrew Jackson and Early Tennessee History* (Nashville, 1920–1921), III, 489; *American Historical Magazine and Tennessee Historical Society Quarterly* (Nashville), IX (1904), 89. The last reference is cited hereafter as *American Historical Magazine.*

14. *Reminiscences of James A. Hamilton* (New York, 1869), pp. 244–245; Hamilton to Jackson, October 20, 1832, *Correspondence of Andrew Jackson,* IV, 289 n. Monroe's denial was taken down by his son-in-law, Samuel L. Gouverneur, on June 19, 1831, and was published in *Writings of James Monroe,* VII, 234–236. Cf. George Morgan, *The Life of James Monroe* (Boston, 1921), pp. 445–452.

1832, while Jackson continued to remain concealed from the public, finding discretion the better part of valor.[15] Gouverneur could gain no satisfaction, and in 1837, having heard that Jackson was still intending to try to read his fable into history, sent the retiring President, as a silent commentary on his depravity, a copy of Rhea's letter to Monroe.[16]

That Jackson was the real author of the slanderous fabrication put forth through Rhea was well understood by interested observers in 1831, who freely expressed for it the contempt which it merited. They likewise easily perceived Jackson's political and personal motives—his desire to prove Calhoun's "treachery" toward him and his desire to place his unauthorized Florida seizure of 1818 in more favorable light before posterity.[17] Calhoun wrote Gouverneur on March 4, 1832: "Should any open move be made in this most nefarious affair by General Jackson . . . it ought to be met directly, and with the indignation, which the character of the transaction is so well calculated to excite. I do not, however, believe any such move will be made. It would not be in character. Crime is cowardly."[18] Jackson was, nevertheless, most anxious to establish his "Rhea letter" story in history. "I have just heard from a respectable source," Calhoun wrote in 1835, "that a book is now writing at Washington under the auspices of Genl. Jackson and to be published when he retires, on the subject of the Seminole affair; in which an attack will be made both on Mr. Monroe's character & my own, and in which the affidavit of John Rhea is to form a

15. Correspondence of Gouverneur and Francis P. Blair, and Duff Green's statements, in *Niles' Weekly Register* (Baltimore), XLIII (1832), 90–94, 104–105, 123; *Washington Globe,* October 4 and 11, 1832; Calvin Colton, ed., *Life and Works of Henry Clay* (New York, 1857), I, 254–256; *United States Telegraph* (Washington), November 7, 1831, June 14, 1832.

16. Gouverneur to Jackson, January 6, 1837, *Correspondence of Andrew Jackson,* V, 448.

17. *Memoirs of John Quincy Adams,* VIII, 404–405; XII, 210; Henry A. Wise, *Seven Decades of the Union* (Philadelphia, 1872), pp. 151–152; Calhoun to Gouverneur, July 14, 1831, March 4, 1832, in J. F. Jameson, ed., *Correspondence of John C. Calhoun,* American Historical Association, *Annual Report,* 1899, II (Washington, 1901), 295, 314; John Floyd's diary, July 16, 1832, in C. H. Ambler, *The Life and Diary of John Floyd* (Richmond, 1918), pp. 192–193; Schouler, "Monroe and the Rhea Letter," pp. 308–322.

18. *Correspondence of John C. Calhoun,* IV, 314.

prominent part."[19] But still Jackson did not come out openly behind the "Rhea letter" tale, and it remained for Benton to publish Jackson's manuscript "Exposition" in 1852, for the first time, in his *Thirty Years' View* (I, 169–189), thus placing Jackson fully in view.

The fact that even some recent writers half credit and others give full credence to Jackson's fictitious story only shows the strength of the traditional belief in Jackson's reputed honesty without which his tale would not have been able to stand on even one leg to this late day. But most historians have glossed lightly over Jackson's version, perhaps sensing that with a close study of the evidence touching it (and of its "minor" discrepancies in their full implications), it would become too grotesque, too detrimental to the myth of Jackson's integrity, and therefore unfit to dwell upon. More recent writers have generally taken their cue from Professor J. S. Bassett, who, in his *Life of Andrew Jackson* (1911), while admitting the falsity of the "Rhea letter" version, held that Jackson was perhaps "honestly mistaken," suggesting that he received a letter from Congressman Rhea in 1818 really pertaining to some other matter but which Jackson erroneously believed to relate and be in answer to his request for authorization from Monroe to seize Florida.[20] Unfortunately, this ingenious effort to shield Jackson from an open exposure of his dishonesty and insidious intriguing is obviously unsuccessful. For the private correspondence between Monroe and Jackson of July–December,

19. Calhoun to Gouverneur, May 22, 1835, *Bulletin of the New York Public Library,* III (1899), 332. From Jackson's manuscript Executive Book (Jackson Mss., Library of Congress) some pages are cut out, and on the adjacent page appears the following note: "Hermitage 21st Decb. 1842. The leaves of this book cut out at this place were cut by me at the request of Genl Andrew Jackson and contained copies of letters from John Rhea to James Monroe from Andrew Jackson to John Rhea and a statement of John Overton's. All in relation to Genl. Jackson's conduct in the Indian War. James A. McLaughlin." Probably Jackson was sending these copies to Amos Kendall, who was then working on a biography of Jackson, which he never finished. See Kendall to Benton, December 29, 1853, Benton, I, 168 n.

20. Professor Bassett stated: "I venture a possible explanation of the discrepancy between the statements of Monroe and Jackson, mostly a conjecture for it cannot be proved." J. S. Bassett, *The Life of Andrew Jackson* (New York, 1911, 1923), I, 249 n.; *Correspondence of Andrew Jackson,* II, 348 n.

1818, in which Monroe directly reproved Jackson for violating his orders and acting on his own responsibility in Florida, and in which the General sought to justify his acts solely on the ground of his military orders of December 23, 1817 (which contemplated merely the quelling of the Seminole Indians), shows conclusively that Jackson had no belief whatever that his acts had been previously secretly authorized or sanctioned by Monroe.[21] This fact appears also in Jackson's letter to Monroe of June 2, 1818, quoted earlier in this paper. Jackson in his correspondence with both Monroe and the War Department in 1818 had pretended that his seizure of the Spanish posts was dictated by the exigencies of the Indian campaign and that he had not formed an intention to occupy them prior to his actual entry into Florida. Thus in his letter of April 26, 1818, to Calhoun, Jackson wrote that, having taken St. Marks and completely put down the Indians, he was about to return to Nashville, the purpose of his campaign having been accomplished—at least so far as the instructions given him by the government were concerned. This letter, to be sure, was but a typical piece of Jacksonian duplicity, anent which the Lacock Committee reported to Congress in February, 1819, after investigating the Seminole War: "It appears, however, by the conduct of the commanding general that he had, at this time, looked to different movements, for, at the time he was writing this letter, as will be seen by the testimony of Captain Call and Surgeon Bronaugh, he had despatched Lieut. Sands to Mobile, to forward on a train of artillery to a given point, to be ready to be made use of in reducing Pensacola and the fort of Barrancas."[22] And soon afterward

21. Correspondence quoted in James Parton, *Life of Andrew Jackson*, 3 vols. (New York, 1860–1861), II, 518–528, and in *Correspondence of Andrew Jackson*, II, *passim*. Jackson's correspondence with the War Department in 1818 was printed in *American State Papers, Military Affairs*, I, 681–709.

22. Jackson to Calhoun, April 26, 1818, in *American State Papers, Foreign Relations*, IV, 600; Lacock Committee report, February 24, 1819, in *American State Papers, Military Affairs*, I, 741. For other instances of Jackson's hoaxing and unscrupulous intrigue see the following papers by the writer: "Jackson, Buchanan and the 'Corrupt Bargain' Calumny," *Pennsylvania Magazine of History and Biography*, LVIII (1934), 61–85; "Jackson, Anthony Butler, and Texas," *Southwestern Social Science Quarterly*, XIII (1932), 264–286; "The Texas Schemes of Jackson and Houston, 1829–1836," *ibid.*, XV (1934), 229–250; and "Jackson's Neches Claim," *South-*

Jackson descended on Pensacola on the Indian pretext, again pretending that his movement was an afterthought.

Jackson's story that he destroyed a letter from Rhea in 1818 is so plainly a deliberate fraud that no further space need be devoted to showing the fact. Its appearance in 1831 was occasioned by Jackson's desire to "prove" the charge of "treachery" which he preferred against Vice-President Calhoun in May, 1830, as a pertext for breaking with him and for seeking his political destruction. Plentiful testimony shows, and Jackson himself finally confessed, that long before this, in the years 1819–1825, he had been informed by various men (whose reliable knowledge in the matter he could hardly have doubted) of Calhoun's true position in Monroe's Cabinet in 1818 on the question as to whether General Jackson should be upheld or punished for his arbitrary conduct.[23] Up to his election as President, Jackson chose to ignore the matter from motives of policy. It appears plainly enough that Jackson's professed "surprise" in the winter of 1829–1830 upon being apprised "for the first time" of the truth of the matter was sheer artful pretense and hypocrisy, assumed as a convenient pretext for making a sudden onslaught on Calhoun, who had grown obnoxious to him and whose political aid he no longer needed. Calhoun did not believe Jackson sincere and wrote a friend on April 10, 1831: "I believe that Jackson was apprized, as far back as 1825, when he and Crawford were reconciled, of the part I took in the Cabinet, through Cobb as fully as he is now, and that the information was repeated in 1828."[24] Calhoun observed later, with much truth, that the real cause of Jackson's animosity toward him and the cause of the one-sided quarrel of 1830 was his, Calhoun's, independence and failure to toady to and flatter Jackson,

---

western Historical Quarterly, XXXIX (1935–1936). The writer is preparing an extensive critique of Jackson's career and character.

23. Jackson finally admitted, in his "Exposition against Calhoun," that he had been informed of the matter, from 1819 to 1825, not only by his own friends but by some of Crawford's most intimate friends, such as Cobb; but Jackson would have us believe that he refused to believe, that he "could not" believe, these informants! *Correspondence of Andrew Jackson,* IV, 233; cf. John Williams to Van Buren, March 22, 1831, *ibid.,* p. 229. This claim of Jackson's stands in strange contrast to his *readiness to believe* in 1829–1830!

24. Copy in the Jackson Mss., LXXIX.

who was ever condescending and eager for adulation and slavish-
ness on the part of those around him.[25] Van Buren's obsequious-
ness toward Jackson and Calhoun's independence (not to forget,
too, *l'affaire* Peggy Eaton, in which *Mrs.* Calhoun's independence
was of some importance in bringing about the breach between
Jackson and Calhoun) may be accounted large factors in shaping
the trend of political affairs in the period after Jackson's accession
to power.[26]

There remains to discuss a point of some interest about the
"Rhea letter" affair, namely, the probable date of Jackson's actual
fabrication of this hoax—the date of his writing the marginal
forgery (as presumptive proof of the story) in his letter book,
"Mr. J. Rhea's letter in answer is burnt this 12th April 1819."
And at this place it may be noted that Jackson's letter book for the
year 1818 has disappeared. In the Jackson Papers we find only
one extant copy of Jackson's letter to Monroe of January 6,
1818—a copy made by and in the handwriting of Andrew Jackson, Jr., and endorsed: "(a true copy) Attest A. Jackson Jr."[27] In
the margin of the letter, opposite Jackson's suggestion that Monroe
send him an authorization to seize Florida through "any channel
(say Mr. J. Rhea)," we find Jackson's marginal note, or forgery;
but it reads: "Mr. J. Rhea's letter in answer is burnt this 12th

25. W. M. Meigs, *Life of Charles J. Ingersoll* (Philadelphia, 1900),
pp. 266–267.

26. Calhoun, who at times during his career had almost prophetic insight
into misfortunes to come, in later life related to his friends the vision that
passed before his mind when his wife told him (in 1829), "Mr. Calhoun, I
have determined not to return Mrs. Eaton's visit": "I have heard that a
drowning man will sometimes see, at a glance, his whole past life, and, at
these words, it seemed as though the future was shown me in as sudden and
as vivid a manner. The rupture with General Jackson; the administration
changing from a Free Trade policy to that of Protection; the failure to
adjust the Tariff difficulties; executive patronage brought to bear upon the
States' Rights leaders; personal property influencing the masses; certain
Nullification by South Carolina, and almost as certain attempt at coercion
by the Federal Government." On recovering from his reverie, Calhoun
merely replied to his wife: "That is a question about which women should
feel, not think. Their instincts are the safest guides. I entirely concur with
you in your decision." Reminiscence of "a prominent South Carolinian" (as
the editor identifies the writer), in the *Southern Review* (St. Louis), XII
(1873), 216–217.

27. Jackson Mss., XLVI.

April 1818." Is this date, "1818," a mere slip in copying on the part of Andrew Jackson's adopted son—or did Jackson date the alleged burning of the Rhea letter "1818" in his original marginal note? As we have not Jackson's original letter book, we cannot answer this question. It may be suggested that if Jackson intended at first to bring forth a simpler version of his story, and date the alleged burning in 1818, he probably decided later to change the date of burning to 1819 (placing it after an alleged interview with Rhea at Washington, thereby to ground it upon Monroe's and Calhoun's request) the better to demonstrate Calhoun's "villainy" toward him.

The evidence provides us two hypothetical dates for Jackson's fabrication of the "Rhea letter" hoax, 1827 or 1830–1831. There is no mention or intimation of a "Rhea letter" in any documents written before May, 1830—at which time Jackson broke with Calhoun and threatened him mysteriously with "evidence" he intended to produce "hereafter, when I shall have more leisure, and the documents at hand . . . which will give a very different view of this subject. . . . I had authority for all that I did" in Florida. Later in the same year Jackson applied to Rhea for perjured testimony. On its face this would strongly suggest that the hoax was conceived by Jackson in 1830, as a means of "framing" Calhoun.

There is some evidence, however, which, though written in 1832, may indicate that Jackson had secretly conceived the self-palliative tale (and concocted the accompanying *pièce de résistance,* the marginal forgery) in 1827, when the circumstances or political background, while somewhat different from those of 1830, were such as would very similarly tempt and inspire Jackson's mind to conceive such a fabrication. In 1830 Jackson's predominant passion was hatred of Calhoun; in 1827 he was angry at Monroe who had been quoted to him as having made an aspersion upon Jackson's conduct in the Southern wars of 1814–1815, and a copy of whose letter to Secretary Calhoun of September 9, 1818, was put into Jackson's hands by Sam Houston in January, 1827. In this letter Monroe, speaking of *their* disagreement with Jackson's view of his military orders in the Seminole War, advised Calhoun to write and ask the General to set down his views fully in writing, so that the positions of both parties should plainly appear in the public archives.[28] Jackson also heard a rumor in the spring of 1827, so he says, that Monroe was engaged in "writing a book" in which he meant to attack Jackson's unauthorized Florida invasions of 1814 and 1818.[29] Though this rumor now seems chimerical, Jackson's letters in 1827 show that he was seemingly upset by the prospect of Monroe's coming out against him in an elaborate exposé, in virtual support of his rival Adams in the then Presidential contest; and he said some harsh things about Monroe. Jackson, in short, may have conceived his "Rhea letter" hoax in 1827, with the aim of bringing it before the world to offset a prospective attack by Monroe in case it should materialize.

In January, 1832, Jackson instructed his "wire-puller," William B. Lewis, to write to Major Henry Lee—who had lived with Jackson at the Hermitage in 1827–1828 while writing campaign pamphlets for him and working on the Old Hero's biography—to ask Lee if when he was staying with Jackson in 1827

he did not have a view of a confidential [letter] of mine to Mr. Munroe . . . dated in January 1818. . . . and whether he did not see marked on the margin of said letter book, that Mr. John Rheas letter in reply to his confidential letter had been burnt on the 12th day of April 1819 . . . and whether Major Lee did not express great astonishment that I should have so destroyed, when I informed [him] it was at the earnest personal request of Mr. Rhea, and Mr. Rhea stated at the earnest request of Mr. Munroe, . . . and having so promised I did burn and made that memorandum on the margin to shew I had complied with my promise, and request the Major to state the month and

28. Calhoun pointed out in 1830 that this letter of September 9, 1818, alone must have shown Jackson as early as 1827 (when it came under his eye), if he had not known long before, that Calhoun had not approved the General's conduct in 1818.

29. See *Correspondence of Andrew Jackson,* III, *passim;* Jackson to R. G. Dunlap, August 29, 1831, *American Historical Magazine,* IX (1904), 102. Lewis stimulated apprehension of Monroe's rumored "book" among Jackson's less intimate friends. That even as late as 1829 some of Jackson's friends feared Monroe's rumored exposé appears in J. Armstrong to Lewis, August 1, 1829, Jackson Mss., LXXIII. Jackson had been angry at Monroe previously, in 1822, without good reason. *Correspondence of Andrew Jackson,* III, 149, 160–161; cf. 362.

year in which he saw my letter to Mr. Munroe with said entry afore-
said on its margin.[30]

Lee, residing at Paris in 1832, was out of favor with Jackson and
avowedly anxious to be restored to good grace, so that his reply to
Lewis' inquiry may well be a deliberate perjury to gratify President
Jackson. Lewis wrote Lee repeating the substance of Jackson's
memorandum. In response Lee wrote Jackson a letter on September 4, 1832, in which, after quoting Lewis' letter at length, he
said:

> My answer to this inquiry is, that I have a distinct recollection of
> finding from a memo. in your letter book while I was investigating
> the Seminole of Florida transactions in Tennessee that you had burnt
> a letter which contained Mr. Monroes approval of your design to
> enter ["occupy" rubbed out] Florida in prosecuting the Seminole War
> and that I expressed to you my surprise at finding you had burnt or
> destroyed so important a paper. I have a less distinct recollection that
> that letter was not from . . .[31]

At this point the extant document ends midway, the concluding
page or pages of Lee's testimony having some time been either lost
or destroyed by Jackson, possibly because Lee remembered something therein not suitable to Jackson's purpose. This testimony if
true would show that Jackson had written the marginal forgery
regarding, and in "proof" of, the alleged "Rhea letter" as early as
1827, for the purpose above suggested. Some color of support is
given to this hypothesis by the veiled threat in Jackson's private
letter to Duff Green of August 13, 1827: "I have said to major
Lee that he can have copies of any correspondence of mine with
the government, not confidential. If, as you intimate, Mr. Munroe
does come out, then these documents may be given to the public. I

30. Jackson's note to Lewis, January 1832, in Jackson-Lewis Mss. (New
York Public Library), published (incorrectly dated "1837") in *Correspondence of Andrew Jackson,* V, 445.

31. Henry Lee to Jackson, near Paris, September 4, 1832, Jackson Mss.,
LXXXI. This testimonial was enclosed by Lee in another letter to Jackson,
of personal nature, dated September 5, 1832, which was published in *Correspondence of Andrew Jackson,* IV, 472.

act on the defensive."[32] In 1831 Jackson wrote similarly of his
apprehension of Monroe's "book" in 1827: "Notwithstanding Mr.
Monroe knew that Mr. Rhea's letter to me was burned, he
perceived from my letter to Southard that I was prepared at every
point, and therefore the project of the Book was abandoned. You
seem to have forgotten that Mr. Monroe had charged me with
transcending my orders. We were at issue on this point, notwithstanding he approved my conduct (as he professed) on a knowledge of the circumstances which attended it."[33]

But, on the other hand, Jackson wrote Calhoun as late as May,
1828: "Majr Lee has never seen Mr. Monroe's private correspondence with me, and . . . is, therefore, left to place such a construction upon the public documents as he may conceive they
justly deserve . . . ; but without his [Monroe's] request I shall

---

32. Jackson to Green, August 13, 1827, *ibid.*, III, 377. Lee had written
Jackson on November 18, 1826: "If you think proper to communicate any
confidential details either of your public or private life, they shall be
sacredly cherished within my own bosom, but they might still enable me to
give a juster and firmer colour to your history." *Ibid.*, p. 318.

Similarly, Jackson tried to make Dr. Robert Mayo, a clerk in the War
Department, a witness in the "Rhea letter" matter. Sometime in 1831–1832,
as Mayo related, Jackson "invited me to his chamber to examine certain
documents (which he took from a large trunk, not a bureau or table
drawer) in relation to his invasion of the Spanish territory of Florida during
Mr. Monroe's administration, and which examination I was invited to make
with the view to establish a charge of falsehood he alleged against Mr.
Monroe." Sensing the spuriousness of the "evidence" shown him by Jackson,
Mayo declined to make an affidavit, and was astonished upon the appearance later, in the *Richmond Enquirer,* of such an affidavit as Jackson
required, made by Samuel Gwin, one of Jackson's parasites and favorites,
and this soon after Gwin's appointment by Jackson to the land office in
Mississippi. It seems that Gwin's testimony did not go to the full extent of
Jackson's desire, for Mayo said: "The asperities of the original design were
much mitigated, however, in that communication, as to the positive induc-
tions of falsehood; but it bore all the other internal evidences of its origin in
the *indications* of the then tenant of the President's mansion." Mayo, *The
Affidavit of Andrew Jackson, taken by the Defendants in the Suit of Robert
Mayo vs. Blair & Rives for a Libel, Analised and Refuted, by Robert Mayo*
(Washington, 1840), p. 11. Indeed, in 1830–1831, Jackson had "Florida" on
the brain, as appears in his hoax of the "Fulton letter" of December 10,
1830, which was exposed by Robert Mayo in 1838–1839, and which the
present writer has discussed in *Southwestern Social Science Quarterly,* XV
(1934–1935), 229–238; XIII (1932–1933), 265–266.

33. Jackson to Dunlap, August 29, 1831, *American Historical Magazine,*
IX (1904), 102.

not expose this correspondence to Majr. Lee, or any one else."[34]
Monroe, however, gave Lee permission in 1828 to see this correspondence, and Jackson may have shown it to Lee some time in
1827–1828. Yet Lee wrote Jackson as late as 1829:

Genl. Armstrong is about publishing a brief historical summary of
the last war, and he had the goodness first to offer it to me, as a material for my promised history of your life; which offer I was compelled
to decline, inasmuch as you took back the memo. you once gave me,
and never did shew me the confidential correspondence with Monroe.
. . . Your withholding of materials from me has involved me in another difficulty for Green (who was to bear my expenses in Tennessee
and then share the profits of the book) has called on me to refund.[35]

It is probable, in the writer's opinion, that in 1827–1828 Lee was
given no intimation by Jackson of the "Rhea letter" story which
was brought forth in 1830–1831, and that Lee's testimony in 1832
was perjured like that of Rhea and Overton. It must be noted that
Jackson's unscrupulous letter to Monroe of January 6, 1818, was
not known to the public until Calhoun published it in paraphrase
in his famous pamphlet of February, 1831. Before he issued his
"Rhea letter" story in June, 1831, Jackson had not been altogether
happy about that private letter of his to Monroe, which so clearly
showed his imperialistic frame of mind on the eve of his Florida
invasion (and which, at the time, had intimated to Monroe's
Cabinet members the real motive behind his operations in Florida).
He considered Calhoun's publication of that letter[36] an additional grievance against the South Carolinian. It is quite possible,
nevertheless, that Jackson secretly contrived his "Rhea letter"

34. Jackson to Calhoun, May 25, 1828, *Correspondence of Andrew Jackson,* III, 404–406; cf. Jackson to Green, August 13, 1827, *ibid.,* p. 377.
35. Lee to Jackson, August 20, 1829, Jackson Mss., LXXIII. Lee complained in other letters to Jackson in 1827–1828 that Jackson had not
facilitated his task by giving him access to his private papers. *Ibid.* Lee's
biography of Jackson was never finished. Author's italics above.
36. Calhoun's *Correspondence between Gen. Andrew Jackson and John
C. Calhoun, President and Vice-President of the U. States, on the Subject of
the Course of the Latter, in the Deliberations of the Cabinet of Mr. Monroe, on the Occurrences in the Seminole War* (Washington, 1831), p. 49.

hoax in 1827 or even earlier,[37] rather than in 1830; but, if so, it is
a little peculiar that he did not at an earlier time solicit a
supporting statement or affidavit from Rhea (who had for years
been on the verge of the grave, and died in the spring of 1832,
shortly after serving as Jackson's tool). In brief, we cannot date
the origin of Jackson's hoax with certainty—having before us only
the result, and not the paths and processes, of his deliberations—
and must leave this among the many unsolved questions which
give history its piquancy.

But whether framed to meet the political exigency of 1827 or
that of 1830, or framed at some earlier time, Jackson's "Rhea
letter" story is a fabrication equally transparent. And his unscrupulous private letter to Monroe of January 6, 1818, upon
which his hoax of afteryears was erected, reminds us

> How oft the sight of means to do ill deeds
> Makes ill deeds done.

37. In his "Exposition against Calhoun," Jackson says that his marginal
entry in his letter book "was seen by several persons many years ago," but
he does not name these "persons." Benton, I, 179. Even if he concocted this
forgery in 1830 Jackson would naturally wish to make it seem that it had
been *known* to have been on record a long time.

THOMAS P. ABERNETHY

✪

Tennessee Nabob

The name of Andrew Jackson is inseparably linked with the rise of
Western democracy, but the biographers of the General have
confined their attention largely to his military exploits and to his
contest for and occupancy of the Presidency. It is not these phases
of his life, however, which connect him most intimately with the
struggle of the pioneer and early Western farmer for political
power. Before he was a General or a Presidential possibility, he
was a Tennessee politician. In this capacity he was closely associated with those events which constituted an integral part of the
democratic movement of the West. A study of this phase of his
career, and of the setting in which he worked, should give a better
idea of the man and of the cause for which his name has come to
stand.

In 1796 Tennessee adopted her first constitution. Jackson was a
member of the committee which drafted it. For its day it was a
liberal document, but among its provisions were two which later
attracted much unfavorable attention. One provided that the justices of the peace should be chosen by the general assembly for life
terms, and that the justices should choose, with a few exceptions,
the other county officials;[1] the second stipulated that all acreage
should be taxed at the same rate, regardless of value.[2]

1. Art. V, Sec. 12; Art. VI, Sec. 1.
2. Art. I, Sec. 26.

Reprinted from *The American Historical Review,* Vol. XXXIII (October
1927), pp. 64–77. Originally published under the title "Andrew Jackson and
the Rise of Southwestern Democracy."

These provisions make it clear that the democracy of the West had not grown to full stature by 1796. The peculiarities of the early frontier go far toward explaining this fact. The familiar portraits of John Sevier show him in military costume of the Continental type, such as officers of the line wore during the Revolutionary War, but in his fighting days he wore a hunting shirt as did the men who followed him as he tracked the elusive Indian through the forest.[3] Distinctions existed on the border, but they were not patent to the eye, and the simple backwoodsman was not alive to them. The voters who elected delegates to the Constitutional Convention of 1796 did not realize to what extent they were smoothing the way for the self-aggrandizement of their leaders, the colonels, the legislators, and the land-grabbers—classifications which greatly overlapped.

The years which elapsed between 1796 and 1812 were years of relative peace and considerable growth for the Southwest, but frontier conditions persisted throughout the period. The settlers, whether in town or country, continued, in the main, to live in log cabins and wear homespun. The acquisition of Louisiana and the final opening of the Mississippi River to the trade of the West was a boon to the country. Such towns as Nashville began to emerge from the primitive and to take on the appearance of civilization. Yet it was only with great difficulty that the rivers could be ascended by keel boats, and the majority of the roads were mere trails through the woods. Money was scarce, and the interchange of goods was difficult and hazardous. Barter was still commonly employed in conducting commercial transactions.[4]

The War of 1812 ushered in a change. Tennessee troops saw considerable service in the campaigns against the Indians and the British, and the supplies necessary for their maintenance were secured largely in the West. This brought ready money into regions which had previously known little of its use,[5] and money meant

3. J. G. M. Ramsey, *Annals of Tennessee* (Kingsport, Tenn., 1926), p. 711.

4. Account book of H. Tatum, merchant, Nashville, 1793–1798, Tennessee Historical Society Mss., Box T–1, No. 5; J. S. Bassett, ed., *The Correspondence of Andrew Jackson*, 6 vols. (Washington, 1926–1933), I, 89–90, 99–101.

5. *Nashville Gazette,* October 29, 1820.

purchasing power, and luxuries, and trade. Moccasins gave place to shoes, and log cabins to brick and frame houses. The Indians caused less trouble after Jackson's conquest of the Creeks in 1813, and large tracts of land were wrested from the natives. The depression suffered by our infant industries as a result of the dumping of British goods on the American market at the end of the long European wars, and the depleted condition of the soils of the South Atlantic states were conditions tending to force population westward.[6] The Cotton Kingdom of the gulf region was planted in these years.[7] The high price of the staple, which reached thirty-four cents a pound in 1817,[8] hastened this movement, and the steamboat came just in time to facilitate the commercial side of the development.[9]

Specie payments had been suspended by the banks south of New England in 1814, and cheap paper money had been one of the elements conducive to the rapid exploitation of the West which followed the war.[10] In 1817 the Second Bank of the United States went into operation, and it was hoped that it would, by bringing pressure to bear upon doubtful state banks, be able to restore the currency of the country to a sound basis.[11] This meant the retirement of much worthless paper money issued by the state banks, and a consequent restraint on speculative operations.

In order to offset this curtailment of currency and credit, Tennessee chartered a "litter" of state banks in 1817.[12] Kentucky did likewise during the next year.[13] At the same time, the legislature of Tennessee prevented the establishment of a branch of

6. A. O. Craven, *Soil Exhaustion as a Factor in the Agricultural History of Virginia and Maryland* (Urbana, Ill., 1926), pp. 118–121.

7. T. P. Abernethy, *Formative Period in Alabama* (Montgomery, 1922), pp. 50–56.

8. U.S. Department of Agriculture, Office of Farm Management, *Atlas of American Agriculture* (Washington, 1918), Pt. V., Sec. A, p. 20.

9. Moore and Foster, *Tennessee, the Volunteer State* (Chicago, 1923), II, 85–86; *Nashville Banner,* April 14, 1827.

10. D. R. Dewey, *Financial History of the United States* (New York, 1920), pp. 144–145.

11. *Ibid.,* pp. 145–151.

12. Tennessee Public Acts, 1817, pp. 163–180.

13. McMaster, *History of the People of the United States* (New York, 1895), IV, 508.

the Bank of the United States within her borders by levying a tax of fifty thousand dollars a year upon any such institution.[14] This prohibitive measure was sponsored by Hugh Lawson White,[15] while the opposition was led by Felix Grundy[16] and supported by William Carroll and Andrew Jackson.[17] Its passage seems to indicate the jealousy felt by local financial interests rather than the influence of constitutional scruples on the subject.

The period of speculation was followed by the Panic of 1819. East Tennessee had largely escaped the financial excesses of the postwar boom,[18] for her valleys were not suited to the culture of cotton, and transportation was so difficult as to make commercial expansion almost impossible. In Middle Tennessee, however, the growing of cotton was far more widespread during these years than it is at the present time. It was, for instance, Jackson's principal crop at the Hermitage, whereas one now has to travel many miles south of Nashville before reaching cotton country. The very high price which the staple commanded from 1815 to 1819 was the primary cause of this expansion, and the result was that thousands of farmers in this section were ruined when the price fell and the panic came on in 1819. Between five and six hundred suits for debt were entered at one term of the court of Davidson County[19] —the county of which Nashville is the seat of justice.

The indications are that the Panic of 1819 hit the small farmers of the Southwest harder than has any succeeding financial disaster. After settled conditions are established and farms are paid for,

14. Tennessee Public Acts, 1817, pp. 138–139.

15. John Catron to Polk, June 17, 1837, Papers of James K. Polk (Library of Congress); Nancy N. Scott, ed., *A Memoir of Hugh Lawson White* (Philadelphia, 1856), pp. 19–23.

16. St. George L. Sioussat, "Some Phases of Tennessee Politics in the Jackson Period," *American Historial Review*, XIV, 60; *Nashville Whig*, February 7, 1818.

17. James Phelan, *History of Tennessee* (Boston, 1888), pp. 394–395; R. C. H. Catterall, *The Second Bank of the United States* (Chicago, 1903), p. 183.

18. Thomas Emmerson to John Overton, October 24, 1820, John Overton Papers (Tennessee Historical Society library); P. M. Miller to Jackson, August 9, 1820, Jackson Papers (Library of Congress); *Nashville Gazette*, June 20, 1820; *Knoxville Register*, June 20, 1820.

19. Jackson to Captain James Gadsden, August 1, 1819, *Correspondence of Andrew Jackson*, II, 421; *Nashville Clarion*, July 13, 1819.

economic crises do their worst only among the trading and speculating classes, but in new country the farmers are the speculators.
The result in this case was that the democracy, for the first time,
rose up to demand legislative relief.

In Tennessee the agitation was led by Felix Grundy, who piloted
through the assembly a bill providing for the establishment of a
loan office.[20] The state was to furnish the capital, the legislature
was to elect the directors, and the loans were to be apportioned
among the counties according to the taxes paid in each. A "stay"
law was also enacted, which provided that any creditor who
refused to receive the notes issued by the loan office, or state bank,
as it was called, would be required to wait two years before he
could enforce collection of his debt.[21] These measures were
passed by the votes of Middle Tennessee, East Tennessee being
opposed.[22] For the first and last time, the debtors of the state were
clearly in the saddle.

Within a few months Kentucky established a loan office similar
to that of Tennessee,[23] and in 1823 Alabama launched a state-
owned bank.[24] Relief legislation was quite general throughout the
states south of New England.[25]

The only prominent men in Middle Tennessee who were conspicuous for their opposition to these measures were Edward Ward
and Andrew Jackson. They addressed a memorial of protest to the
assembly, which that body refused to accept on the ground that its
language was disrespectful to the lawmakers. The memorial did, in
fact, charge the members who voted for the loan office act with
perjury since they had taken an oath to support the Constitution of
the United States, and now assented to a law which made something besides gold and silver a tender in payment of debts.[26]

In 1821 Tennessee experienced one of her most exciting gubernatorial elections. The candidates were Edward Ward and William
Carroll. The former was he who had, together with Jackson,

20. *Knoxville Register,* July 18, 1820.
21. Tennessee Public Acts, 1820, p. 13.
22. Tennessee Assembly, *Journal of the House,* 1820, p. 129.
23. *Nashville Gazette,* December 9, 1820.
24. Abernethy, p. 99.
25. Thomas H. Benton, *Thirty Years' View* (New York, 1854), I, 5.
26. *Nashville Clarion,* July 25, 1820; *Knoxville Register,* August 15, 1820.

protested against the loan office; he was a native of Virginia, a man of education and wealth, and a neighbor to General Jackson.[27] The latter was a merchant from Pennsylvania who had opened the first nail store in Nashville. He was a young man of energy and address, and Jackson had befriended him in his early days. As Major General of Tennessee militia he had served with signal distinction at the Battle of New Orleans, but a break, the causes of which are obscure, developed between him and Jackson in 1816.[28]

In the contest of 1821 Jackson used his influence in support of Ward, and looked upon Carroll and his friends as a group of demagogues.[29] The press of the state entered heartily into the campaign and Carroll was touted as a man of the people—an unpretentious merchant, without wealth and without social prestige—whereas Ward's wealth, his slaves, and his education were held against him. He was pictured in the press as a snobbish representative of the aristocracy of the planters.[30]

Both candidates were opposed to the loan office of 1820. Ward advocated a centralized state-banking system in place of it,[31] whereas Carroll simply stressed a policy of retrenchment.[32] The people appear to have discovered that the legislative relief was no panacea for their financial ills, and they were ready to accept Carroll's harsher doctrine of economy. They were beginning to understand that farmers, whose profits did not often run above five per cent, could not afford to borrow from banks at six per cent. Carroll carried every county in the state except two,[33] and the mere magnitude of the victory indicates that his success was due to his reputation for democracy rather than to his merchant-class economic ideas.

27. Hale and Merritt, *A History of Tennessee and Tennesseans* (Chicago, 1913), II, 267.

28. Jackson to Coffee, February 2, 1816, Papers of John Coffee (Tennessee Historical Society library).

29. Jackson to Coffee, July 26, 1821, *ibid.;* Jackson to Captain John Donelson, September 2, 1821, Jackson Papers.

30. *Knoxville Register,* July 17, 1821; *Nashville Clarion,* July 18, 1821.

31. *Nashville Gazette,* June 2, 1821; *Nashville Clarion,* June 13, 1821; *Knoxville Register,* June 16, 1821.

32. *Nashville Clarion,* June 27, 1821.

33. *Ibid.,* August 15, 1821.

With the exception of a one-term intermission made necessary by the state constitution, William Carroll presided over the government of Tennessee continuously until 1835. He was the most constructive Governor who ever held office in the state, for, curiously enough, it was he who, staunchly opposed by Jackson, established "Jacksonian democracy" within her borders. He believed in government of, for, and by the people, but he also believed in a financial policy of specie payments and legislative noninterference between debtor and creditor. Under his leadership, Tennessee disavowed the kind of democracy which had mounted into the saddle on the heels of the Panic of 1819, and of which Felix Grundy had been the protagonist.

In his first message to the general assembly, the new chief magistrate outlined his policy. He stuck tenaciously to his program throughout his twelve years in office, and, though it was slow work, nearly every item of his platform was finally carried into effect. In 1821 he advocated the erection of a penitentiary and the abolition of the use of the whipping post, the pillory, and the branding iron. These changes were finally brought about in 1831.[34] Imprisonment for debt was abolished at the same time.[35] In 1821 the "stay" law of 1820 was held unconstitutional by the supreme court of the state.[36] In 1826 the law of 1817 which prevented the establishment of a branch of the Bank of the United States in Tennessee was repealed with few dissenting votes in the lower house of the legislature,[37] and accordingly that institution established an office in Nashville during the following year. In 1831 the loan office of 1820 was abolished upon Carroll's recommendation,[38] and in 1832 and 1833 several important privately owned banks of the usual commercial type were established.[39]

34. See messages of 1821 and 1823, Tennessee Assembly, *Journal of the Senate,* 1821, pp. 86–99; *Journal of the House,* 1823, pp. 9–15.

35. Tennessee Public Acts, 1831, p. 56.

36. Townsend *v.* Townsend *et al., Tennessee Reports* (Peck), pp. 1–21.

37. Tennessee Public Acts, 1826, p. 18; Tennessee Assembly, *Journal of the House,* 1826, pp. 173–174.

38. Tennessee Assembly, *Journal of the Senate,* 1831, pp. 6–9; *Journal of the House,* 1831, pp. 41 *et seq.*

39. Tennessee Public Acts, 1832, pp. 2–13, and 1833, pp. 30–42; Phelan, pp. 267–268.

The sales of the public lands belonging to the state, which had been put upon a credit basis in 1819, were put upon a cash basis in 1823,[40] and the prices were graduated according to the principle later advocated in Congress by Thomas H. Benton.[41] Finally, after several unsuccessful attempts had been made in the legislature to bring the question before the people, a referendum was held and a constitutional convention assembled in 1834.[42] The new instrument of government which was now drawn up and adopted provided for a revision of the judicial system which would facilitate the collection of debts, for popular election of county officials, and for the taxation of real estate according to its value. Thus democracy won its victory in Tennessee, and the guiding spirit was that of William Carroll.

Up to this time, the state had gone through three distinct political phases. The first, extending from 1796 until the Panic of 1819, was a period during which the people gratefully and implicitly accepted the leadership of a group of outstanding citizens. The frontiersman was busy with his clearings and he gladly accepted the services of such energetic men as would organize governments and fight the Indians. The fact that these same men were usually land speculators did not disturb him even if he knew it. Land was cheap.

The second period was that of the Panic of 1819, during which economic ills aroused the people to a consciousness of their political power. Felix Grundy was the first to see the possibilities of the situation and to organize the movement for his own advancement. He was the first, but by no means the last, demagogue of Tennessee. Carroll won the people away from him and inaugurated the third period, which was one of constructive social and conservative economic legislation. It is noteworthy that until 1829 both Carroll and the legislature favored federal as well as state banks, nor does anything in the history of the state indicate

40. Whitney, *Land Laws of Tennessee* (Chattanooga, 1891), pp. 387–394.
41. *Ibid.,* pp. 398–400; see also Sioussat, pp. 54–58.
42. The question of calling a convention was voted on by the assembly and defeated in 1821, 1823, and 1826. It was finally carried by the assembly and ratified by popular vote in 1833.

that there was any general feeling against such institutions before Jackson became President.

It was well for Tennessee that Carroll remained so long in office, for the demagogue was not dead. The people had been aroused and Grundy had taught a lesson to the politicians. Public office was eagerly sought by the young lawyers and others, and electioneering, unknown in the earlier days, grew rapidly in vogue during the period following 1819. Stump speaking came to be an art and cajolery a profession, while whisky flowed freely at the hustings. The politicians could most easily attain their object by appealing to the prejudices of the masses. Colleges were said to exist for the rich, and the ignorant were asked to elect the ignorant because enlightenment and intelligence were not democratic.[43] America, to say nothing of Tennessee, has not outlived his brand of democracy.

It was during the years of Carroll's supremacy that the Jackson Presidential boom took shape and ran its course. The relation between this movement and the rise of Western democracy is of considerable interest for the reason that the two have ordinarily been considered as amounting to practically the same thing. The truth of the matter is that Jackson had little to do with the development of the democracy of the West. The movement made him President, but he contributed to it not one idea previously to his election in 1828. He rode into office upon a military reputation and the appeal which a self-made man can make so effectively to self-made men.

It did not take as astute a politician as Aaron Burr to see the possibility of making the Hero of New Orleans President of the United States. Not only Burr, but Edward Livingston and others saw it shortly after January 8, 1815.[44] In fact, the General himself probably saw it, but did not admit it. He at least began

43. For suggestions on this topic see J. W. M. Breazeale, "Satirical Burlesque upon the Practice of Electioneering," *Life as It Is* (Knoxville, 1842), pp. 158–226; and "An Address to Farmers and Mechanics," *Works of Philip Lindsley* (Philadelphia, 1866), III, 265–316.

44. J. S. Bassett, *The Life of Andrew Jackson* (New York, 1925), p. 279; William Carroll to Jackson, October 4, 1815; *Correspondence of Andrew Jackson*, II, 217–218; James Parton, *Life of Andrew Jackson* (Boston, 1887), II, 350.

taking a keen interest in national politics and set himself the agreeable task of helping Monroe keep Crawford out of the chief magistracy,[45] for the enmity between the General and the Secretary dates from 1816. It arose as a result of an agreement which Crawford negotiated with the Cherokees during that year, according to the terms of which the Indians were allowed to retain three million acres of land which the Creeks had claimed and which had been ceded to the government by Jackson's treaty of 1813. The Cherokees were also allowed damages for depredations alleged to have been committed by Jackson's troops during the course of the Creek campaign.[46] The General considered this a slur on his military reputation, and the author of it was duly condemned. It was also good political material, for Crawford was made to appear an enemy of the Western heroes and an opponent of westward expansion. It was only after the election of 1820, however, that the friends of Jackson could tactfully avow their intention to make him President, and the movement did not actually take shape until after his retirement from the Governorship of Florida in 1821.

At the time when Jackson resigned this commission and returned to the Hermitage to spend his declining years "surrounded by the pleasures of domestic felicity," a little group of friends in Nashville was forming to make plans of campaign for their distinguished fellow-townsman. The leaders of this group were William B. Lewis, John Overton, and John H. Eaton.

The first-named was a planter and Jackson's neighbor. He was a close personal friend and adviser of long standing, but he was not a man of large affairs. Parton has overestimated his importance because he obtained much of his information on the campaign from Lewis himself.[47] John Overton was a former member of the supreme court of Tennessee and one of the richest men in the

45. A. P. Hayne to Jackson, January 21, 1819, Jackson Papers; Hayne to Jackson, March 6, 1819; Jackson to Governor Clark of Georgia, April 20, 1819; *Correspondence of Andrew Jackson,* II, 412, 416; Address of Enoch Parsons, March 25, 1819, Jackson Papers; Jackson to Coffee, April 3, 1819, Coffee Papers.

46. Parton, II, 355–356; Bassett, *Life of Andrew Jackson,* p. 281; *Nashville Whig,* July 31, 1819; Jackson to Monroe, October 10, 1823, Jackson Papers; Jackson to Crawford, June 10, 13[?], and 16, 1816, *Correspondence of Andrew Jackson,* II, 243–250.

47. Parton, III, 17.

state. At that time he and Jackson were partners in a large land deal: namely, the establishment of a trading town on the Mississippi by the name of Memphis.[48] They were closely associated in Jackson's political venture, too, and Overton later burned the papers relating thereto so that the curious might not pry into its details.[49] In 1816 John H. Eaton, then comparatively unknown in Tennessee, undertook to complete a biography of Jackson.[50] In 1818 he was appointed to the United States Senate,[51] and in 1819 he defended the General when the Seminole campaign was before that body for investigation.[52] From his vantage point in Washington he served as field agent for the little group of Nashville managers.

Both Overton and Eaton were accused of having entertained Federalist opinions in their early days.[53] There was certainly nothing in the background or the connections of the group to tie it up with the democratic movement which was in full tide about them. In 1823 a former judge who had sat with Overton in the supreme court of the state wrote to him: "True republicanism must supersede the Democracy of the present day before public employment will be suited to my taste. . . . There are too many who would prefer a directly contrary state of things."[54] At about this time Jackson himself was keenly interested in a legal scheme to throw open to question the titles to about half the occupied lands in Tennessee. This, of course, was in the interest of speculators like himself. The legislature however set itself against the plan and it failed miserably.[55]

48. Phelan, p. 317.
49. W. W. Clayton, *History of Davidson County, Tennessee* (Philadelphia, 1880), p. 99.
50. *Nashville Whig,* June 4, 1816.
51. C. A. Miller, *Official and Political Manual of the State of Tennessee* (Nashville, 1890), p. 173.
52. Jackson to William Williams, September 25, 1819, *Correspondence of Andrew Jackson,* II, 430.
53. *Nashville Clarion,* January 5, 1819; Phelan, p. 241.
54. Thomas Emmerson to John Overton, May 25, 1823; see also Emmerson to Overton, December 26, 1823, and June 3, 1824, Overton Papers.
55. This had to do with a decision of the state supreme court which overruled former decisions and declared that titles to land, in order to be valid, must be connected by an unbroken chain with the original grant, and that occupiers might be ejected even though they held under color of title.

The General had no personal dealings with either Grundy or Carroll during the early years of his candidacy, and though Grundy, with an eye to personal advancement, refused to break with him politically, and Carroll was later reconciled, it is significant that the latter is the only outstanding Tennessee Democrat who did not, sooner or later, receive federal recognition at the hands of Jackson's party.

Yet Jackson's political views were little known outside Tennessee at the time when he began to be looked upon as Presidential timber. His strength lay in his military reputation, in his connection with the expansion of the West at the expense of the Spanish and Indians, and in the fact that he was not closely connected with the intrigue of Washington politics. A movement to turn out the "Virginia dynasty" and to forestall Crawford, the "heir apparent," was inevitable. The dissatisfied element in the Southern and Middle states instinctively turned to Jackson as the logical instrument for this purpose, and certainly no role could have been more congenial to the General than one which cast him in opposition to William H. Crawford.

The first statement that he was being definitely considered for the Presidency came from Pennsylvania in 1821, where the leaders were said to have canvassed the situation and found that he was the logical man.[56] North Carolina followed the lead of Pennsylvania,[57] and word came from Virginia that the people were for Jackson, but that leadership was needed in order that the politicians be overthrown.[58]

The movement in Tennessee was brought to the surface in 1822 when it was proposed that the general assembly present the General's name to the nation as a suitable candidate for the

---

The legislature added another justice to the court, and John Catron, afterward Justice of the United States Supreme Court, was appointed to fill the place in order that this decision might be annulled. Jackson had a personal interest in the matter and denounced the action of the legislature. See Jackson to Coffee, April 15 and May 24, 1823, Coffee Papers. For the legal phase of the question, see Barton's Lessee *v.* Shall, *Tennessee Reports* (Peck), p. 172.

56. S. R. Overton to Jackson, August 1, 1821, Jackson Papers.
57. A. D. Murphy to John H. Eaton, January 16, 1824, Overton Papers.
58. Thomas G. Watkins to Jackson, March 13, 1822, Jackson Papers.

Presidency. The proposition was carried by that body without a dissenting vote.[59] This in the face of the fact that Jackson's candidate for the Governorship had been defeated during the previous year by an overwhelming majority. This apparently conflicting vote merely shows that national and state politics were not closely related at that time. The General had been repudiated in no uncertain manner as a state politician, but as a national hero he was a success. Discredited because of his conservative stand in the state, he was chosen to lead the progressive movement in the nation.

A sidelight on the situation is afforded by an incident which occurred during the next year. Colonel John Williams, of Knoxville, had represented Tennessee in the United States Senate since 1815, and had attacked Jackson during the Seminole investigation of 1819.[60] His term expired in 1823, and he was up for re-election with excellent prospects of success. Jackson's friends decided that his Presidential prospects would be blighted by the election of one of his bitterest enemies to the Senate from his own state, and when no other candidate could develop sufficient strength to defeat Williams, the General himself was, at the last minute, induced to run.[61] A number of the members of the legislature had already pledged their votes to Williams and could not change, but the ballot, when counted, stood twenty-five to thirty-five in favor of Jackson. The names of those voting were not recorded in the journal—a significant omission. Tennesseans would not permit Jackson to dictate to them, but his personal prestige was great, and there were few who dared stand against him face to face.

Jackson went to the Senate against his will. Back in 1798 he

59. Jackson to Dr. J. C. Bronaugh, August 1, 1822, and S. R. Overton to Jackson, September 10, 1822, Jackson Papers; *Nashville Whig,* July 31, 1822. See also Grundy to Jackson, June 27, 1822, Jackson Papers.

60. Jackson to William Williams, September 25, 1819, *Correspondence of Andrew Jackson,* II, 430.

61. Thomas L. Williams to Overton, September 10, 1823, Overton Papers; William Brady and Thomas Williamson to Jackson, September 20, 1823, and Jackson to Brady and Williamson, September 27, 1823, Jackson Papers; Jackson to Coffee, October 5, 1823, Coffee Papers; *Knoxville Register,* October 10, 1823.

had resigned from that body after a year of uncongenial service. He was now returned to the national forum at the behest of friends who had previously devoted their best efforts to keeping him quiet. Yet it was not because he was afraid to speak his mind that he shrank from the Senate. Above all things, save perhaps a good fight, the General liked to speak his mind. That he gave in so often to his advisers shows that he was not devoid of political discretion. His real objection to Washington, as he so often stated, was its partisan intrigue. There was too much competition in the capital.

There was no doubt but that, before the Presidential election, Jackson's hand would be revealed in regard to the important questions which were agitating the country. It was a brave stand for a General in politics to take, but he took it unequivocally. He voted consistently for internal improvements and for the tariff of 1824.[62]

Jackson posed as a Jeffersonian, as did nearly all the Southern Republicans of his day, and in 1822 he had written to Monroe congratulating him upon the veto of the Cumberland Road bill.[63] Yet Tennessee needed internal improvements and ardently desired them. As late as 1825 James K. Polk advocated federal aid for such purposes.[64] In voting as he did in 1824, Jackson represented the interests of his constituents, but during the same year he expressed the opinion that the consent of the state should be secured before the national government should give assistance.[65] During 1827 his supporters in the Tennessee legislature were said to have opposed a federal aid project because of the effect that the agitation of such a question by them might have upon the Presidential election in Pennsylvania and Virginia.[66] Finally, when the General became President, he vetoed the Maysville Road bill on the ground that the thoroughfare in question was one of only local importance. The fact was, however, that it was the main highway —an extension of the old Cumberland Road—along which the

62. Bassett, *Life of Andrew Jackson,* pp. 344–345.
63. Jackson to Monroe, July 26, 1822, Jackson Papers.
64. Phelan, p. 396.
65. Jackson to James W. Lanier, May [?] 1824, Jackson Papers; Jackson to Polk, December 4, 1826, Polk Papers.
66. *Knoxville Enquirer,* January 9, 1828.

Eastern mail was, at the very time, being carried to Nashville and the Southwest.[67]

In his stand on the tariff question in 1824, Jackson stressed the military importance of domestic manufactures, and also argued for the development of a home market for agricultural products.[68] In this matter he doubtless voiced his personal convictions. The home-market argument had an appeal for the grain farmers of the West, and there were more grain farmers in Tennessee than there were cotton planters, yet Jackson himself belonged to the latter group and protection was not popular with them as a class. Furthermore, despite the rise of democracy, the wealthy cotton planters still had a large share in the creation of public opinion, and there were, in Tennessee, few active advocates of a high tariff before 1840.[69]

In regard to the Bank of the United States, Jackson's views were not developed until after the period of his Senatorial services. He certainly did not take a stand against that institution before 1826. In 1827 he began making unfavorable comments on it, but public opposition did not develop until after his election to the Presidency.[70] This was clearly not a question of long-standing prejudice with him, and the evidence seems to point to Van Buren as the source of his opinions on the subject.[71] In addition to this, Jackson knew that most of the branches of the Bank were in the hands of his opponents and had good reason to believe that their influence was used against him during the election of 1828.[72] It was entirely Jacksonian for him to form his opinion upon such grounds.

Jackson had once been a merchant and he was still a man of business affairs. He had long been a believer in a sound currency and the rights of the creditor. His early economic ideas were in

67. J. P. Bretz, "Early Land Communication with the Lower Mississippi Valley," *Mississippi Valley Historical Review*, XIII, 27–29.

68. Jackson to Coffee, May 7, 1824, and Jackson to John Overton, June 18, 1824, Coffee Papers; Parton, III, 35–36.

69. Phelan, p. 425.

70. Catterall, pp. 183–184.

71. R. L. Colt to Biddle, January 7, 1829, June 10, 1830, and Henry Clay to Biddle, June 14, 1830, R. C. McGrane, ed., *The Correspondence of Nicholas Biddle*, pp. 66–67, 104, 105.

72. William B. Lewis to Biddle, October 16, 1829, pp. 79–80, and Biddle to George Hoffman, November 22, 1829, *ibid.*, pp. 87–88.

accord with those of William Carroll, and there was nothing here to bring him into conflict with the Bank of the United States. The motives of his opposition were political, not economic.

No historian has ever accused Jackson, the great Democrat, of having had a political philosophy. It is hard to see that he even had any political principles. He was a man of action, and the man of action is likely to be an opportunist. Politically speaking, Jackson was certainly an opportunist. If he gave any real help or encouragement before 1828 to any of the movements which, under men like Carroll, aimed at the amelioration of the condition of the masses, the fact has not been recorded. He belonged to the moneyed aristocracy of Nashville, yet he was a self-made man and devoid of snobbishness. He thought he was sincere when he spoke to the people, yet he never really championed their cause. He merely encouraged them to champion his.

It seems clear that Jackson's political habits were formed in the period of the early settlement of the Southwest when a few leaders were able to shape the public mind and use their official positions as an aid to their exploitation of the land. He never failed, for instance, to use the patronage of office for the promotion of the interests of his friends. The democratic awakening which took such hold upon the people of Tennessee after the Panic of 1819 failed to enlist his sympathy. He was called upon to lead the national phase of this movement, but played no part in the formulation or promotion of its constructive program. He did, however, in 1824, represent the needs of the West for improved commercial facilities, and he was a nationalist from early conviction. After 1824 he came under political influence—that of Van Buren, it seems, being paramount[73]—which caused him to change his earlier opinions in several respects. This accounts for the fact that his Presidential policy favored the seaboard staple growers rather than the grain producers of the West. Yet he failed, in the main, to capture the support of the cotton planters of the South, for many of them either sympathized with nullification or desired a United States bank and internal improvements. He was a political

---

73. Bassett, *Life of Andrew Jackson,* pp. 484–489; *David Crockett's Circular,* pamphlet in Library of Congress (Washington, 1831), pp. 2–5.

hybrid—too strong a nationalist for some, too strong a states-rights man for others. On the other hand, he held to the end the loyalty of the small farmers, for the Jacksonian tradition was deeply rooted in them, and Jackson's bank policy looked to them like democracy. Banks often worked to their disadvantage, and they could manage without commercial facilities. They constituted the rank and file of the Democratic party in the South until the Whig organization went to pieces and the planters were thereby forced to accept, at a late date, the bait which Jackson had proffered them in vain.

✪

Boom for President

The contagious enthusiasm for General Andrew Jackson that in 1824 swept thousands of voters for the first time out of their accustomed tutelage to the established leaders demands careful study as a major phenomenon in the history of political democracy. It demands study also as an example of the frequently neglected influence of local political maneuvers on national developments. Though a few historians have intimated that Old Hickory's popularity could not have been converted into an electoral plurality without the aid of disgruntled politicians pursuing conventional factional and personal advantages in the various states,[1] little attention has been paid to the Tennessee politicians who brought him before the country in the first place.

The accepted interpretation assumes that the men behind Jackson's candidacy—principally Judge John Overton, Senator John H. Eaton, Felix Grundy, and Major William B. Lewis—were moved by sincere admiration and affection for their friend. They are also credited with a shrewd perception that the groundswell of democratic discontent building up beneath the surface of American politics might be mobilized to make the popular General

1. See especially Philip S. Klein, *Pennsylvania Politics 1817–1832: A Game without Rules* (Philadelphia, 1940), pp. 117–124.

Reprinted from "Jackson Men with Feet of Clay," *The American Historical Review*, Vol. LXII (April 1957), pp. 537–550. Supplemented with parts of Charles Sellers, "Banking and Politics in Jackson's Tennessee, 1817–1827," reprinted from *The Mississippi Valley Historical Review*, Vol. XLI (June 1954), pp. 75–81, 83–84.

President.[2] A close scrutiny of the events of 1821–1823 in Tennessee reveals, however, that the objectives of Judge Overton and most of his associates were by no means so large and disinterested. There is evidence to show that Jackson was nominated for the Presidency only in order that specific local political advantages could be achieved and that "the original Jackson men" actually favored other nominees.

When General Jackson retired to private life in the winter of 1821–1822, seven years had elapsed since his victory over the British at New Orleans had made him a national hero. The sporadic talk that he might be a Presidential possibility had never been entertained seriously in any responsible quarter, and Jackson himself had never taken it seriously. President-making was still left exclusively to the political leaders, and they were already grooming more than enough entries for the Presidential sweepstakes of 1824. Already in the field, or soon to be there, were the major contenders: President Monroe's Secretary of State, John Quincy Adams of Massachusetts; the Secretary of the Treasury, William H. Crawford of Georgia; the Secretary of War, John C. Calhoun of South Carolina; and the Speaker of the national House of Representatives, Henry Clay of Kentucky. Among the long shots being mentioned were Congressman William Lowndes of South Carolina, soon to be removed by death, and Governor DeWitt Clinton, leader of the opposition to Martin Van Buren's pro-Crawford Bucktail faction in New York.

Jackson's attitude toward these candidates was dictated mainly by personal considerations. Grateful to Adams and Calhoun for their defense of his violent incursion into Spanish Florida in 1818, he was hostile to Crawford and Clay, whose friends had attacked the Florida expedition in Congress. Crawford was slated by the old-line Republican leaders to receive the nomination of the regular Congressional caucus, but Jackson declared that he "would support the Devil first."[3] The Georgian had earlier impugned some of

2. Cf. James Parton, *Life of Andrew Jackson* (New York, 1861), III, 11–23; J. S. Bassett, *The Life of Andrew Jackson* (New York, 1911), I, 326–329; Marquis James, *The Life of Andrew Jackson* (Indianapolis, 1938), pp. 335–353.

3. Jackson to James Gadsden, December 6, 1821, draft copy, Jackson Papers (Library of Congress).

Jackson's Indian treaties, and he was being supported by the General's personal and political enemies in Tennessee.

The exigencies of factional politics largely controlled the attitudes of Tennesseans generally toward the Presidential candidates. Overton, Eaton, and Lewis were associated with a faction that had dominated Tennessee for most of its history. Founded by William Blount, the architect of a fabulous land speculation involving most of the acreage in the state, this faction had been concerned primarily with making good its land claims and later with exploiting the possibilities of the banking business. Jackson had worked with this loosely knit group in his early days of political activity, and he was still personally intimate with Overton, now its unofficial leader, Eaton, Lewis, and their principal allies in East Tennessee, Overton's brother-in-law, Hugh Lawson White, and Pleasant M. Miller, a son-in-law of William Blount.

John Sevier had led the opposition to the Blount-Overton faction in the state's first years; more recently his mantle had fallen on a group of vigorous men who were all deadly personal enemies of Andrew Jackson. They included Senator John Williams and several Congressmen, while their principal strategist was a Middle Tennessee planter and land speculator, Colonel Andrew Erwin, with whom Jackson was, in 1822, engaged in a bitter litigation that brought Erwin to the brink of financial ruin.[4]

Since Erwin and his friends were solidly in the Crawford camp, the Blount-Overton men were certain to be anti-Crawford, and Jackson undoubtedly hoped to line them up behind Adams or Calhoun. This hope was threatened, however, when Henry Clay entered the Presidential competition as the first Western candidate in the history of the office, attracting strong support that cut across factional lines in Tennessee. Judge Overton had visited Clay in the summer of 1821, and as soon as the Kentuckian became a candidate, the Judge promised him Tennessee's electoral votes. Clay got additional support from another important Tennessee politician, Felix Grundy, who a decade before had worked closely with him as one of the Congressional War Hawks in precipitating

4. Charles G. Sellers, Jr., "Banking and Politics in Jackson's Tennessee, 1817–1827," *Mississippi Valley Historical Review*, XLI (June 1954).

the War of 1812. Grundy, like Overton, had been in communication with Clay during 1821, urging him to become a candidate and assuring him of Tennessee's support. Still another Clay backer was Governor William Carroll.[5]

Overton, Grundy, and Carroll spanned the political spectrum in Tennessee, and a union of their followers for the Kentuckian would have insured his success in the state. Overton and his faction had been in eclipse since the Panic of 1819, which had generated a storm of public resentment against the banks they operated. Grundy, the only important Tennessee politician not identified with either major faction, had shrewdly capitalized on this popular discontent to become the dominant figure in the legislature, while veering back and forth between the two factions. Carroll was the ultimate beneficiary of the panic-generated discontent. Running as the Erwin faction's candidate for Governor in 1821, he won a smashing victory over the Blount-Overton candidate. It was, in fact, the Overton men's desperate efforts to regain their ascendancy that led to Jackson's nomination for President.

The accounts left by Major Lewis and Judge Overton both indicate that the movement to nominate Jackson developed in the winter of 1821–1822, hard on the heels of Carroll's election. According to Lewis, the General's friends around Nashville "began now to speak of him as a candidate and, in *good earnest,* to take the necessary steps to place his name prominently before the country." The first public manifestation of the movement, Lewis continues, was an article in one of the Nashville newspapers in January, 1822, and soon afterward the *Nashville Gazette,* organ of the Blount-Overton faction, "took the field openly and boldly for the General."[6]

Overton's account is similar, but he claims credit for originating the movement. Early in 1822, says the Judge, "it forcibly struck me that he [Jackson] ought to be the next President and by proper

5. Overton to Clay, January 16, 1822, Henry Clay Papers (Library of Congress); *Nashville Constitutional Advocate,* September 17, 1822.

6. Lewis to Governor Lewis Cass, undated letter, probably written in the 1840's (Henry L. Huntington Library).

means might be made so." Overton goes on to recall that he had "praises thrown out" in the *Nashville Gazette*. "They were lightly thought of," he says, "but that made no difference with me."[7]

Contemporary evidence makes it clear, however, that Overton was not the first to envision Jackson as a Presidential candidate. Indeed, even after the Jackson talk had started, the Judge preferred another. In a letter of January 16, 1822, he assured Clay that "as far as I know the public mind, you will get all the votes in Tennessee in preference to any man whose name has been mentioned." Though Overton reported "some whispering conversation here that Jackson would suffer himself to be run," he was "almost certain that he will not, and my information is derived from good authority." The Judge added that Jackson could probably "beat you himself" in Tennessee, but that the General could not induce the voters to prefer Adams or Calhoun over Clay. Overton particularly requested Clay to keep his remarks confidential. "Inasmuch as I, and our family have always been friendly with Jackson," he wrote, "I should not like him to know of any interposition of mine on this subject."[8]

The apparent conflicts in the foregoing evidence are not irreconcilable. It would seem that the Jackson-for-President talk actually started with a group of politically ineffectual men around the General, most notably Major Lewis, that Overton was converted to the idea shortly after he wrote to Clay, and that Overton then instructed the *Gazette*'s editor to launch the public campaign. If things happened this way, Overton's claim that he initiated the movement is essentially valid, since without his support it would never have gotten beyond the stage of talk. At any rate, the movement was certainly being pushed "in *good earnest*" by February, when Jackson's wife complained that "Major Eaton, General Carroll, the Doctor and even the Parson and I can't tell how

7. Overton to his nephew, February 23, 1824, quoted in a sketch of Overton by Judge John M. Lea, a newspaper clipping in the Overton Papers on microfilm (Joint University Library, Nashville). In the letter, Overton dates these events in early 1821, but this is an obvious slip, since he speaks of them as immediately preceding the legislature's nomination of Jackson, which did not occur until 1822.

8. Overton to Clay, January 16, 1822, Clay Papers.

many others—all of his friends who come here—talk everlastingly about his being President."[9]

Why did Overton throw his great influence behind the Jackson movement? Much of the answer to this question may be found in a letter he received about the time he must have been making his decision. On January 27, Pleasant M. Miller of Knoxville, leader of the Blount-Overton forces in the lower house of the legislature, wrote to the Judge suggesting that Jackson should be run for Governor in 1823.[10] Though Miller's epistolary style was highly ambiguous, the most casual reader could hardly miss his reiterated suggestions that Jackson's popularity might be used to effect certain local political objectives. Overton would have had no trouble understanding Miller's intimations that Governor Carroll, whose overwhelming strength was the chief obstacle to a Blount-Overton comeback, might thus be defeated at the state elections of 1823, that a new legislature purged of Jackson's enemies from the Erwin-Carroll faction might be elected at the same time, and that the various legislative purposes of the Blount-Overton men might thus be achieved.[11]

A single paragraph of Miller's long letter will sufficiently suggest its tone:

1st is there any man whose personal popularity is so likely to assist in fixing the seat of government permanently at any given point as Andrew Jackson, if so why should he not be the next governor, or why should this not be wish[ed] for by those who desire this result. I am satisfied that this cannot be done with the present legislature.

A more reliable legislature could be elected along with Jackson in 1823, Miller was suggesting. Even in Bedford County, Andrew

9. Augustus C. Buell, *History of Andrew Jackson: Pioneer, Patriot, Soldier, Politician, President* (New York, 1904), II, 157–158.

10. Miller to Overton, January 27, 1822, John Overton Papers (Claybrooke Collection, Tennessee Historical Society, Nashville).

11. Among the issues to which Miller alluded were the location of the state capital and a proposed penitentiary, land legislation in which the speculators were vitally interested, and revision of the state judiciary. The judicial question was related to the land issue, the state supreme court having recently made a ruling disastrous to the speculators, and Overton was anxious to return to the supreme bench for the purpose of rectifying matters. See Patrick H. Darby to Jackson, July 4, 1821, Jackson Papers.

Erwin's stronghold, Miller was confident the Jackson question
would be potent enough to insure the right kind of representation.
In addition, Senator John Williams, whose term was expiring,
could be replaced by a reliable Blount-Overton man. Miller had
himself in mind for this position, as subsequently appeared.

At the time Miller wrote, there was talk of calling a special
session of the legislature to meet during the summer. This legislature, having been elected along with Carroll the previous year, was
untrustworthy from the Blount-Overton point of view. Hence
Miller was anxious to prevent a special session, or if it were called,
to keep it from acting on the matters he mentioned.

Miller had got wind of the talk about running Jackson for
President, and he was by no means opposed to the idea, his
comments implying that the General had no chance to be elected,
but that his candidacy might yield certain collateral advantages.
Miller was reported to favor Adams for the Presidency about this
time,[12] and though his meaning is obscure, his letter of January
27 seems to suggest that Tennessee and other Southern states
cooperate with the smaller Northeastern states in electing the New
England candidate. Jackson's nomination would actually help
Adams in the Electoral College by depriving Crawford and Clay of
votes from Tennessee, Alabama, Mississippi, and Louisiana, in
most of which the New Englander had no chance anyhow. Crawford's defeat would aid in prostrating the Erwin-Carroll faction in
Tennessee. Miller knew that Grundy "has different views at the
called session," which doubtless meant a plan to nominate Clay.
But, he told Overton, "I know that if you fall in with my notions
that you will know how to act." He particularly urged the Judge to
"take time to consider of these matters so far as they concern our
local affairs & ascertain how far certain persons will act on them,"
and concluded by promising to visit Nashville in March, when "we
can converse more freely."

Overton's desertion of Clay and endorsement of the Jackson
movement was substantially a fulfillment of Miller's hope that the
Judge would "fall in with my notions." The project of running

12. Statement of Hugh Lawson White, *Nashville Union,* September 25,
1835.

Jackson for Governor was found impracticable, but his nomination for President was to serve the same purposes. Although it was Miller who actually conceived the essential strategy first, Overton was doubtless responsible for abandoning the plan to run Jackson for Governor and concentrating on his Presidential candidacy. Early in the spring, Miller made his promised trip West to concert strategy with Overton. The special session had now been called for July, and it was agreed that this body should nominate Tennessee's hero formally.

Miller's subsequent letters to Overton throw further light on the motives of Jackson's two principal managers. "I have Jackson's interest deeply at heart," he wrote on June 8.[13] "I think I know how bringing him forward is to operate upon the next congressional election &c. &c. I should not have went to the west when I did but with this view, & I think the effects of my visit will shew itself in some shape." The time had come, he thought, "for the papers to come directly forward" and call on the legislature to nominate Jackson at the special session. "Tell Jackson to come up Wednesday of the first week while people are all in a good humour—ask his friends to see him," Miller advised. "He can say he feels proud he has once returned to private life. If he has any redgmental coat were it, put on little milletary dress &c. You know more I need say no more."

Miller did not hesitate to admit that "I have motives for this matter." Jackson's nomination was the best way of frustrating Senator Williams' plan to win re-election at the special session. "There ought not to be an election for Senator at this time," Miller insisted, "—these good people must be held in check & this is all the hold we have—in a state of excitement publick opinion will keep them down unless that election is over." Should Williams be re-elected, he predicted, there would be "a prodigious struggle" to realign Tennessee's Congressional districts so as to favor Erwinite Congressmen who "will in caucus vote for you knowho [Crawford]. I believe however I understand this matter tolerable well & expect to frustrate these views," Miller continued. "If I fail it will be the first time[.] keep your eye on [the] fidler & work even a head & let me alone for the rest." Almost parenthetically he

13. Miller to Overton, June 8, 1822, Overton Papers.

reported talk that "I am a candidate for the Senate, & that my visit to the west was to promote that view."

Several weeks later, Miller wrote again,[14] in terms indicating that he and Overton were working closely together toward mutually agreeable objectives. "I have rec[eive]d your two letters," he told the Judge, "& things will be attended to to your satisfaction in part or in whole. I am using all my exertions to bring old hickory to view during the approaching session."

Meanwhile Overton and Miller had acquired an important recruit. Felix Grundy had become estranged from the Erwin-Carroll men and, in danger of political isolation, was ready to jump aboard any bandwagon that happened along. The Jackson movement offered him a perfect opportunity to reinstate himself in the good graces of the Blount-Overton faction, and he did not hesitate. It was Grundy who on June 27 signed the note asking Jackson whether he had any objection to the proposed nomination.[15] Jackson seems not to have replied, but silence was as good as open assent.

The last possible obstacle removed, Overton, Miller, and Grundy now made their final preparations, and the Nashville newspapers endorsed the plan for a legislative nomination. State pride kept even the Erwin-Carroll men from opposing Jackson publicly,[16] though the editorial of endorsement in their organ, the *Nashville Clarion,* had a sarcastic ring. When the special session assembled on July 22, Miller was able to push his nominating resolutions through the lower house promptly, though the Erwin-Carroll men delayed action in the Senate for two weeks.[17]

14. Miller to Overton, June 25, 1822, *ibid.*

15. Grundy to Jackson, June 27, 1822, Jackson Papers. Grundy was probably enlisted during Miller's visit to Nashville in the spring. Miller had even foreseen Grundy's cooperation, having informed Overton in his letter of January 27 that Grundy had "abandoned the head of department at Nashville [Governor Carroll] & said that he would stick to me."

16. Andrew Hynes (an associate of Carroll) to Henry Clay, June 30, 1822, Clay Papers; James, p. 351.

17. James, pp. 352–353. Though inaccurate in details, Overton's account, cited in n. 7 above, illuminates the roles of the principals. "The Legislature met," says the Judge, "and then I communicated to a leading member my views which he gave into, communicated them to Grundy, who at first seemed a little surprised, but gave into the measure of recommending him by our Legislature which was done unanimously. The resolutions were

The reactions to Jackson's nomination by well-informed politicians outside the circle of Jackson managers were significant. All the comments that have been discovered agree in predicting that Jackson would not remain in the race as a serious contender. A month before the nomination, one of Governor Carroll's associates, Colonel Andrew Hynes, had informed Clay that Jackson had no hope of being elected and that he was being brought forward "not so much with view of promoting his own elevation, as to subserve an Eastern or Northern interest."[18] The same explanation was advanced as late as the summer of 1823 by that astute politician, Thomas Hart Benton, following a two-month tour of Tennessee in the interest of Clay. "Jackson out of the way the state will go for you," Benton told the Kentuckian, "and there is hardly anyone who thinks he has any chance, and many see in his offering nothing but a diversion in favor of Adams."[19]

During the special session of 1822, Colonel Hynes discovered an additional explanation for the nomination. According to a "secret rumor that is afloat in the air," he informed Clay, Jackson's nomination was designed mainly to affect the Senatorial election.[20] This was corroborated by a Colonel McClung, one of the leading citizens of Knoxville, who asserted that Pleasant M. Miller had "played off this manouvre to bring Jacksons name to bear, & make a point in the election of Senator." McClung was confident that Williams would be re-elected by the special session despite the Jackson movement and that "so soon as the election of Senator is over, we shall hear no more of a Tenn. candidate for the office of President."[21] McClung's judgment was wrong, for Miller's strategy succeeded in blocking Williams' re-election at the special session, and the Senatorial election was postponed to the regular session of 1823.

---

preceded by a speech which I wrote for a member." Most of these negotiations took place, as we have seen, some time before the legislature met. The "leading member" was unquestionably Miller.

18. Hynes to Clay, June 30, 1822, Clay Papers.
19. Benton to Clay, July 23, 1823, *ibid*.
20. Hynes to Clay, July 31, 1822, *ibid*.
21. McClung's remarks were reported by one of Clay's correspondents, George C. Thompson. Thompson to Clay, August 12, 1822, *ibid*.

Meanwhile, Governor Carroll was spreading reports that Jackson would probably not remain long in the running and telling Clay that he still had a good chance for Tennessee. The Governor also informed the Kentuckian that Grundy had promised to support him "if the prospects of Jackson became hopeless . . . and that he would indeavour to have you nominated at the next meeting of our legislature."[22] About the same time, Colonel Hynes was in New Orleans assuring the Louisiana politicians that Tennessee would ultimately go for Clay.[23]

Skepticism about the seriousness of Jackson's candidacy was also expressed by one of his sincere admirers. "Whatever may be the estimate in which he is held by the people of this State (and surely even here he is very differently estimated)," wrote Thomas Claiborne to a friend in Virginia, "I confess that I fear he will not be likely to unite sufficient strength in other States to secure his election. There are too many great men in other States to suffer a man from the young & small State of Tennessee at the present day to be made President of the United States."[24]

Whatever their ultimate purposes or expectations, Miller and his allies did everything they could to raise a Jackson excitement in the state campaign of 1823. Meetings to endorse Jackson were organized all over the state; pro-Jackson candidates for Congress and the legislature were put up in most districts; office-seekers were called upon to say whether they would vote against Williams for Senator and for Jackson in the Presidential election; and an unsuccessful effort was made to induce Jackson to aid his supporters by touring East Tennessee.[25]

One of the hottest contests was in the Knoxville district, home of Williams, Miller, and Judge Hugh Lawson White, where Miller had entered a Doctor Wiatt as the pro-Jackson candidate for the

22. Carroll to Clay, February 1, 1823, *ibid.*

23. *Ibid.;* Isaac L. Baker to Jackson, March 3, 1823, Jackson Papers.

24. Claiborne to David Campbell, September 9, 1822, David Campbell Papers (Duke University Library).

25. Samuel Martin to Jackson, June 17, 1823, Jackson Papers; John Williams to Rufus King, November 19, 1823, Rufus King Papers (New York Historical Society); James Campbell to David Campbell, April 3, 1823 [misplaced 1825], Campbell Papers.

legislature against the Senator's brother, Thomas L. Williams.[26] This placed Judge White in a particularly embarrassing position. One of Jackson's oldest friends, a brother-in-law of Overton, and long a leader of the Blount-Overton faction, White was also related to Senator Williams and reluctant to oppose him. When he took the Williams side in the Knoxville legislative campaign, he and his sons became involved in such a bitter personal broil with the Miller-Wiatt party that several duels were barely averted.

"If Genl Jackson has any wishes or prospects of success, I never was more disposed to aid him than now," White explained to Overton; "but I will not, as far as I can prevent it, permit scoundrels by the use of his name, to effect their dishonest or dishonorable purposes." White never doubted that Miller's Senatorial aspirations lay at the root of the Jackson-for-President movement. "The whole cry is that Jackson must be President," he complained. "They have no more notion of trying to make him President than of making me. If he had a wish that way, and there was any prospect of success no three persons in this State would aid him more zealously than me and my sons; but I will not consent that scoundrels under a pretense of that kind shall rule, or tyrannize, over me and mine."[27] Recalling these events later, White maintained that Wiatt was in reality for Clay, while Miller wished "to use the name of Gen. Jackson, only for the purpose of securing the election of Mr. Adams, by dividing the western vote."[28]

When the state election finally occurred in August, 1923, the results were inconclusive. The Williamses defeated Miller's pro-Jackson candidate for the legislature in the Knoxville district, but Andrew Erwin lost to a pro-Jackson candidate for Congress, and a pro-Jackson legislator was elected in Erwin's bailiwick, Bedford County.

Meanwhile there had been two important new developments. First, an astonishing and unprecedented upsurge of grass-roots

26. J. G. M. Ramsey to Francis P. Blair, October 5, 1835, Blair-Lee Papers (Princeton University Library).

27. White to Overton, January 30, 1823, Overton Papers. White expressed similar sentiments in a letter to David Campbell, June 19, 1823, Campbell Papers.

28. Quoted in the *Nashville Union*, September 25, 1835.

support for Jackson had manifested itself in various places outside Tennessee. A veritable "contagion" of Jacksonism was spreading over Alabama, as an alarmed Clay backer had to admit, and it rapidly attained sufficient proportions to block the expected election of a Crawford man as United States Senator.[29] Major Lewis had been sounding out North Carolina and Mississippi politicians with surprisingly gratifying results.[30] Most startling of all was the outburst of Jackson sentiment in Pennsylvania, stemming, as one of Calhoun's lieutenants sneered, from "the grog shop politicians of the villages & the rabble of Philadelphia & Pittsburgh."[31] But contempt quickly turned into intense concern when the swelling Jackson enthusiasm prevented the anticipated nomination of Calhoun by the state Republican convention in March.[32] Major Lewis was virtually the only member of Jackson's inner circle who seems to have anticipated anything like this. As early as October, 1822, he had predicted that Jackson's popularity with the masses would give him such states as Pennsylvania and North Carolina, that Calhoun would be forced to withdraw, and that Jackson would fall heir to the South Carolinian's following.[33] At the time it was written, Lewis' estimate had been the wildest optimism, but by the summer of 1823 it was a sober statement of a reality that was daily becoming more apparent.

Simultaneously with these surprising indications of his national strength, Jackson began demonstrating a disturbing independence of the Blount-Overton faction on state issues. . . . Students of the period have been misled by the interpretation of Jackson's role in Tennessee politics set forth in studies by Thomas P. Aber-

29. James, p. 370; Charles R. King, ed., *The Life and Correspondence of Rufus King* . . . (New York, 1900), VI, 494.

30. Albert Ray Newsome, *The Presidential Election of 1824 in North Carolina, James Sprunt Studies in History and Political Science*, XXXIII, No. 1 (Chapel Hill, 1939), 90–91; Lewis to George Poindexter, October 10, 1822, J. F. H. Claiborne Papers (Mississippi Department of Archives and History) (copy furnished the writer by Dr. Edwin Miles).

31. George McDuffie to Charles Fisher, January 13, 1823, Charles Fisher Papers Department (Southern Historical Collection, University of North Carolina Library).

32. James, p. 370.

33. Lewis to George Poindexter, October 10, 1822, Claiborne Papers.

nethy.[34] According to Professor Abernethy: "No historian has ever accused Jackson, the great Democrat, of having had a political philosophy. It is hard to see that he even had any political principles. He was a man of action, and the man of action is likely to be an opportunist. . . . He belonged to the moneyed aristocracy of Nashville, yet he was a self-made man and devoid of snobbishness. He thought he was sincere when he spoke to the people, yet he never really championed their cause. He merely encouraged them to champion his."[35] Had he not been the most violent critic of Grundy's popular state bank? Did he not support the aristocratic Ward against Carroll in 1821? Were not the land speculators and bankers of the Overton coterie his most intimate friends? Was it not these very men who brought him out as a candidate for President? Jackson, concludes Professor Abernethy, "was not a progressive politician. . . . He always believed in making the public serve the ends of the politician. Democracy was good talk with which to win the favor of the people and thereby accomplish ulterior objectives."[36]

It is true that Jackson had won early prominence in Tennessee through the favor of William Blount, and none of the frontier nabobs of the Blount group had been more assiduous than he in land and mercantile speculations based on paper credit. But Jackson's landholdings had been swept away in the Panic of 1797, and his mercantile business had dragged him deeper and deeper

34. Thomas P. Abernethy, *From Frontier to Plantation in Tennessee* (Chapel Hill, 1932), especially pp. 238–249; Abernethy, "Andrew Jackson and the Rise of Southwestern Democracy," *American Historical Review,* XXXIII (October 1927), 64–77; Allen Johnson, Dumas Malone, and Harris E. Starr, eds., *Dictionary of American Biography,* 21 vols. (New York, 1928–1944), IX, 526–534. Even Arthur M. Schlesinger, Jr., who takes sharp issue with Professor Abernethy's general view of Jackson, argues only that "no amount of inference based on what Jackson was like before 1828 can be a substitute for the facts after 1828." *The Age of Jackson* (Boston, 1945), p. 44.

Although this paper dissents from the view of Andrew Jackson drawn by Professor Abernethy, the writer wishes to acknowledge the indebtedness of himself and every other recent investigator of early Tennessee history to Professor Abernethy's pioneering work.

35. Abernethy, "Andrew Jackson and the Rise of Southwestern Democracy," p. 76.

36. Abernethy, *From Frontier to Plantation in Tennessee,* p. 249.

into debt, until in 1804 he was forced to sell his fine plantation, abandon his political career, and retire to a new plantation where he struggled for years to regain solvency. The experience was a chastening one, and never again was Jackson to engage in any considerable speculative ventures.[37] True, he remained close to the leaders of the Overton faction, but this does not mean that he continued to share their proclivities for land and banking speculations. It must be remembered that personal relationships were just giving way to issues as the major factors in determining political alignments, and that the leaders of the Erwin-Carroll party were Jackson's implacable personal enemies.

Jackson's connection with the Burr conspiracy and the subsequent reluctance of the Madison administration to utilize his services in the War of 1812 had tended to align him with the Tertium Quid or Old Republican members of Jefferson's party. That he absorbed some of their distaste for the nationalizing and pro-business tendencies of latter-day Republicanism is indicated by his congratulations to President Monroe for vetoing the Cumberland Road bill of 1822.[38] The same thing is more conclusively demonstrated by Jackson's relation to the banking issue in Tennessee.

Did Jackson's opposition to Grundy's state bank in 1820 reflect the interests of his banker friends, or did it grow out of an Old Republican hostility to the social effects of a paper system of any kind? His own words answer the question. "You know my op[in]ion as to the Banks," he wrote Lewis while the measure was pending, "that is, that the constitution of our State, as well as the constitution of the united [*sic*] States prohibits the establishment of Banks in every State."[39] The emphatic memorial he sent to the legislature predicted that if the proposed bank were established, "the imprudent speculator may be enabled to extricate himself from his pecuniary embarrassments but the burthen must ultimately fall upon the honest farmer and industrious tradesman."[40]

37. James, pp. 76, 80–81, 98–101.
38. Jackson to James Monroe, July 26, 1822, Jackson Papers.
39. Jackson to William B. Lewis, July 16, 1820, Ford Collection (New York Public Library).
40. *Nashville Whig,* July 26, 1820.

Nor is it surprising that Jackson should have refused to line up with his own bitter enemies and the friends of Grundy's state bank in support of Carroll in the gubernatorial campaign of the next year. Under the circumstances it was natural for him to back Ward, his old friend and neighbor.

Jackson's hostility to the banking system was well known in Tennessee. A member of the legislature that elected him to the Senate in 1823 reported that "the commonality . . . thought him the only man . . . [to] revise what they thought a corrupt system of government, Meaning the caucus—the treasury and Bank influences."[41] Ten years later Jackson assured James K. Polk that "every one that knows me, does know I have been always opposed to the U. States Bank, nay all Banks."[42] Again, in a letter to Thomas H. Benton, he reiterated his long-held views: "I have been opposed always to the Bank of the U. S. as well as all state banks of paper issues, upon constitutional grounds believing as I do, that Congress has no constitutional power to grant a charter. The states are prohibited from granting charters of paper issues. Their powers retained are to charter banks of deposit, discount, & exchange."[43] The truth of Jackson's assertions was attested by John Bell, speaking in support of the National Bank in 1832. "I have no doubt," Bell told the House of Representatives, "it will be found that he has, throughout his whole life, been opposed to the whole paper system and the extensive credits which grow out of it, and that all his prepossessions are, and have ever been, in favor of what has been significantly called a *hard money government*."[44] . . .

Much of the indictment of Jackson as a land speculator is concerned with his suit against Andrew Erwin, himself a land operator of no mean proportions. As the result of a complicated legal tangle Jackson found himself in possession of a claim on twenty-five thousand acres of exceedingly valuable lands held by his old enemy, at the very time that Erwin and his associates were

41. Pleasant M. Miller to Charles Fisher, January 3, 1824, quoted in James, p. 395.
42. Jackson to Polk, December 23, 1833, Polk Papers.
43. Jackson to Thomas H. Benton [n.d.], draft, Jackson Papers.
44. *Nashville Republican,* April 14, 1832.

trying to ruin Jackson's reputation by charges concerning the Seminole campaign. Abernethy condemns Jackson for prosecuting this claim, though even Erwin's political allies considered it legally unimpeachable. Despite the strength of his case, Jackson eventually accepted a compromise so lenient that his associates in the suit complained, and he finally gave up his share of the award altogether when Mrs. Erwin pleaded in tears that payment would mean ruin for her family.[45]

But Jackson's ruthlessness as a land speculator, in Professor Abernethy's view, was even more conclusively demonstrated by the support which he gave to Patrick H. Darby, his lawyer in the Erwin case. Once a carpenter, Darby had educated himself sufficiently to secure an attorney's license. His specialty, bringing suit against doubtful land titles, had not made him popular in a state long dominated by speculators with a casual attitude toward legal formalities.[46] The holders of doubtful titles, however, found a champion in Judge John Haywood, who began a campaign to

45. Abernethy, *From Frontier to Plantation in Tennessee,* pp. 262–269; Arda S. Walker, "Andrew Jackson: Frontier Democrat," East Tennessee Historical Society, *Publications,* No. 18 (1946), 83–85; Alfred Balch to Jackson, March 12 and 20, 1823, and James Jackson to Jackson, October 21, 1823, Jackson Papers. Eighty-five thousand acres of land were involved in this case, of which Erwin had obtained twenty-five thousand from the original owners and Jackson five thousand. Jackson had long since disposed of his portion when he discovered that the title to all the land was invalid and that he was responsible for the current value of the land he had sold. It was to protect himself and give a good title to those who had purchased from him that he was obliged to obtain a relinquishment to himself of the entire eighty-five thousand acres. It was in this way that he secured a claim to Erwin's land. Marquis James holds that Jackson showed "attributes of courage and of honest impulse" by his course in this case, and that "he imperilled his fortune beyond hope of extrication to protect his personal honor." Pp. 133–134. For other speculative interests of Erwin, see *Nashville Whig,* October 30, 1822, and Erwin to George Swain, November 11, 1822, David L. Swain Epistolary Correspondence, Ms., Vol. III (North Carolina Collection, Library of the University of North Carolina, Chapel Hill).

46. *Nashville Constitutional Advocate,* September 3 and 10, 1822. Grundy had once tried to have Darby disbarred; but Darby had been able to get enough incriminating evidence against Grundy to force him, along with most of the leading lawyers of Middle Tennessee, to attest that Darby's conduct had always been open and honorable. For indications that Darby was an opportunist see Easter to Jackson, May 10 and June 25, 1821, Jackson Papers.

reinterpret a statute of limitations of 1797 so that it would protect even those claims that could not be traced back to an original grant. Haywood was voted down again and again by his colleagues on the state supreme court, but, in 1822, Grundy induced the legislature to increase the size of the court and pack it with judges who would agree with Haywood. Already, at the previous session, Grundy, Overton, and Pleasant M. Miller had pushed through a champerty law, with some of its provisions aimed directly at Darby. In self-defense, Darby purchased the *Nashville Clarion,* renamed it the *Constitutional Advocate,* and declared war on his assailants.[47]

It is clear that the opposition to Darby was led by the land-speculating and banking group, supported by persons who had purchased doubtful titles from the speculators. Although Jackson's suit against Erwin was not affected by the more liberal interpretation of the statute of limitations, he backed Darby vigorously. Jackson's earlier bankruptcy had made him a fervent foe of all kinds of speculation—whether land, mercantile, or banking—especially where the law was being set aside. "The attempt by few to inveigle a legislature to pack a court" he thought contemptible.[48]

Darby's slashing attacks on the bankers and speculators soon made his newspaper the most popular and influential in the state, and he was put up in the Nashville district as an anti-Overton candidate for the legislature in 1823. The bank issue was again before the voters, and in the course of the campaign Darby uncovered evidence that Stephen Cantrell, president of the Nashville Bank and War Department agent for disbursing pensions to Revolutionary veterans, had been selling the government's specie funds to his bank and paying the pensioners in depreciated bank notes. To Jackson this was just another indication that "our society has been much demoralized by our paper banking system." Its corrupting influence, he thought, "has been no where felt more

47. *Nashville Constitutional Advocate,* July 30, August 29, and September 3, 1822; Overton to Miller, April 13, 1823, draft, Overton Papers.

48. Jackson to John Coffee, April 15, 1823, J. S. Bassett, ed., *The Correspondence of Andrew Jackson,* 6 vols. (Washington, 1926–1936), III, 194–195.

seriously and banefully" than in Tennessee, and he applauded Secretary Calhoun for dismissing Cantrell promptly.[49]

Darby opened his appeal for votes by promising to serve the people, not the banks. He was sure the people would not consent to alter the constitutional provision for gold and silver coin. But, he asked the voters, "Are you willing to allow that constitutional law to be changed by the practice of a few corporate companies, who speculate on money for private gain, & in which not one in fifty of the people have any interest?" He was positive that the banks could not resume specie payments and thought they should be forced out of business. He favored one more trial with the state bank alone, but if that institution proved unable to maintain a sound currency, he would abolish it also "and return to those days that are past, when we lived happy without banks, and knew what our money was worth without paying a broker to tell us."[50] But the speculators and bankers were too powerful in the wealthy Nashville district, and Darby and his running mate lost the election to the Overton candidates, Grundy and Andrew Lytle. Darby's Jacksonism and the enmity of the Erwins prevented him from getting the full anti-Overton vote.[51]

The significant thing about this election is Jackson's recognition that personal friendship was no longer an adequate basis for political alliance. His anger against activities of his banking and speculating friends had led him to support a man sharing his own hostility to the speculative system, though to do so he had to oppose the very leaders who were at this time managing his candidacy for the Presidency. . . .

Thus by the time the new legislature met in 1823, Jackson's conservative managers were in a dilemma. Their candidate had begun to display his dangerous tendencies just at the moment when he unexpectedly became a major contender. Most mortifyingly of all, they had initiated the whole business. But Jackson's candidacy might still be killed. John Williams' re-election to the Senate would

49. Jackson to John C. Calhoun, [n.d.], *ibid.,* III, 202. See also Jackson to Coffee, May 24, 1823, *ibid.,* III, 198; *Nashville Constitutional Advocate,* August 19, 1823; *Nashville Whig,* June 17 and 23, and July 14, 1823; Benton to Clay, July 23, 1823, Clay Papers.
50. *Nashville Constitutional Advocate,* July 15, 1823.
51. *Ibid.,* August 12, 1823.

indicate that Jackson did not control his own state and keep worried politicians in states like Pennsylvania from jumping aboard the Jackson bandwagon. Even Tennessee might be held for Clay after all.

The crucial importance of the Tennessee Senatorial election was appreciated far beyond the borders of the state. Senator Ninian Edwards came down from Illinois to represent Calhoun's interests, while Thomas Hart Benton of Missouri spent several months in Tennessee on a similar mission for Clay.[52] When the legislature assembled at Murfreesborough in September, the little village was crowded with "extra members," who had flocked in from every part of the state to influence the legislators in the Senatorial election. Judge White had come from Knoxville to "spread himself against Jackson,"[53] and was frequently seen with Senator Williams "in deep consultation on the woodpiles about the square."[54] The pro-Jackson delegation on hand to insure Williams' downfall included Senator Eaton, Major Lewis, Thomas Claiborne, fresh from his defeat for the legislature on the anti-Grundy ticket, and Sam Houston, the dashing young lawyer who had just won a seat in Congress as Jackson's protégé.

During the preceding weeks, John Williams had been touring the state to line up his supporters, and despite Miller's active campaign the Senator reached Murfreesborough with the assurance of a comfortable majority over the announced opposition. Much of his advantage arose from the fact that Miller was not the only politician hoping to ride into the Senate on Jackson's coattails. William G. Blount, son of the great speculator and a former Congressman from East Tennessee, threatened to enter the race, while Jackson's old crony, the veteran East Tennessee politician John Rhea, had actually abandoned his seat in Congress to offer as a candidate. Neither Miller nor Rhea would withdraw, and the Jackson men were forced into desperate efforts to stave off the election until they could unite on one of their two candidates. The least division would insure the election of Jackson's notorious

52. Elihu B. Washburne, ed., *The Edwards Papers* (Chicago, 1884), p. 207; John Williams to Rufus King, November 19, 1823, King Papers; Benton to Clay, July 23, 1823, Clay Papers; Jackson to [Eaton ?], October 4, 1823, draft copy, Jackson Papers.
53. J. G. M. Ramsey to F. P. Blair, October 5, 1835, Blair-Lee Papers.
54. *Nashville Union,* September 22, 1836.

enemy and almost certainly destroy his Presidential prospects.[55]

There is strong evidence that Overton and Grundy were now working for just this result, with the important assistance of Judge White. Since January, Senator Williams had been writing familiarly to Overton about his chances,[56] and now Thomas L. Williams implored Overton to come to Murfreesborough and help his brother. "As the friends of our opponents assemble to influence members and to promote the views of their favourite I think ours should be permitted an equal liberty," he wrote, betraying not the slightest doubt of Overton's sympathy. "Will you come up next week."[57]

Grundy, meanwhile, was leading the fight to bring on the election at once. "His vote had been firmly fixed from shortly after his arrival here," a newspaper reported him as saying in debate; "previous to that time a difficulty had existed with him on the subject which but one man [John Williams] could remove; and he now could say that the difficulty had been removed fully and satisfactorily, and he was now ready to give his vote."[58] This was merely part of a concerted effort to convince members that Williams was not unfriendly to Jackson and would not oppose his Presidential aspirations. Simultaneously, Grundy introduced resolutions instructing Tennessee's Senators to do their best to prevent the Congressional nominating caucus. All of this convinced Jackson's friends that Grundy was leading the Williams forces and had introduced his caucus resolutions to obviate the most serious objection to Williams, the expectation that he would attend the caucus and help nominate Crawford.[59]

The suspicious Jackson men now sent a delegation to question Williams on his attitude toward the General, and when he equivocated, they dispatched a messenger urging Jackson to hasten to Murfreesborough and save the situation. Jackson refused to come,

55. John Rhea to Jackson, June 18, 1823, Jackson Papers; R. G. Dunlap to Jackson, July 2, 1823, *ibid.;* John Williams to Rufus King, November 19, 1823, King Papers; *Correspondence of Andrew Jackson,* III, 201 n.; Tennessee Assembly, *Journal of the House,* 1823, pp. 20, 76–77; *Journal of the Senate,* 1823, pp. 29–30, 37, 59–60.

56. John Williams to Overton, January 14, 1823, Overton Papers.

57. Thomas L. Williams to Overton, September 20, 1823, *ibid.*

58. *Nashville Whig,* September 22, 1823.

59. William Brady and Thomas Williamson to Jackson, September 20, 1823, Jackson Papers.

but he did insist on Williams' defeat and denounced Grundy and the other "schemers of the opposition."[60] By this time, as Governor Carroll reported to Clay, the situation was extremely "strange and uncertain."[61] When it became clear that Miller had too many personal enemies to overcome the well-organized Williams forces, the Jackson men persuaded the General to endorse Rhea, but even this left them three votes short of a majority. Jackson again refused to come personally to their aid, and the election could be staved off no longer.

Finally, in desperation, Eaton and Lewis had Jackson's name placed before the legislature as Williams' competitor for the Senate. When the messenger bearing this news reached the Hermitage, Jackson mounted up and left posthaste for Murfreesborough, arriving in the middle of the night preceding the election. Even with Jackson as a candidate and present at the election, Williams was beaten and Jackson elected Senator by a vote of only thirty-five to twenty-five.

In Washington the following winter, Senator Jackson charmed friend and foe alike. Pennsylvania soon endorsed Tennessee's hero, most of Calhoun's support shifted to Jackson when the South Carolinian was forced to withdraw, and everywhere the popular enthusiasm for Old Hickory mounted.

Though Grundy, Overton, Miller, and White now joined Lewis and Eaton in the five-year campaign that carried Jackson into the White House, their situation was ironical. A movement started by obscure Tennessee politicians for their own local purposes had unexpectedly been caught up by a deep groundswell of democratic aspiration. The original Jackson promoters found themselves uncomfortably astride a whirlwind of their own devising.

None of these conservative men were fundamentally sympathetic to Jackson's social philosophy, as it began to manifest itself in the 1820's or as it was implemented in the 1830's. Old Hickory was hardly inaugurated before Miller went into opposition. Overton and Eaton evidenced their discomfort by trying to block Van Buren's Vice-Presidential nomination in 1832. Overton died

60. Jackson [to William Brady and Thomas Williamson], September 27, 1823, draft copy, *ibid.; Nashville Union,* September 22, 1836.
61. Carroll to Clay, October 1, 1823, Clay Papers.

shortly afterward, while Eaton opposed the Jackson party covertly in 1836 and openly in 1840. Major Lewis dissembled from about 1833 on, professing friendship to Jackson but actually aiding his enemies. Judge White ran for President against the Jackson party's candidate in 1836. . . .

Jacksonian democracy was left to be defended in Tennessee mainly by such veterans of Carroll's anti-Bank campaign as James K. Polk, Aaron V. Brown, and Cave Johnson, together with Felix Grundy, who decided that continued loyalty to the President would be most to his own advantage.[62] Carroll himself had previously supported the National Bank on moderate hard-money grounds as the best instrument to remedy the evils of state banking, and he eventually found it comparatively easy to side with Jackson against national as well as state banks.[63] . . .

Jackson was much more thoroughgoing in his hard-money views than William Carroll. Family connections and hostility toward the Overton banking interests had caused a considerable number of the Nashville merchants to support the Erwin-Carroll party, and Carroll was sympathetic to their demands for commercial credit. Some of this credit was for a time supplied by the firm of Thomas Yeatman, a son-in-law of Andrew Erwin and probably the wealthiest merchant in the state. During the 1820's his company had begun to carry on a private banking business and issue notes without benefit of a state charter. In 1825, Jackson induced his friends in the legislature to propose a bill outlawing private banking, but Carroll came to Yeatman's defense, and the Erwin-Carroll forces defeated the measure.[64]

62. Cave Johnson had originally supported William H. Crawford for President in 1824, but had switched to Jackson when Crawford's health failed. Clement L. Grant, "The Public Career of Cave Johnson" (Ph.D. dissertation, Vanderbilt University, 1951), p. 23. In the campaign of 1833, Johnson denied that Congress had the constitutional power to charter a bank and contended that "a metalic currency is the only one contemplated by the Constitution." *Nashville Republican,* March 1, 1833. Grundy even managed to come out for the hard-money doctrine. *Murfreesboro Central Monitor,* September 6, 1834.

63. See Carroll's letter to William Jones, October 3, 1817, denouncing the unstable state-bank currency and requesting a Nashville branch. *Senate Documents,* 23rd Congress, 2nd Session, No. 17, p. 227.

64. *Jackson* (Tennessee) *Gazette,* December 17, 1825; John P. Erwin to Clay, December 12, 1825, Clay Papers.

When the old banks closed their doors the next year, the merchants complained that Yeatman alone could not supply enough credit, and an effort was made to have the legislature repeal the fifty-thousand-dollar tax of 1817, so as to secure a branch of the National Bank. There was no advance notice of this attempt in the newspapers—Jackson called it "a secrete & combined movement of the arristocracy"[65]—but the General rushed to Nashville as soon as he heard of it. The bill had by this time passed the lower house, and despite Jackson's expostulations with the members of the Senate it was approved on its final reading by the margin of a single vote. Shortly thereafter, on petition of Carroll and his allies, a branch was opened at Nashville, and it was soon financing most of the crop and commercial transactions of Middle Tennessee.[66] . . .

The question of government policy toward banks was the key issue of the period which saw new parties taking the place of the old factional organization of politics. But the banking issue's real significance is as an index to the underlying assumptions that actually divided Whigs, who contended for a neo-Hamiltonian alliance between government and business, from Democrats, who would attempt to maintain equal access for all to the new opportunities generated by the economic revolution. Andrew Jackson had been quicker than most of his contemporaries to sense that the changes in American society revealed by the Panic of 1819 dictated a shift from politics based on personal friendship to politics based on convictions about public policy. His central conviction, that government should afford "equal protection and equal benefits,"[67] had determined his attitude on Tennessee issues a decade before his celebrated Bank veto expounded it to the nation.

65. Jackson to Benton, [n.d.], draft, Jackson Papers.
66. *Ibid.;* Catterall, p. 183 n.; St. George L. Sioussat, "Some Phases of Tennessee Politics in the Jackson Period," *American Historical Review,* XIV (October 1908), 62–63.
67. Jackson's phrase, from the Bank veto message, in James D. Richardson, comp., *A Compilation of the Messages and Papers of the Presidents, 1789–1902,* 10 vols. (Washington, 1905), III, 590. For an unusually perceptive discussion of Jackson's own political philosophy see Marvin Meyers, "The Jacksonian Persuasion," *American Quarterly,* V (Spring 1953), 3–15.

✪

Winning the Presidency

The people who were jammed into the galleries of the House of Representatives that snowy February afternoon in 1825 strained to hear what the Speaker was saying. It was difficult for them to catch every word because the acoustics in the hall were so "vile." Sounds skidded around the walls before ascending and disappearing into the great dome ceiling that rose sixty feet above the floor.

And it was important that they hear each word, for the Representatives of Congress on that ninth day of February were about to select the next President of the United States. A House election had taken place only once before, in 1801; in another hundred and more years it would not occur again.

Addressing the Representatives, the distinguished Speaker, Henry Clay, looked supremely self-confident; but then Clay never looked anything less than self-confident when he appeared in public. Tall, gaunt, with great hollows gouged in both cheeks and a thin, almost invisible line marking the location of his mouth, this fiercely ambitious, hard-drinking, gambling man from Kentucky knew the full measure of his worth. Critics said he was a hail fellow all wet—a rather sarcastic acknowledgment of his many social triumphs—but their judgment was obviously distorted by partisan distemper.

Right up to the last minute prior to Clay's arrival at the Speaker's desk, managers of the several candidates scurried about

Abridged from the book *The Election of Andrew Jackson* by Robert V. Remini. Copyright, ©, 1963 by Robert V. Remini. Reprinted by permission of J. B. Lippincott Company.

the hall in a desperate effort to corral stray votes. There were signs that the contest would be close, and the political strategists were taking no chances on losing by default. Each state cast a single ballot, determined by the delegation, and a majority of states was necessary for election.

Above the confusion and noisy excitement Clay was heard calling for order. Then, in a voice that matched the solemnity of the occasion, he directed each delegation to poll its members.[1]

The election of 1824, held the previous fall, had failed to determine President James Monroe's successor because the electoral ballots were split among four candidates, none of whom had a majority. Thus, according to the Twelfth Amendment to the Constitution, the House of Representatives was required to select the chief executive from among the three men with the highest electoral count. In 1824 these three included the Senator from Tennessee, Andrew Jackson, who had 99 votes; the Secretary of State, John Quincy Adams, with 84 votes; and the Secretary of the Treasury, William H. Crawford, who received 41 votes. The fourth candidate, Henry Clay himself, was eliminated since his total floored the list at a meager 37 ballots.

Had the amended Constitution not designated so precisely the number of candidates permitted in the House, Clay might have won the Presidency because of his enormous influence over many state delegations. Instead, he held the balance of power, or thought he did. He had a pretty good suspicion that the man to follow Monroe into the executive mansion would be the lucky individual he chose to favor with his support. So for the next few weeks he struggled with his conscience. He examined and re-examined the claims of the three candidates. He was importuned by every manager and political string-puller in Washington, but he resisted the pressures in an effort to render an independent decision, one beneficial to the country and one compatible with the ambitions of Henry Clay.

1. Benjamin F. Butler to his wife, Harriet, May 7, 1823, Benjamin F. Butler Papers (New York State Library, Albany); George Dangerfield, *The Era of Good Feelings* (New York, 1952), pp. 331–345. John C. Fitzgerald, ed., *The Autobiography of Martin Van Buren,* American Historical Association, *Annual Report,* 1918, II (Washington, 1920), 142–156.

Coming from Kentucky, though born in Virginia, the Speaker might have acknowledged Western aspirations by awarding the prize to Andrew Jackson. The great General of the Battle of New Orleans was unquestionably popular with the electorate—frighteningly popular, worried some—for he was one of the few genuine American heroes still living. On the other hand, his experience in government was negligible. Most of his detractors (which is to say the managers and supporters of the other candidates) wrote him off as a "military chieftain" with no acceptable qualification for the Presidency. And, as far as Clay was concerned, the Hero was a rival for Western votes; so in terms of future political advantage, it seemed wiser to exclude him from the contest.

To some commentators Jackson's candidacy was a terrible judgment on the times, in that an uneducated, untrained, uninformed, and inexperienced Indian fighter would presume to challenge tried and tested statesmen for the highest office in the nation. What could he possibly offer the American people except the achievement of the battlefield? And was it not obvious that the framers of the Constitution had endeavored to protect the executive branch from such "adventurers" as well as from popular, democratic control? In providing an Electoral College they expected thoughtful and dedicated men from the different states to select the President from a number of possible contenders, each of whom had previously earned a national reputation as a wise and just man, devoted to public service.

Andrew Jackson's career could not remotely measure up to such standards, thought Clay. The Hero had demonstrated a remarkable talent for slaughtering Indians and Englishmen—and sometimes American militiamen when they got out of line or temporarily forgot the rules of military discipline—but that was all. While the populace might thrill to such exploits, responsible citizens understood that the Presidency demanded loftier credentials. To be sure, he had served short terms as a member of the House of Representatives, a judge, Governor of the Florida Territory, and currently as Senator from Tennessee; nevertheless, these services were singularly undistinguished.

Still, as Clay understood full well, it was not easy to dismiss Andrew Jackson. His electoral count in 1824 was impressive, representing solid backing from the South, Pennsylvania, most of the West, and substantial political pockets in several Middle Atlantic states. Equally impressive was his appearance. Tall and slender, he carried himself with military stiffness. His face was long, accentuated by a sharp lantern jaw, and lighted by clear blue eyes. His gray-white hair bristled with electricity and stood nearly as erect as the General himself. If apppearance meant anything, Jackson was the most Presidential-looking of the three candidates. There was an air and grace about him that signaled the presence of a leader.

The Hero was born of poor Scotch-Irish parents in the Carolina back country and later moved to Tennessee, where he became a lawyer, small businessman, land speculator, and planter. But he was no crude or simple frontiersman—not Andrew Jackson. By any standard of the time he was a gentleman, and, as a Tennessee planter of moderately good income who owned slaves and resided in a handsome mansion called the Hermitage, he lived like one. He was naturally warm and affectionate toward his family and close associates; at the same time he could be harshly vindictive toward political adversaries, and vindictive for unreasonably long periods of time. He was stubborn and quick to take offense and, when angry, easily lost his self-control. The canings he administered to a few unfortunate men were marks of his lively temper. It was not a light thing to cross him, but by 1824 Clay was well along toward making a habit of crossing Andrew Jackson. . . .[2]

After many consultations with his friends, Clay finally made up his mind. On January 8, 1825, in spite of official instructions from the Kentucky legislature to back Jackson, he tapped John Quincy Adams as the man privileged to receive his support. Two weeks later his decision was announced to the public. He invited other Congressmen to imitate his example and deployed agents among the delegations to start the bandwagon rolling. . . .

Poor Jackson. He had had a plurality of electoral votes and was

2. Clay to Francis Brooke, January 28, 1825, and Clay to Francis P. Blair, January 8, 29, 1825, Calvin Colton, ed., *The Private Correspondence of Henry Clay* (New York, 1856), pp. 109–112.

seemingly the choice of the country, yet he was denied the prize he felt was his right. At first he took his defeat with gentlemanly good grace. At a reception given by James Monroe on the night of the election he exchanged pleasantries with the President-Elect.

"How do you do, Mr. Adams," said the Hero. "I hope you are well, sir."

"Very well, sir," replied Adams. "I hope General Jackson is well!"

As this civilized conversation clearly indicates, the mood in Washington immediately following the contest was one of quiet acquiescence to the will of the Congress. The Speaker reported correctly that the election, in every way, "was creditable to our institutions and to our country."

Then came the explosion. Adams announced his intention of appointing Henry Clay as his Secretary of State. It was foolish of him to offer the post, but it was political suicide for Clay to accept it. Howling their indignation, the Jacksonians set up a cry that a "corrupt bargain" had been struck between the two men just prior to the election, that the will of the people, expressed in November, had been criminally subverted by Washington politicians. "So you see," wrote Old Hickory in an impassioned outburst, "the *Judas* of the West has closed the contract and will receive the thirty pieces of silver." To cynical voters around the country who were prone to believe that politics was a dirty business at best and that "deals" were normal in the operation of government, the accusation required no proof so long as it was repeated at regular intervals; others wondered whether the spirit of the Constitution had not been violated by arrogant men who presumed to tell the people what was best for them. . . .[3]

When the Congressional session ended, the disappointed Hero of New Orleans headed for his home in Tennessee by way of West Alexandria, Pennsylvania. As he reached the little town, an old

3. Ben: Perley Poore, *Perley's Reminiscences of Sixty Years in the National Metropolis* (Philadelphia, 1886), p. 26; Clay to Brooke, February 10, 1825, Clay, *Correspondence,* p. 114; Jackson to William B. Lewis, February 16, 1825, Miscellaneous Jackson Papers (New York Historical Society).

comrade by the name of Edward McLaughlin came up to him and
offered his sympathy over the results of the House election. "Well,
General," he said, "we did all we could for you here, but the
rascals at Washington cheated you out of it."

"Indeed, my old friend," rumbled the Hero, "there was *cheat-
ing,* and *corruption,* and *bribery* too."

With each mile that took him closer to home, Jackson's anger
mounted. Over and over he recalled the scene when James Buchanan stood before him, winking at him, beckoning him to betray
the people's trust. He remembered Buchanan's words, something
the Clay men had said about ending the election in an hour if he
would expel Adams from the Cabinet. Suddenly it struck him.
That "Judas," Henry Clay, had authorized an "arrangement" and
sent Buchanan as the emissary, and when there was no response
the deal was made with Adams.

In Brownsville, Jackson repeated his tale of skulduggery in
Washington, only this time he added several embellishments. To
all who would listen—and there were many—he accused Henry
Clay personally of attempted bribery.

Almost as swiftly as Jackson's anger turned to fury, his indictment of the coalition spread to neighboring towns. When he
reached his next stop the citizenry surrounded his carriage and
asked if Clay had truly dared to corrupt America's great Hero.
"Yes, sir," stormed the General, "such a proposition was made. I
said to the bearer—Go tell Mr. Clay, tell Mr. Adams, that if I go
into that chair, I go with clear hands and a pure heart, and that I'd
rather see them together with myself, engulphed to the earth's
centre, than to compass it by such means."

In Frankfort, Kentucky, Jackson re-enacted his outrage, but his
words had been sharpened in the meantime to a finer political
point. *"The people* [have] *been cheated,"* he bellowed. ". . .
*Corruptions and intrigues at Washington . . . defeated the will of
the people."*

So what started as suspicion in Jackson's mind ended as conviction: that he had been betrayed, abused, and cheated by a wicked
coalition. Not himself alone but the people, too.

By the time he reached his home in Tennessee, a well-marked
trail of political propaganda reached back to Washington right

into the halls of Congress. Jackson had placed the Adams-Clay coalition on notice. The campaign for the Presidency in 1828 had already begun.[4]

The work of Calhoun, Ritchie, and Van Buren was essential to the creation of a new national party, but without the name, reputation, popularity, leadership, and political wisdom of Andrew Jackson, they were all wasting their time. From the very beginning of the attempts to organize an opposition, the Hero was the head of the party—without question and without doubt.

At his home in Tennessee the General carefully watched the events occurring in Washington through the information supplied him by a corps of devoted Congressmen. The "various communications from Eaton White and Houston," he wrote, "with a great run of company has occupied all my time." Although he had voluntarily relinquished his Senate seat and presumably had retired from public life, Jackson was a busy man, attending to his voluminous correspondence, meeting the delegations of politicians who called upon him regularly, and generally keeping himself in the public eye as the innocent victim of the corrupt bargain. He was the first Presidential candidate to engage actively and publicly in his own campaign, violating what many regarded as a near-sacred tradition among Presidential aspirants to remain silent during the canvass. "I regretted," he wrote to one friend, "that . . . so much of my time was taken up by the calls of my friends abroad, and here, for documents and statements." As he became more active and more vocal in directing the campaign, several party leaders, including Van Buren and Eaton, urged him to be *"still,"* implying that his conduct was most unseemly. "Candidates for the Presidency," pontificated one Radical, ". . . ought not to say one word on the subject of the election. Washington, Jefferson, & Madison were as silent as the grave when they were before the American people for this office."

But Jackson had special problems in seeking the Presidency. It was difficult for him as a man without office to engage public interest in his candidacy without violating that tradition. Despite

4. Letters reprinted in *Niles' Weekly Register,* July 5, 1828.

his popularity as a great national hero, he knew from his experience in 1824 that popularity alone was not enough to capture the White House, at least not while sinister men lurked in the corridors of the Congress. Aside from that, when his wife was viciously slandered in the newspapers, "it was more than my mind could bear to hear it, and not redress it," he argued, "with that punishment it deserved."

During 1827 and 1828 hardly a month passed without the newspapers printing a long letter by the General answering some charge brought against his public and private life. Many of these letters, it is true, were written by others. Since Jackson had a rare talent for mangling the English language, he had to exercise extreme caution in releasing statements for publication lest they prove the coalition's contention that his "illiteracy" disqualified him for the Presidency. Nevertheless, most of these letters were written under his supervision or were the corrected versions of his own compositions. Writing, he admitted, was "laborious," but like the fiercely determined man he was he kept working at it, asking his many friends for editorial assistance. Painfully, he struggled to improve his communications with the public, and in the end he succeeded admirably. Adams, on the other hand, was dismayingly inarticulate, despite a Harvard degree.[5]

Like all sensible politicians, Jackson sought the widest possible audience for his opinions and public statements. By the last year of the campaign he had become expert in reaching every quarter of the Union where his ideas could be used to advantage. For example, in March, 1828, he instructed Major William Lewis to send "one hundred extras [of a newspaper containing an important pronouncement] to every printer & Jackson Committee [in] Ohio, Indiana, Illinois, Mississippi, Louisiana, and Alabama

5. Jackson to John Coffee, March 16, 1827, Jackson to Richard K. Call, May 3, 1827, Eaton to Jackson, January 21, 1828, and Van Buren to Jackson, September 14, 1827, J. S. Bassett, ed., *The Correspondence of Andrew Jackson,* 6 vols. (Washington, 1926–1933), III, 348, 354–355, 382, 390; John Campbell to James Campbell, August 23, 1827, Campbell Papers (Duke University Library); Jackson to Coffee, May 12, 1828, and Jackson to Lewis, July 28, 1828, Jackson, *Correspondence,* III, 403, 416; Jackson to Grundy, May 30, 1826, Grundy Papers (University of North Carolina Library).

—and to the north Pennsylvania, Virginia, Maryland, New Jersey, New York and New Hampshire. Those you may send me I shall distribute in Virginia and Kentucky," he added.

In seeking this publicity the General operated directly through correspondence committees in the states, newspaper editors, Congressional leaders, and—most important of all—his own Central Committee in Nashville. This committee, called the Whitewashing Committee by the friends of the administration, was set up in the spring of 1827 for the avowed purpose of detecting and arresting "falsehoods and calumny, by the publication of truth, and by furnishing either to the public or to individuals, whether alone or associated, full and correct information upon any matter or subject within their knowledge or power, properly connected with the fitness or qualification of Andrew Jackson to fill the office of President of the United States." Major Lewis put it more succinctly. The Central Committee was formed, he told the Ohio party, "for the purpose of corresponding with other Jackson committees in the different sections of the union."

The announcement of the committee's formation sent the administration newspapers bawling their indignation. "When its organization was first announced," raged the *Washington National Journal* on May 22, "it struck us as a matter of surprise, that any man, presenting himself to the nation as a candidate for the chief magistry, should think it necessary to form so extraordinary an association for the purpose of promoting his views." But for an astute politician like Jackson there was nothing extraordinary about it at all. Aside from "promoting his views," it also helped to unite the state organizations, after they formed, into something resembling a national party.

Of the eighteen members comprising the Central Committee, Overton, Lewis, Balch, George W. Campbell, Tom Claiborne, John Catron, Robert Whyte, John McNairy, William L. Brown, and Robert C. Foster, who sometimes acted as the chairman pro tem, were the most important. In letters introducing these men to the central committees of the other states, Lewis described Overton as "an old & intimate friend" of the General; Campbell, he ventured, "is well known to the nation"; Foster, in March, 1827, was the speaker of the Tennessee Senate; Whyte and Catron were two judges of the state supreme court; Brown was a former judge and "now at the head of the Bar"; while McNairy was the federal district judge for western Tennessee. The activities of this committee, though normally directed by Overton and Lewis, were carefully superintended by Jackson himself. "I should have been down this week to have seen you," he wrote Lewis early in May, 1827, "but . . . I do not wish to be seen mingling with the members of the Committee, *now*." Shortly thereafter he was in full command of their operations. For example, when he was accused of participation in the Burr conspiracy, he snapped his friends to attention. "If the Committee are not ready to come out (if they do intend)," he said, "the great necessity that some notice should be taken in todays Republican [newspaper]. . . . This will give time for me to make an address to the public, but the Committee under all circumstances ought to say something on the subject first."

Along with directing the Central Committee and the Junto, Jackson frequently assigned specific tasks to his friends in Congress. On one occasion, when a partisan informed him that an Ohio newspaperman named Charles Hammond had been to Kentucky to see Henry Clay to gather materials for a low-swinging broadside, the General asked Eaton in Washington to check into it. Eaton confronted the scowling Clay with a demand for an explanation, but the Secretary had no idea what the Senator was talking about. Clay frankly admitted seeing Hammond in Lexington but denied giving the editor any documentary information. However, when Hammond later published an article charging Mrs. Jackson with adultery, the General was certain that Clay was responsible. At another time Jackson asked Sam Houston, on his return to Congress, to question a Dr. Wallace and a Colonel Grey about a statement made by the Secretary of the Navy, Samuel Southard, at a dinner in Fredericksburg, Virginia. Houston was to obtain the statement in writing, retain the original, and forward a copy to Nashville. This done, Houston was told to present himself to Southard, hand the Secretary a note from Jackson, and wait for a reply. Do this quickly, commanded the Hero, for the department heads had been "secretely [*sic*] intimating slanderous things of me. This I mean to expose, and put down, one after the other, as I can obtain the positive proof."

Jackson also had a small band of men traveling through the country eagerly campaigning for him. They conferred with state leaders, kept tabs on organizational developments, and reported their findings directly to the General or to the Central Committee. "In N. York I saw many of your friends in various parts of the State," wrote John Eaton, the Hero's chief roving ambassador. "I was in Ohio some time . . . and in Indiana." Major Henry Lee was another "circulating medium" who scouted the Middle Atlantic and New England states and submitted comprehensive reports on party operations in Connecticut and New York. Occasionally the work of the "mediums" was supplemented by local leaders. Caleb Atwater of Ohio, for example, took a carefully planned excursion through the Eastern and Northeastern states, following a long and confidential meeting with Jackson at the Hermitage. "I have visited our friends every where," he told the Hero. Later, Duff Green, Calhoun, Clinton, Edward Livingston, Thomas Ritchie, Samuel D. Ingham, and others stumped various sections of the country, each submitting statements of their success to Lewis, Overton, Jackson, or the Central Committee.[6]

In directing all these varied activities, the General committed only one serious blunder. He still remembered James Buchanan's confused story about a bargain, the details of which he sent to Duff Green, editor of the *Telegraph,* with instructions to investigate.

6. Jackson to Lewis, March 8, 1828, Jackson Papers (Morgan Library, New York City); Lewis to E. Haywood, March 28, 1827, Jackson-Lewis Papers (New York Public Library). The first notice concerning the Nashville Central Committee appeared in the *Telegraph* on April 9, 1827. The committee included Overton, Lewis, Campbell, Claiborne, Balch, Catron, Foster, Brown, Whyte, Joseph Philips, Daniel Graham, Jesse Wharton, Edward Ward, Felix Robertson, John Shelby, Josiah Nichol, William White, and John McNairy. Jackson to Lewis, May 5, 1827, August 19, 1828, and Jackson to Coffee, September 25, 1826, Jackson, *Correspondence,* III, 314, 355, 428; James Parton, *Life of Jackson,* 3 vols. (New York, 1859–1860), III, 147; Clay to Hammond, December 23, 1826, Miscellaneous Clay Papers (Duke University Library); *Telegraph,* May 27, 1828; Jackson to Houston, November 22, 1826, Jackson, *Correspondence,* III, 319; Eaton to Jackson, August 21, 1828, Lee to Jackson, August 12, 1828. Caleb Atwater to Jackson, September 4, 1827, and February 28, 1828, and Green to Jackson, October 22, 1827, Jackson Papers (Library of Congress); William B. Hatcher, *Edward Livingston* (University, La., 1940), p. 319; Charles N. Hunt, *Life of Edward Livingston* (1864), pp. 318–322; Livingston to Jackson, August 12, 1828, Jackson Papers (Library of Congress).

Green contacted Buchanan and asked if he had been authorized by Clay to approach Jackson with an offer. Buchanan replied that he had had no such authorization, and requested that the unfortunate incident be forgotten. He said he was making excellent progress in organizing the Jackson party in Pennsylvania and did not wish to be "provoked into a public statement." Green accepted the disclaimer and agreed to let the thing alone. But not Jackson. Every politician who visited him at the Hermitage he chilled with a dramatic account of the dark deed. According to the General, a "congressman of high respectability" came to him in the dead of night with an offer from Clay's friends. Like the pure-of-heart he was, he "indignantly" rejected the offer. So he was cheated of the Presidency.

One of the men who heard Jackson's tale of corruption in high places was a Virginian named Carter Beverley who later published the story in the *Fayetteville Observer* in North Carolina. Demands for confirmation followed, and the General, always ready to remind the people of his and their betrayal, replied in a letter to Beverley dated June 5, 1827, in which he confirmed the essential points of the story. Henry Clay answered this with a "direct, unqualified, and indignant denial" of the charges, swearing that no friend of his had been authorized to approach Jackson on any matter.

As the furor mounted, there were calls for the name of the "congressman of high respectability." Never one to duck a challenge, Jackson named James Buchanan and claimed that Buchanan told him—and also told Eaton and Kremer—that the Adams men had definitely offered Clay the State Department in exchange for House votes.

Now it was up to Buchanan to confirm or deny Jackson's words. Now he must pay the price for his stupid meddling. On August 8, 1827, he addressed a letter to the editor of the *Lancaster Journal,* reconciling, as far as he was able, the points of conflict between what actually happened and what Jackson reported. But no matter how he tried to shield the Hero behind a flimsy veil of words, the gist of his letter was his reasonably clear denial that emissaries from Clay ever came to him with an offer. Earlier, he told Green he had no authority from Clay or Clay's friends to go to Jackson on any matter. Yet the impression he left with the General—an impression no one could have missed, insisted the Hero—was that he represented the Kentuckian.

Jackson was livid with rage over the letter. The blinking, sniveling, little busybody had dared to trifle with him. "The outrageous statement of Mr. Buchanan will require my attention," he threatened. Meanwhile the unhappy meddler, who really meant no harm, apologized profusely to the Hero. "I regret beyond expression," he wrote, "that you believed me to be an emissary from Mr. Clay. Since some time . . . I have been your ardent, decided, & perhaps without vanity I may say, your efficient friend." Indeed, he was an efficient friend and too important to the Pennsylvania party to be reprimanded or (as some demanded) expelled from Jackson's ranks. So the Hero calmed down and the Nashville Junto agreed to "touch" Buchanan's statement with "tenderness" in order to "preserve his friendship and needful influence." The task of applying the tender touch was turned over to Eaton, who, in a letter to the public dated September 12, 1827, contradicted nothing Buchanan had written except the time of the interview.

The unfortunate outcome of this incident in no way lessened Jackson's enthusiasm to charge into the public prints whenever he could lash the coalition with the sharp words of one of his assistants. Besides initiating, supervising, or approving public letters, pamphlets, and handbills and studying the findings of his "travelling corpsmen," the General personally kept up a vast correspondence with state leaders and Congressmen. He was the natural center of the party organizations just beginning to emerge in each community to block Adams' re-election. "I have given you the annexed list," wrote one of his correspondents, "for the purpose of enabling you, if you should think proper, to write to certain men in this state, and at the same time, to give you the best data now at command, from which to estimate your present strength in Kentucky." If the Hero did not himself write to these "certain men," most assuredly someone on the committee did so in his behalf.[7]

7. Buchanan to Ingham, August 16, 1827, Buchanan Papers (Pennsylvania Historical Society); the letters of Beverley, Jackson, Clay, Buchanan,

At first, few of Jackson's contemporaries recognized what a superb politician he really was, a politician straight to the bone whose natural instincts for the game were probably refined by his many years in the army. Even historians have failed to credit him sufficiently for his political astuteness. Not only do they downgrade his importance in conducting this election, but during his administration, later on, they tend to overemphasize Van Buren's role in shaping public policy, especially in the Bank war and in the decision to read John C. Calhoun out of the party. Actually Jackson's control of his own administration was unshared with any other public officer.

Very early in this campaign—even before he was formally renominated by the Tennessee legislature—the Hero made it clear that he regarded himself as the candidate of the people, as the man "taken up" by the electorate to defend justice and virtue, as a popular champion sent against an entrenched elite who viewed the government as a private operation restricted to certified gentlemen. There was nothing hypocritical or cynical in this pose. He sincerely believed what he said. Probably most really good politicians think this way, whether true or not, and in Jackson's case there was more than an element of truth in what he said.

There was also a touch of craft and guile in the old General. No sooner did Calhoun and Van Buren draw close to him than Jackson began repeating that he was much too old and ill to serve *two* terms as President. (He was sixty in 1827, the same age as John Quincy Adams.) Four years as chief executive was all he wanted; then he would turn the reins of government over to younger men. His protestations of feebleness had Calhoun quivering with anticipation, to say nothing of Martin Van Buren. Perhaps the Hero meant what he said; but whether he did or not, his words were perfectly calculated to swell the loyalties of several important and ambitious men in Washington.

Jackson always insisted that he would not electioneer for the

---

and Eaton in *Niles' Weekly Register,* July 7 and 21, August 11 and 18, October 6, 1827; Jackson to Lewis, September 1, 1827, Jackson Papers (Morgan Library); Buchanan to Jackson, August 10, 1827, Jackson Papers (Library of Congress); *National Journal,* October 6, 1827; Major Allan Campbell to Jackson, February 4, 1827, Jackson, *Correspondence,* III, 333.

Presidency, but every letter he wrote, every delegation of visitors he entertained at the Hermitage, every politician he sent off on an assignment in different sections of the nation, was part of a careful campaign to wrest the Presidency from John Quincy Adams. His trip to New Orleans in January, 1828, to celebrate his victory over the British was electioneering in the grand manner. Ostensibly nonpartisan, the celebration happily combined national pride in a great historical event with the political ambitions of the man who was responsible for that event.

Around this popular and politically wise old gentleman other men were now constructing a new national party; yet as long as he lived Andrew Jackson remained its head and vital force.

As Van Buren had promised earlier, once re-elected to the Senate in February, 1827, he really got down to the work of forging a "new political combination." Characteristically, he began his task by calling a series of conferences among Jacksonian Congressmen, where, according to one opposition report, "schemes [were] devised, questions debated & the minority was ruled by the majority." It was said that the conferees agreed to commence their "labors" to elect Jackson on July 4, 1827, "in every part of the Union at once." There may have been no such agreement as reported, but conferences were held and the formal canvass did begin on the assigned date. "Little squads in the North and East, West and South," in recognition of Independence Day, "made toasts of egregious length" to the election of Old Hickory and to the restoration of liberty.

Present at Van Buren's conferences were representatives from most of the large states, including Calhoun; Senators Benton, Eaton, Dickerson of New Jersey, Johnson of Kentucky, and McLane of Delaware; and Representatives Buchanan, Moore, Ingham, and Houston. Reportedly, they met several times a week, although that sounds a bit excessive even for such a caucus-minded politician as Van Buren. Whatever the frequency, the meetings were extremely fruitful in initiating plans for the "substantial reorganization of the old Republican party." . . .[8] Most

8. *Catawba Journal* (Charlotte, N.C.), May 1, 1827, quoting *National Intelligencer; National Journal,* July 24, 1827; Benton to Balch, February

important of all, however, they forged the essential political "combinations for electing Gen. Jackson"—so said Representative John Floyd of Virginia, who participated in the forging. And, by the spring of 1827, he advised his Virginia cronies that those "combinations" were "nearly complete."

Partly by design and partly by accident, Floyd's words leaked to the administration newspapers, and a horrendous cry went up about the "unnatural alliances" being concluded in Washington "under the standard of a new cabalistic party organization." . . .

Now that the Adams newspapers were privy to the so-called "combinations," they demanded to know on what terms the agreement had been arranged, apparently without realizing that the sole condition required by some men was certainty over Jackson's ability to win the election. These editors jumped to the conclusion, of course, that Van Buren was the only politician slick enough to unite so many disparate groups. "The masterspirit with his magic wand," they said, "cast a spell over the heterogeneous mass, and the wolves and kids mingled together in peace and love!" But how long would this love-spell last? Can Senator Dickerson, the advocate of protection, cooperate with his Southern colleagues, asked the *National Journal?* Can John Randolph and Littleton W. Tazewell unite with the men whose opinions on improvements collide with their own? "Can the Tennessee and Kentucky and Virginia Hotspurs long coalesce with their new allies who desire to oust the present Administration because of alleged hostility to federal men and federal measures?" Surely such excellent men as McLane, Ingham, Buchanan, Houston, Drayton, and Macon, continued these editors, owed it to the public to "announce the terms and conditions of the agreement that has been made."

There were indeed many differences of opinion dividing the Jackson men, both in and out of Congress. The problem of settling on terms and conditions was complicated by the necessity of creating a national voting majority out of a patchwork of conflict-

---

8, 22, 1827, February 14 and April 30, 1828, Jackson Papers (Library of Congress); Benton to Van Buren (n.d.), Levi Woodbury Papers (Library of Congress).

ing interest groups, classes, and factions. These groups ranged from farmers and mechanics to planters, businessmen, and bankers. They included Republicans and Federalists, nationalists and states' righters, conservatives and liberals. Some Jacksonians in Pennsylvania, New York, Ohio, Indiana, and Kentucky called for a protective tariff, a system of national roads and improvements, and the continued support of the Second National Bank; others, often from the same states, objected to these proposals and urged a freer capitalistic system, unhampered by governmental controls.

Undoubtedly, if these Congressmen had attempted a settlement on national issues, the alliances would have been stillborn. Because they represented a wide range of diverse interests among coalescing Jacksonians, no basic statement of purpose and direction seemed wise or feasible. Their first objective was to win the election, nothing more. What the administration editors by their questions were really trying to do, therefore, was prove to the public that the Democrats were irresponsible opportunists bound together by little else than a will to oust Adams, even if that meant supporting an incompetent and illiterate military chieftain.

The problem of the Jacksonian Congressmen was, to a degree, solved by the General himself. When asked specifically about certain issues, he responded by following one of several alternatives: either he took Benton's advice and referred to his voting record in the Senate, or he refused a direct answer on the ground that it might be interpreted as electioneering (and no gentleman would ever electioneer for the Presidency), or he wrote long, highly ambiguous replies that could be interpreted several ways, or he ignored the question and simply struck a pose as the Hero of New Orleans cheated of the Presidency in 1825.

Yet for all his double talk and concern for his public image, Jackson did subscribe to a national program, one he vaguely alluded to during the campaign (very vaguely) but one he later outlined in detail to Amos Kendall, editor of the Kentucky *Argus of the West*. As he subsequently defined it, his program was neo-Jeffersonian and conservative, leaning toward states' rights and the economics of *laissez faire,* but so bland and inoffensive that those previously disposed to follow him could not seriously object to a single point.

In the first place, Jackson told Kendall, he intended to reduce the patronage of the federal government. (By interpreting his words as loosely as the rules of language allow, this could mean a policy of economy, though the General did not say so specifically.) The Hero believed that Adams had used the patronage to pay off the men responsible for "stealing" the Presidency in 1825, a belief documented to his entire satisfaction by the report on executive appointments submitted to the Senate by Thomas Hart Benton. Hence, Jackson saw as his first duty the wholesale removal of these coalitionists, along with anyone else who campaigned for Adams' re-election. "All men in office," he assured Kendall, "who are known to have interferred in the election as committee men, electioneers or otherwise . . . will be unceremoniously removed. So also will all men who have been appointed from political considerations or against the will of the people, and all who are incompetent." Throughout the campaign this issue became a favorite theme with Jacksonian editors and politicians, who assured the people that the removals were necessary in order to "purify the Departments" and "reform the Government." "Let the cry be JACKSON and REFORM," they thundered. But obviously the word "reform" was hardly more than a euphemism for political head-chopping.

Next, Jackson informed Kendall that he favored a "middle and just course" with respect to the tariff question. As he had stated several years before in a letter to Littleton H. Coleman, he thought the rates of protection should be "judicious," a remark that prompted Henry Clay to declare his preference for an "*in*judicious" tariff. In an Albany speech Martin Van Buren seconded Jackson's position by calling for a tariff that would be "wise" and "just" and "salutary." One man in the audience cheered the speech and then turned to his neighbor and asked: "On which side of the Tariff question was it?"[9]

9. *Telegraph,* October 20, 1827; Kendall to Blair, February 3, 1829, Blair-Lee Papers (Princeton University Library); Houston to Jackson, January 5, 1827, Jackson, *Correspondence,* III, 331; *Whig* (Richmond), February 16 and March 16, 1827; *National Journal,* March 1, April 10 and 15, 1827;

Jackson may have preferred the "middle course"—wherever that was—but his friends frequently reshaped his preference to conform to local prejudice. In "protection-mad" Pennsylvania, Samuel D. Ingham assured his people that Old Hickory would "raise the tariff everytime he touched it." Yet in the South the *Richmond Enquirer* and the *Raleigh Register,* among others, expressed amazement that anyone could claim Jackson as a friend of protection. He favored a tariff, they wrote, only as a source of revenue and a means of strengthening the national defense and liquidating the national debt. Any other interpretation was unjustified. To clarify the matter the Indiana legislature pressed Jackson during the campaign for a more precise declaration, but the General refused to be drawn out. "Not, sir, that I would wish to conceal my opinions from the people upon any political, or national subject," the foxy Hero replied, "but as they were in various ways promulgated in 1824, I am apprehensive that my appearance before the public, at this time, may be attributed, as has been the case, to improper motives." The Hoosiers were delighted with his clarification and expressed their complete satisfaction with it. One report insisted that it even converted three Adams committees within the state!

The General did not double talk all the issues, however. Regarding federally sponsored public works, he straightforwardly admitted his opposition. Then he modified his statement slightly by proposing to distribute surplus revenues to the states to permit them to undertake their own improvements. After all, the issue was important to the people of Kentucky, Ohio, Indiana, and Illinois, and it was necessary to relieve their minds about his intentions without antagonizing, at the same time, the people of New York and Virginia. Once again his attitude about the question was reshaped to accord with varying sectional opinions. In Pennsylvania, Jackson's partisans went so far as to declare that "His triumph will give expansion to the 'American System.'"

National Intelligencer, March 10, 13, 20, and 22, 1827; Kendall to Blair, March 7, 1829, Blair-Lee Papers (Princeton University Library); *Telegraph,* January 24, February 9, and June 23, 1828; *Statesman* (Boston), March 19 and October 24, 1828; *National Journal,* June 9, 1828; Van Buren, *Autobiography,* pp. 171, 240; *Argus* (Albany), July 3, 10, and 13, 1827.

The final point in his program was the most startling of all. He actually told Kendall he was looking for "plain, business men" to assist him in running his administration. Presumably, these hard-headed realists would help restore the government to fiscal and ethical soundness. No Cabinet officer, he concluded, could be a candidate for President, and all members must concur in his "policies."

One additional policy might be added to this list, though Jackson did not include it himself. It concerned the Indians and their removal to the West, an issue that developed when Georgia renewed her efforts to despoil the Creek nation. When President Adams negotiated a treaty with the Creeks by which the Indians were to cede their land in Georgia except for a strip west of the Chatahoochee River, Governor George M. Troup of Georgia objected. He wanted all the land. Defying both the President and the Secretary of War, he threatened to use his militia if they attempted to carry out the terms of the treaty. Adams responded to the verbal cannonade by vowing to employ "all means under his control to maintain the faith of the nation."

Jackson, whose affection for the Indian about equaled his affection for Henry Clay, unreservedly endorsed the policy of total removal. "Say to them [the Indians]," he once wrote, "their Father, the President will lay off a country of equal extent, transport them to it . . . and give them a free [*sic*] simple title to the land." But, as the General's friends in Georgia understood only too well, it was less important to tell the Indians anything than it was to assure the electorate of the Hero's commitment to removal.

Meanwhile the Jacksonian-controlled Senate appointed a committee, headed by Thomas Hart Benton, to investigate the administration's trouble with Governor Troup. As expected, Benton's final report faulted the government for its unwarranted interference in the internal affairs of Georgia and justified everything the Governor had been "compelled" to do to protect the interests of his state. But long before Benton's report was published, Adams was "politically dead" in Georgia, and the stench arising from the corpse permeated the entire Southwest. In the Georgia 1828 race, both sets of electors pledged themselves to Jackson.

These policies, as Jackson liked to call them, revealed his excellence as a politician of compromise and accommodation; they explain in part why so many discordant groups could unite behind him in his campaign for the Presidency, why the wolves and kids could mingle together in peace and love. For some people, of course, the issues had nothing to do with their decision to join the General's party. Far more important than a meaningless program was the energy, leadership, and exciting personality they felt Jackson could bring to the Presidency—qualities that make history, not simply wait upon it. Others had an even more basic reason for supporting the Hero. He "is the man," commented one politician, "that alone can be run with success."[10]

10. William E. Dodd, "Andrew Jackson and His Enemies," *Century,* CXI (1926), 736; *Register* (Raleigh), April 28, 1827; *National Journal,* July 14, 1827; *Niles' Weekly Register,* May 3, 1828; Kendall to Blair, March 7, 1829, Blair-Lee Papers (Princeton University Library); *National Journal,* July 14, 1827; Samuel Flagg Bemis, *John Quincy Adams and the Union* (New York, 1956), pp. 79–87; Jackson to Colonel John D. Terrill, July 29, 1826, Jackson, *Correspondence,* III, 308; *National Journal,* May 26, 1827; Saunders to Yancey, January 20, 1827, Bartlett Yancey Papers (University of North Carolina Library).

JOHN SPENCER BASSETT

✪

A Remarkable Man

At this point we turn from Jackson's conflicts and problems and consider the man himself. His enemies hated him and rarely saw his good qualities; his friends loved him and reluctantly admitted his failings; and in a sense each was right. Some of the good things he did are excellent and some of the bad things are wretched. His puzzling personality defies clear analysis, but we must admit that he was a remarkable man. He lacked much through the want of an education, and he acquired much through apparent accident, but it was only his strong character which turned deficiency and opportunity alike to his purpose and made his will the strongest influence in his country in his time.

The secret of his power was his adjustment to the period in which he lived. Other men excelled him in experience, wisdom, and balanced judgment; but the American Democrats of the day admired neither of these qualities. They honored courage, strength, and directness. They could tolerate ignorance but not hesitancy. Jackson was the best embodiment of their desires from the beginning of the national government to his own day.

Jackson accepted democracy with relentless logic. Some others believed that wise leaders could best determine the policies of government, but he more than anyone else of his day threw the task of judging upon the common man. And this he did without cant and in entire sincerity. No passionate dreamer of the past was

From John Spencer Bassett, *The Life of Andrew Jackson* (New York: Macmillan, 1911), Vol. II, pp. 700–715, 748–750.

more willing than he to test his principles to the uttermost. "You know I never despair," he said; "I have confidence in the virtue and good sense of the people. God is just, and while we act faithfully to the Constitution, he will smile upon and prosper our exertions."[1]

Mere military glory will not explain his hold on the nation. It undoubtedly had much to do with his introduction into national politics, but it soon gave place to a popularity resting on other qualities. In fact, his peculiar character shone behind his military fame and recommended him to the people. They liked his promptness in invading Florida in 1818 and his abrupt bridling of the dallying Callava in 1821 as much as his victory at New Orleans. Other generals won victories in the war, but they did not become political forces through them. To the people the old government seemed weak and unequal, and Jackson, the man who solved difficulties, was elected to reform it. When the process of reform began his capacity as a political leader showed itself. Probably he could have been re-elected in 1832 independently of his war record.

Much has been said about his honesty. The historical critic and the moralist know this for a common virtue. Most of Jackson's contemporaries were as honest as he, but he excelled them in candor, which is frequently pronounced honesty. He was apt to speak his mind clearly, although he could on occasion, as has been seen, be as diplomatic as a delicate case demanded. Van Buren said in apparent sincerity that he believed "an honester or in any sense a better man was never placed at the head of the Government."[2]

Many citations and incidents . . . witness Jackson's lack of restraint and fair judgment. They seem to suggest habitual errors of mind; but we are assured that such was not the case. Even Calhoun, in the bitterness of the final quarrel, admitted that in ordinary matters and when not irritated by some unusual thing he was fair and reasonable. The explosions of anger for which he was noted were incident to a tense natural temperament; and they were

1. Jackson to Van Buren, November 1, 1830, Van Buren Mss. (Library of Congress).
2. Van Buren to John Randolph, April 13, 1831, Van Buren Mss.

apt to come when he was off his guard. In dangers which were anticipated he was extremely cool. Thus at New Orleans he broke into violent rage when he saw the column on the west bank falling back, although when the lines were assailed two hours earlier he was complete master of himself. In the long struggles against his political enemies he was never surprised into some rash explosion, although many efforts were made by opponents to lead him into such a situation. "He was," says Van Buren, "in times of peculiar difficulty and danger, calm and equable in his carriage and always master of his passions."[3]

But Van Buren would not claim that he was fair toward an opponent. "The conciliation of individuals," he said, "formed the smallest, perhaps too small a part of his policy. His strength lay with the masses, and he knew it. He first, and at last in all public questions, always tried to be right, and when he felt that he was so he apprehended little, sometimes too little, from the opposition of prominent and powerful men, and it must now be admitted that he seldom overestimated the strength he derived from the confidence and favor of the people."[4]

In England Van Buren came into contact with the Duke of Wellington, then a leader of the conservatives there; and he made the following comparison between the Duke and Jackson:

There were many points in which he and General Jackson resembled each other. In moral and physical courage, in indifference to personal consequences, and in promptness of action there was little if any difference in their characters. The Duke was better educated and had received the instruction of experience upon a larger scale, but the General in native intellect had, I think, been more richly endowed.[5]

But there was a marked dissimilarity which Van Buren over-looked. The Englishman was cautious, steady, and persistent; the American was aggressive, incautious, and disposed to throw all his strength into a frontal attack. Wellington was a conservative by nature, Jackson was a radical; Wellington in politics led the party

3. *Autobiography*, Van Buren Mss., V, 84.
4. *Ibid.*, III, 52.
5. *Ibid.*, IV, 167.

of privilege, Jackson led the party of equality. Neither could have performed the task of the other.

When Jackson became President it was expected that he would fall under the influence of favorites. His inexperience in national affairs made it essential that he should take advice freely, and he himself was conscious of it. But he was never a tool. In all his important measures he was the dominant figure. The Maysville veto was, perhaps, the affair in which another had most part, but even here Van Buren, who suggested the measure, was careful to base it on Jackson's known opposition to the invasion of states' rights and to the exploitation of the public treasury by private parties. He approached the matter most cautiously and used his best tact to conceal his purpose.

Other Presidents were dependent on advice, but they usually consulted their Cabinet. Jackson, when a General, rarely held military councils; when President he rarely held Cabinet meetings. A formal Cabinet decision limited him; he preferred to consult whom he wished, informally and without responsibility. Out of such conditions grew the "Kitchen Cabinet." This group did not control him outright; all its members approached him with great caution, and they accomplished their ends only by tact and insinuating appeals to his feelings.

If his policies were his own his documents were usually prepared by others. He was not a master of writing or argumentation, but he knew well what he would fight for. His private letters show crude reasoning to support objects which are dictated by common sense. His best documents are his military proclamations, where there is room for the play of such strong feelings as courage, endurance, and loyalty—qualities in which he was at his best.

His lack of political knowledge made him in cases where knowledge was essential a bad judge of men. In 1834 he expressed a desire to appoint Cuthbert, of Georgia, to the Supreme bench, upon which Van Buren observed that there were two Cuthberts in Georgia, Alfred, of whom he had never heard that he was a lawyer, and John, whom he did not think equal to the position.[6]

6. Jackson to Van Buren, October 27, 1834, and Van Buren to Jackson, November 5, 1834, Van Buren Mss.

Jackson took the rebuke in good spirit, and appointed another man.

Van Buren's anxiety to escape blame for participating in the removal of the deposits has been alluded to; but we are hardly prepared for the following audacious utterance made the day after the order to remove went into effect:

You will see by the inclosed, that the opposition have commenced the game I anticipated. They have found by experience that their abuse of you is labour lost, and they conclude wisely that if they could succeed in shifting the Bank question from your shoulders to mine, they would be better able to serve the Mammon than they are at present. Now, although I cannot grumble at the service they are rendering me with the people, by identifying me with you in this matter, it will not do for us to expose the great measure to prejudice by doing anything that would tend in the slightest degree to withdraw from it the protection of your name.[7]

The object of this peculiarly insidious flattery probably never suspected its nature. To the faults of a friend he was singularly blind.

Of associates other than Van Buren, Lewis seems to have had influence chiefly in personal affairs. He was at home in the Eaton intrigue, the exclusion of Calhoun, and the nomination of Van Buren in 1832. He lived in the President's house and encouraged the impression that he held the key to his favor. He was able by this means to exert a wide influence among the office-seekers. Jackson used him freely in matters high and low. At one time he wants him to stay in Washington to keep an eye on the situation during the President's absence: at another he gives him all kinds of minor commissions, as writing papers and selling cotton.[8] Kendall had more to do with policies, but his influence came comparatively late. He was powerful in the Bank controversy, a strong supporter of Jackson's anti-Bank views, and after that war was won his influence survived in general matters. Blair, who came into touch with the administration in 1830, became after a while a

7. Van Buren to Jackson, October 2, 1833, Van Buren Mss.
8. Illustrations are found in the Ford Mss. See calendar in *Eulletin of New York Public Library,* IV, 295–302.

warm personal associate; but he was not a man of creative power. He loved Jackson and fought faithfully for him, but the many letters which passed between them show no evidence that he sought to modify the President's political life.

But Blair gave a rich friendship. He had the homely virtues of the West. His home on Pennsylvania Avenue opposite the President's house was presided over by a wife who to a larger culture added the reliable virtues of Mrs. Jackson. It was a haven of comfort to the tired spirit and body of the harassed and pain-racked Jackson, and he made touching references to it as long as he lived. To Mrs. Blair on the eve of his departure from Washington he wrote the following characteristic words:

I cannot leave this city without presenting you my grateful thanks for the great kindness you have extended to me and my family whilst here. When sick you visited us and extended to me and our dear little ones all comforts within your power. We all part with you and your dear husband and amiable family with sincere regret; but I trust a kind providence that I may reach home and be spared until I have the pleasure of seeing you and Mr. Blair and your dear Eliza at the Hermitage. You will receive a good welcome. I beg you to accept as a memento of my regard a heifer raised by me since my second election. She will bring you in mind of my fondness for good milk, and how I was gratified in this fondness from your liberal hands.[9]

If he had the failings of suspiciousness, narrowness, and vindictiveness, he had also the calmer virtues of domesticity and personal honor. He was peculiarly gentle with the weak. Women were pleased with his protecting chivalry. They admired his grave dignity and warm emotions. For children he had a tender heart, and the cry of an infant aroused his warm sympathy. His letters contain many expressions of pride in the developments of the children of his adopted son and of distress over their suffering. Into his relations with his relatives storms rarely entered. To them he was the clan leader and defender.

With true Southern feeling he took every woman seriously. In 1833 a New Haven spinster appealed to Van Buren to introduce

9. March 6, 1837, Jackson Mss. (Library of Congress).

her to Jackson, so that she might win his affection and become his wife. Her letter was forwarded to Jackson, who wrote in the finest possible strain, and with his own hand:

Whatever may be her virtues, I could make but one answer to any partiality they could form for me, and that is, my heart is in the grave of my dear departed wife, from which sacred spot no living being can recall it. In the cultivation of the sentiments of friendship, which are perhaps rendered more active by the loss I have sustained, I trust I shall always be able to produce suitable returns for the favor of my acquaintants; and if therefore I ever meet this lady I shall hope to satisfy her that I appreciate as I ought her kindness, tho' I cannot for a moment entertain the proposition it has led her to make.[10]

Much of the affection of his old age centered in the family and person of his adopted son, a man whose business failures brought much sorrow. For the son's wife, Sarah York Jackson, the father had a strong affection which was well deserved by her calm and faithful care of his old age. His fatherly instinct was marked. It appears with many other virtues, in the following letter to Andrew Jackson, Jr., written from Washington, March 9, 1834, after paying many of the young man's debts:

My dear son, I recd yesterday your letter of the 16th ultimo, and have read with attention, and am more than pleased that you have taken a just view of that fatherly advice I have been constantly pressing upon you, believing as I do, that unless you adopt them you cannot possibly get well thro life and provide for an increasing family which it is now your duty to do, and have the means of giving them such education as your duty to them as a parent requires, and their standing in society, merits.

My dear son, It is enough for me that you acknowledge your error, it is the error of youth and inexperience, and my son I fully forgive them. You have my advice, it is that of a tender and affectionate father given to you for your benefit and that of your dear and amiable family, and I pray you to adhere to it in all respects and it will give peace and plenty thro life and that of your amiable Sarah and her dear little ones. Keep clear of Banks and indebtedness, and you live a freeman, and die in independence and leave your family so.

Before this reaches you, you will have received my letter enclosing

10. Van Buren to Jackson, July 22, 1833, and Jackson to Van Buren, July 25, 1833, Van Buren Mss.

Mr. Hubbs note, cancelled; and as soon as you furnish me with the full amount of the debts due by the farm, with any you may have contracted in Tennessee, and the contract with Mr. Hill for the land purchased, I will, if my means are equal to the object, free you from debt and the farm, when the farm with the aid of your own industry and economy must support us, and after I am gone, you and your family. Hence it is, and was, that I was and am so solicitous to be furnished with the full information on all the points required of you. Those who do not settle all their accounts at the end of the year, cannot know what means he really possesses, for the next; and remember, my son, that honesty and justice to all men require that we should always live within our own means, and not on those of others, when it may be, that those to whom we are indebted are relying on what we owe them, for their own support. Therefore it is unjust to live on any but our own means honestly and justly acquired. Follow this rule and a wise and just providence will smile upon your honest endeavours, and surround you with plenty, so long as you deserve it by your just and charitable conduct to all others.[11]

In 1829 many persons thought that a democratic President would rob the office of its dignity. Their fears were only partially realized; for although the new party gave a touch of crudeness to life in Washington generally, the manners of the democratic President on formal occasions were all that could be desired. Francis Lieber, who visited him, spoke admiringly of his "noble, expressive countenance," and said: "He has the appearance of a venerable old man, his features by no means plain; on the contrary, he made the best impression on me."[12]

Tyrone Power, the actor, gives this account:

As viewed on horseback, the General is a fine, soldierly, well-preserved old gentleman, with a pale, wrinkled countenance, and a keen clear eye, restless and searching. His seat is an uncommonly good one, his hand apparently light, and his carriage easy and horseman-like; circumstances though trifling in themselves, not so general here as to escape observation. . . . Both the wife and sister of an English officer of high rank, themselves women of remarkable refinement of mind and manners, observed to me, in speaking of the President, that

11. Jackson Mss.
12. Thomas Sergeant Perry, ed., *The Life and Letters of Francis Lieber* (Boston, 1882), pp. 92, 93.

they had seldom met a person possessed of more native courtesy, or a more dignified deportment.[13]

A more critical and less friendly observer was Nathaniel Sargent, who said:

In any promiscuous assembly of a thousand men he would have been pointed out above all the others as a man "born to command," and who would, in any dangerous emergency, be at once placed in command. Ordinarily, he had the peculiar, rough, independent, free and easy ways of the backwoodsman; but at the same time he had, whenever occasion required, and especially when in the society of ladies, very urbane and graceful manners.[14]

John Fairfield, Congressman from Maine, said of him:

He is a warm-hearted, honest old man as ever lived, and possesses talents too of the first order, notwithstanding what many of our Northern folk think of him. He talks about all matters freely and fearlessly without any disguise, and in a straightforward honesty and simplicity of style and manner which you would expect from what I have before said of him. I wish some of our good folks North could hear him talk upon a subject in which he is interested, say the French question, which he talked about on Monday evening. I think their opinions would undergo a change.[15]

Life in the President's house now lost something of the good form of the Virginia regime, but it lost nothing of the air of domesticity. Throughout most of the two administrations the household was directed by Mrs. A. J. Donelson, a woman of firm and refined character whom the people of Washington greatly respected. Her husband, a private secretary of more than ordinary ability, was related to Mrs. Jackson. Their presence in the White House gave something of the Hermitage feeling to the place. Politicians came and went as freely in office hours as in any

13. Tyrone Power, *Impressions of America* (London, 1836), I, 279, 281.
14. Nathaniel Sargent, *Public Men and Events* (Philadelphia, 1875), I, 35, 246.
15. John Fairfield to his wife, December 9, 1835, Fairfield Mss. in the possession of Miss Martha Fairfield, Saco, Maine.

exterior public office in the city. Intimates like Van Buren, Eaton, and Blair dropped in at any time, before breakfast, or in the evening, as inclination prompted; and the industrious Lewis for a large part of the administrations lived in the house. Ordinarily the President and his family made one group in the evenings. If a Cabinet member, or other official, appeared to talk about public business, he read his documents or otherwise consulted with Jackson in one part of the room, the ladies sewing or chatting and the children playing meanwhile in another part.[16]

The levees were as republican as Jefferson could wish. George Bancroft thus describes one he attended in 1831:

> The old man stood in the centre of a little circle, about large enough for a cotillion, and shook hands with everybody that offered. The number of ladies who attended was small; nor were they brilliant. But to compensate for it there was a throng of apprentices, boys of all ages, men not civilized enough to walk about the room with their hats off; the vilest promiscuous medley that ever was congregated in a decent house; many of the lowest gathering round the doors, pouncing with avidity upon the wine and refreshments, tearing the cake with the ravenous keenness of intense hunger; starvelings, and fellows with dirty faces and dirty manners; all the refuse that Washington could turn forth from its workshops and stables. In one part of the room it became necessary to use a rattan.[17]

Bancroft was ever a precise gentleman and in his own day in the capital his entertainments were models of propriety, but we cannot doubt that the people at the levee he attended were absolutely rude. Fortunately he was at a select reception and his impressions of it were better. "The old gentleman," he said, "received us as civilly as any private individual could have done; he had me introduced to all the ladies of the family, and such was the perfect ease and good breeding that prevailed there, they talked to me as though I had been an acquaintance of ten years' standing. . . . I received a very favorable impression of the President's personal

16. For Van Buren's praise of Jackson's love of family, see *Autobiography,* IV, 82.
17. M. A. DeWolfe Howe, *The Life and Letters of George Bancroft,* 2 vols. (New York, 1908), I, 196.

character; I gave him credit for great firmness in his attachments, for sincere kindness of heart, for a great deal of philanthropy and genuine good feeling; but touching his qualifications for President, avast there—Sparta hath many a wiser than he."[18]

Of a reception at the President's, December 24, 1835, we have this description: "More than three hundred guests were invited, and there was on this evening much scurrying of the innumerable hacks on Pennsylvania Avenue to take guests to the mansion. Entering the door we leave our wraps, cross a large empty room, pass another door to a room in which Jackson meets his guests. He receives his company by shaking hands with each, which is done in a very kind, courteous and gentlemanly manner, and sometimes with friendly warmth, according to the personage." We may loiter in this room if we will, but we probably pass on to the "blue room," whose light is so trying to the complexion that few ladies will linger a moment in it. Beyond that is the brilliantly lighted "east room," in which the guests promenade, and it fills with people intermingling informally, a lively "scene of bowing, talking, laughing, ogling, squinting, squeezing, etc." In the room are many of the notables of the city, Congressmen with their wives, Senators, army and naval officers with swords and uniforms, and persons of distinction. The ladies are handsome, or not, as nature made them, but they are uniformly dressed with elegance, mostly in satin gowns with here and there a mantle of rich silk and velvet. Ices, jellies, wine, and lemonade are passed continually among the guests; and at eleven o'clock supper is served. Into a large dining room enter the guests. A table, or counter, surrounds the space set so as to allow the company to sit outside of its perimeter, next the wall. Within this square is a smaller table from which food and drink are served. Of each sort there is an abundance. "I can't describe this supper," says our informant; "I am not capable of it. I can only say it surpassed everything of the kind I ever saw before, and that we had *everything*. This party could not have cost the President much short of $1,500."[19]

Jackson's dinners were generous and in good form. General Robert Patterson, of Philadelphia, gives us this impression of one

18. *Ibid.,* I, 192.
19. John Fairfield to his wife, December 25, 1835, Fairfield Mss.

he attended: "At 4 o'clock, we went to the President's. The party was small, comprising only the General's family and ourselves. The dinner was very neat and served in excellent taste, while the wines were of the choicest qualities. The President himself dined on the simplest fare; bread, milk and vegetables. After dinner took a walk through the grounds about the 'White House' which are laid out with much neatness and order, and filled with a number of shrubs and flowers."[20]

The following items from his personal accounts of 1834 will show how amply his table was spread: October 1, he had twelve pounds of veal, forty-nine of beef, and nineteen cents' worth of hog's fat. October 2, he had eight pounds of mutton, forty pounds of beef, and twenty-five cents' worth of sausages. October 3, it was twenty-two pounds of mutton and twenty pounds of beef. October 4, he had six pounds of sweetbreads, sixteen pounds of mutton, three pounds of lard, $1.10 worth of beef, and twenty-five cents' worth of veal. For drink he was charged on October 13, with one barrel of ale and half a barrel of beer, and on October 31, with another barrel of ale. October 1, he bought three gallons of brandy, two gallons of Holland gin, and one gallon of Jamaica spirits. October 13, he bought three bottles of Château Margeaux, a like quantity of Château Lafitte, and a dozen bottles of London porter. October 22, he had two gallons each of brandy, Jamaica spirits, and Holland gin.[21]

Some idea of the furnishing of the President's house under Jackson may be had from an inventory made March 24, 1825. The contents of each room appear in faithful description and are here reproduced because I know of no other such reliable account. In the entrance hall were four mahogany settees, two marble consul tables, two elegant brass fenders, one oilcloth carpet, one thermometer and barometer, and one "lamp with branches wants repair." In the large levee room were four large mahogany sofas and twenty-four large mahogany armchairs—all "unfinished"— eight pine tables, one door screen, one paper screen partition, one mahogany map stand, one "common" washstand, basin, and ewer, one pine clothespress, and a bookcase in three sections. In the

20. General Patterson's diary, in possession of Mr. Lindsay Patterson, Winston-Salem, North Carolina.
21. Jackson Mss.

"Elliptical Drawing Room" were one "large glass and gilt chandelier, elegant," two gilt brown mirrors, one gilt consul table, marble top, two china vases, one elegant gilt French mantel clock, four bronze and gilt candelabras with eagle heads, pair of bronze and gilt andirons, two sofas—gilt and satin—with twenty-four chairs, four settees, and five footstools to match a large French carpet, double silk window curtains with gilt eagle cornices and six small curtain pins, and with two fire screens in gilt and satin, two bronze candlesticks, and shovel and tongs. Besides the two rooms mentioned, there were on the first floor a "Yellow Drawing Room," a "Green Drawing Room," large and small dining rooms, a china closet, a pantry, and a porter's room. There were a "first service" of two hundred and seventy pieces of French china, a "second service, dessert," of 157 pieces of crimson and gilt china, a service of white and gilt china of 232 pieces, a white and gilt French china tea service containing 156 pieces, a blue china dinner service of 66 pieces. The solid silver consisted of 28 dishes in three sizes, one coffeepot, two teapots, one urn, two large tureens with buckskin cases, one sugar dish, eight castor rolls, one set of castors, five nutcrackers, with spoons, forks, fish knives, etc. Among these was one large chest with 167 pieces, most of which were solid silver. Another case had 150 pieces of French plate, and there was a French gilt dessert set of 140 pieces. In the basement were the kitchens, the steward's rooms, the servants' hall, servants' rooms with the scantiest furniture, this being a sample: "No. 1, one cot, worn out, one mattress, worn out, one short bench." On the second floor were the family sleeping quarters with six furnished bedrooms, and private drawing and dressing rooms. No mention is made of bathrooms, and the illumination of the house was by candles and lamps.[22]

Jackson was never a careful spender, and through this trait as well as by an abundant hospitality he used all his Presidential salary, twenty-five thousand dollars a year. When he left Washington he was poorer than he entered it. "I returned," he said, "with barely ninety dollars in my pockets, Beacon for my family and corn and oats for the stock to buy, the new roof on my house just rebuilt leaking and to be repaired. I carried $5,000 when I went to

---

22. See inventory in the House of Representatives Library of Congress.

Washington: it took of my cotton crop $2,250, with my salary, to bring me home. The burning of my house and furniture has left me poor."[23] The Hermitage with its contents was burned in 1834.[24] He ordered it rebuilt, according to the old plans. His receipts from his farm during his absence were very small.

As his administration progressed Jackson became deeply engrossed in its controversies. Visitors were liable to have from him hot outbursts of wrath against Biddle, Clay, or Calhoun. His particular friends learned to ignore such displays, but other persons found them disagreeable. A caller who alluded to contemporary politics might have a harangue on the decay of liberty.[25] It soon dawned on the public that the President was feeling the effects of the strain on him. Victor as he was, sorrow pressed him down, and he was much alone. Defiantly he watched his beaten foes, who dared not renew the battle as long as he was in power.

The two terms of the Presidency brought him continued ill health. Chronic indigestion made it necessary to diet strictly, and but for an iron will he could hardly have lived through the period. Beside this, he suffered continually from the wounds he received in the Benton and Dickinson duels. For his most distressing attacks his favorite remedy was bleeding, and he insisted on using it even when he could ill afford the weakening effects. The winter of 1832–1833 was very trying; and in the following spring and summer its difficulties were increased by the death of Overton and Coffee, two of his oldest and best-loved friends. More than this, the period saw the culmination of the nullification movement and the opening of the controversy over the removal of the deposits. Together they brought great depression. "I want relaxation from business, and rest," he said, "but where can I get rest? I fear not on this earth."[26] Of Coffee's death he said: "I mourn his loss with the feelings of David for his son [*sic*] Jonathan. It is useless to mourn. He is gone the way of all the earth and I will soon follow him. Peace to his manes."[27] . . .

23. See endorsement on Rev. A. D. Campbell to Jackson, March 17, 1837, Jackson Mss.
24. Jackson to Van Buren, October 27, 1834, Van Buren Mss.
25. Sargent, II, 21; Howe, I, 193.
26. Jackson to Van Buren, January 6, 1833, Van Buren Mss.
27. Jackson to Van Buren, July 24, 1833, Van Buren Mss.

In Jackson's old age he fulfilled the promise he had long since made to his wife to join the Presbyterian Church. This he did early in the year 1839 at the end of a series of revival services and with the usual manifestations of conversion. For thirty-five years before he became President, he said, he was accustomed to read at least three chapters of the Bible daily.[28] Such a man could not have been at any time indifferent to religion as an intellectual fact, however little it may have affected his outward conduct. While President he attended the Presbyterian Church regularly. Mrs. Calhoun, mother-in-law of the distinguished South Carolinian, once said that if Jackson were elected President in 1824, she would spend the following winter in Washington, in order to see a President who would go to church. Of her, it was once said that she and Jackson were "the only independent characters" in Washington.[29] In the passages in this book quoted from his letters are abundant evidences of a pious attitude in bearing sorrow and of dependence on God in times of great danger. These feelings increased with old age and with the approach of death: they do not seem to have been more frequent after the date of his conversion. Nor is there any noticeable decrease after that date in the angry epithets he hurled at his opponents. Clay and Adams to the day of his death were unforgiven, and some of his last utterances were to pronounce them falsifiers. Religion was only one of his emotions.

Next to his devotion to his wife Jackson's best friendship was with Blair. From the beginning of his retirement to the end of his life he wrote regularly to his friend in Washington. Hardly a week passed without a letter. In 1842 both Blair and Lewis visited the Hermitage, and Van Buren came also on his tour in the South. The visits brought cheerfulness for a time; but the progress of disease prevented real happiness. Eyes failed, dizziness and weakness became more notable, and at last in the winter of 1844–1845 came dropsical symptoms. To the doctors it indicated a failure of functions which precedes the end. They knew not how to control them, and the dropsy developed throughout the spring.

28, James Parton, *Life of Andrew Jackson,* 3 vols. (New York, 1859–1860), III, 633. See also, B. F. Butler to Jackson, March 16, 1839, Jackson Mss.

29. Rev. E. S. Ely to Jackson, January 28, 1829, Jackson Mss.

The letters to Blair witness in many ways the advance of the disease. . . . The last letter of the series is dated May 26, two weeks before he died. It contains some information for C. J. Ingersoll, in regard to the invasion of Florida, and after that comes to his health. Describing it he says: "This is my situation, and in what it may result God only knows. I am resting patiently under the visitations of providence, calmly resigned to his will. It would be a miracle should I be restored to health under all these afflictions. The Lord's will be done."

June 8, 1845, he died peacefully and two days later was buried by the side of his wife in the Hermitage garden. The long illness had attracted the attention of the whole country, and many friends came to say farewell. By his own wish the funeral was as simple as possible. An Oriental sarcophagus popularly said to have once contained the bones of Alexander Severus, the Roman emperor, was offered him in March, 1945, for his own body. He refused it, saying: "My republican feelings and principles forbid it, the simplicity of our system of government forbids it." Memorial services were held by his friends in many cities. Some bitter partisans would not attend them, even as he himself would not attend a similar meeting in honor of John Marshall. But with the majority of the people his death was a genuine sorrow. To them he was a real hero—a personification of a great cause, and the passing of his influence was a national loss.

Time has softened some of the asperities of the epoch in which he lived. The American who now knows how to estimate the life of the Jacksonian era will take something from the pretensions of his enemies and add something to the virtues hitherto accorded his partisans. Jackson's lack of education, his crude judgments in many affairs, his occasional outbreaks of passion, his habitual hatred of those enemies with whom he had not made friends for party purposes, and his crude ideas of some political policies—all lose some of their infelicity in the face of his brave, frank, masterly leadership of the democratic movement which then established itself in our life. This was his task: he was adapted to it; he did it faithfully, conscientiously, ably. Few American Presidents have better lived up to the demands of the movement which brought them into power.

✪

An Impressive Mandate and the Meaning of Jacksonianism

Who was General Andrew Jackson, the new popular favorite? To the nation he was known primarily as a military hero. In the Revolution, an English officer had slashed him with a saber for refusing to clean a pair of boots. In the War of 1812 he had shown great energy and resource in putting down some Indian uprisings, and in 1815, after the treaty of peace had been signed, he won at New Orleans the greatest American victory of the war. His nominal profession was the law, and he had served in the House of Representatives and Senate of the United States, as well as on the Tennessee supreme court. For the decade past, his life had been mainly that of a Tennessee gentleman, living on a fine plantation near Nashville, entertaining his friends, racing his horses, and heatedly talking politics. In 1828 he was sixty-one years old.

His immense popular vote in 1824 came from his military fame and from the widespread conviction of his integrity.[1] His actual politics were somewhat vague. In 1808 he had sympathized with the schismatic movement of Randolph and Macon, but in a letter to President Monroe in 1816 he recommended a policy of reconciliation with the war Federalists (accompanied by characteristic

1. John C. Fitzpatrick, ed., *The Autobiography of Martin Van Buren,* American Historical Association, *Annual Report,* 1918, II (Washington, 1920), 449.

From *The Age of Jackson* by Arthur M. Schlesinger, Jr., by permission of Little, Brown and Co. Copyright 1945, by Arthur M. Schlesinger, Jr.

regrets that the leaders of the Hartford Convention had escaped hanging). Seven years later in the Senate, his votes indicated an attitude of at least tolerance toward the American System. He favored what he called enigmatically a "judicious" tariff in order to end dependence on foreign nations for war materials, but at the same time he committed himself definitely against the premises of Federalism. "I am one of those who do not believe that a national debt is a national blessing," he said, "but rather a curse to a republic; inasmuch as it is calculated to raise around the administration a moneyed aristocracy dangerous to the liberties of the country."[2]

In Tennessee, he normally acted with the landholding aristocracy both against the financial aristocracy and the canebrake democracy. When the depression of 1819 gave Tennessee a relief system similar to Kentucky's, Jackson vainly opposed it, not in order to protect the banks, but on the correct conviction that inflation would not solve the problems of the debtors. Yet he also supported a dubious adventure which would have despoiled many small farmers of their lands for the benefit of speculators. His experience neither in national nor in state politics afforded any clear indication of what could be expected from him once in power.[3]

Nor could much be inferred from the nature of his backing in 1824. Persons of every political faith endorsed him, including even many former Federalists who never forgave John Quincy Adams for deserting the party; and he was specifically opposed by the guardians of Virginia orthodoxy. Jefferson himself is supposed to have told Daniel Webster, "He is one of the most unfit men I know of for such a place. . . . he is a dangerous man."[4] John Taylor

2. Jackson to L. H. Colman, April 26, 1824, James Parton, *Life of Andrew Jackson,* 3 vols. (New York, 1859–1860), III, 35–36.

3. For Jackson in Tennessee, W. M. Gouge, *A Short History of Paper Money and Banking in the United States* . . . (Philadelphia, 1833), Pt. 2, p. 135; St. George L. Sioussat, "Some Phases of Tennessee Politics in the Jackson Period," *American Historical Review,* XIV, 60–61; T. P. Abernethy, "Andrew Jackson and the Rise of Southwestern Democracy," *ibid.,* XXXIII, 64–77.

4. Daniel Webster, *Private Correspondence,* Fletcher Webster, ed. (Boston, 1856), I, 371. Cf. also George Ticknor to George Bancroft, December 26, 1824, Bancroft Papers (Massachusetts Historical Society). Mr. Jefferson

(who rather desperately favored Adams) and James Madison shared this mistrust. Martin Van Buren, the chief Crawford manager in 1824, brought the Virginians timidly into the Jackson fold by 1828. There they remained in constant fear of his indiscretion. According to Van Buren, Thomas Ritchie of the *Richmond Enquirer* "scarcely ever went to bed . . . without apprehension that he would wake up to hear of some *coup d'état* by the General."[5]

Jackson did indeed bear the reputation of being intemperate, arbitrary, and ambitious for power. As a General he had tended to do necessary things with great expedition and to inquire afterward into their legality. His political opponents, building ardently upon incidents of his military past, managed almost to read into the records of history a legend of his rude violence and uncontrolled irascibility.

In the Republic's early years, martial reputation had counted little for future political success. But the broadening of the suffrage, the thrill of surging nationalism, and the declining glamour of the old ruling class created a favorable atmosphere for new idols, and the War of 1812 promptly produced the military hero. The old aristocracy resented such vulgar and parvenu prestige, and a man with Jackson's credentials was almost forced into the opposition. Moreover, while the newly enfranchised and chauvinistic masses regarded the military hero with wild enthu-

---

"expressed his unwillingness to see Genl. Jackson in the chair of state, as decidedly as any New-Englander of us all." When Monroe asked Jefferson whether it would be a good idea to appoint Jackson to the Russian mission, Jefferson burst out, "Why, good God! he would breed you a quarrel before he had been there a month!" John Quincy Adams, *Memoirs*, C. F. Adams, ed., 12 vols. (Philadelphia, 1874–1877), IV, 76.

On the other hand, it is fair to state that Webster's original notes of his conversation with Jefferson, which Senator Hoar republished with the flat comment that Webster's record of the talk was "published in full from these *memoranda*," do not include any mention of Jefferson's attack on Jackson; and Webster failed to make public his account of the conversation till after Jefferson's death, when it served his political purpose. George F. Hoar, "Daniel Webster," *Scribner's Magazine*, XXVI (August 1899), 215. Professor Bassett points out that Webster's statement is hard to reconcile with the tone and content of Jefferson's letter to Jackson of December 18, 1823. J. S. Bassett, *The Life of Andrew Jackson* (New York, 1928), p. 329.

5. Martin Van Buren, *Inquiry into the Origin and Course of Political Parties in the United States* (New York, 1867), p. 322.

siasm, to the old aristocracy, raised on classical analogies, no figure could seem more dangerous to the Republic. The warnings of Cicero and the example of Caesar supplied ample documentation for their worst misgivings. This background, in addition to Jackson's own record, accounted for the singular consternation which greeted his candidacy.

Yet, in actual fact, virtually all the direct testimony agrees in describing the Jackson of these later years as a man of great urbanity and distinction of manner. His presence in Washington as Senator in the winter of 1823–1824 did much to dispel the impression that he was some kind of border savage. As the elegant wife of the editor of the *National Intelligencer* put it, the General "appears to possess quite as much *suaviter in modo* as *fortiter in re*." Even Daniel Webster, later to become a sedulous promoter of the Jackson legend, commented in 1824, "General Jackson's manners are more presidential than those of any of the candidates. . . . My wife is for him decidedly."[6]

Tall and thin, his white hair pushed straight back from his forehead, his long face reamed with wrinkles, his eyes sharp and commanding, Jackson was a noble and impressive figure. On foot, with firm military step, compressed lips and resolute expression, or on horseback, where his seat was excellent, his hand light, and his carriage easy, he had a natural grandeur which few could resist. Many in this bitter day shared the emotions of the conservative Boston merchant who watched out of his window to catch a glimpse of the old General, "regarding him very much as he might

6. Letter of Sarah Gales Seaton, December 1823. She continues, "He is, indeed, a polished and perfect courtier in female society, and polite to all." Josephine Seaton, *William Winston Seaton of the "National Intelligencer"* (Boston, 1871), p. 161. Webster's comment appeared in a letter to Ezekiel Webster, February 22, 1824, Webster, I, 346. Cf. the remarks of Elijah H. Mills, an old Massachusetts Federalist, in a letter to his wife, January 22, 1824, *Proceedings of the Massachusetts Historical Society,* XIX, 40–41: "He was considered extremely rash and inconsiderate, tyrannical and despotic, in his principles. A personal acquaintance with him has convinced many who held these opinions that they were unfounded. He is very mild and amiable in his disposition, of great benevolence, and his manners, though formed in the wilds of the West, exceedingly polished and polite. Everybody that knows him loves him, and he is exactly the man with whom *you* would be delighted."

have done some dangerous monster which was being led captive past his house." When Jackson finally appeared, his hatred abruptly collapsed. Exclaiming, "Do some one come here and salute the old man!" he thrust his small daughter forward to wave her handkerchief. Jackson, as Josiah Quincy said, "wrought a mysterious charm upon old and young."[7]

By 1829 he was technically a sick man—many thought dying. His head throbbed with splitting pains apparently produced by years of tobacco chewing, and his lean frame shook with a hacking consumptive cough. Yet, while his face grew whiter and more haggard, his spirit was grim and indomitable.

At White House receptions he remained urbane, though reserved and somewhat formal. Among his intimates he cast off his gravity, becoming sociable and sympathetic. He smoked with fierce energy, usually an old Powhatan bowl pipe with a long stem which he rested on his crossed legs, while he puffed out great white clouds until the whole room was "so obfuscated that one could hardly breathe." Or, after the Tennessee custom, he would chew and spit at regular intervals, while carrying on conversation or even conducting the affairs of state.[8]

He spoke quickly and forcibly, often emphasizing his points by raising a clenched hand in a brief, sharp gesture. "He obviously had a hidden vein of humor," reported Henry A. Wise, for many years a bitter foe, "loved aphorism, and could politely convey a sense of smart travesty. If put upon his mettle, he was very positive, but gravely respectful." When his mind was made up, he would draw down the left corner of his mouth, giving his face, as one observer noted, "a peculiar 'G—d damn me' expression."[9]

But he was not particularly dogmatic. Though accustomed to

7. The merchant was Daniel P. Parker; Josiah Quincy, *Figures of the Past* (Boston, 1882), p. 363. This essay contains an attractive account of Quincy's own surrender to Jackson's magnetism.

8. The quotation is from Henry A. Wise, *Seven Decades of the Union* (Philadelphia, 1872), pp. 110–111. See also Edward Everett to his wife, January 1, 1834, Everett Papers (Massachusetts Historical Society), and Theodore Sedgwick, Jr., to Theodore Sedgwick, February 6, 1835, Sedgwick Papers (Massachusetts Historical Society).

9. The quotations are from Wise, pp. 98–99, and J. B. Derby, *Political Reminiscences, including a Sketch . . . of the "Statesman Party" of Boston* (Boston, 1835), p. 57.

maintain his own position with pertinacity, he yielded gracefully when convinced of his error. No man, as Benton said, knew better the difference between firmness and obstinacy. "Of all the Presidents who have done me the honor to listen to my opinions, there was no one to whom I spoke with more confidence when I felt myself strongly to be in the right." The testimony on this point is fairly conclusive. "I never knew a man," commented Van Buren, "more free from conceit, or one to whom it was to a greater extent a pleasure, as well as a recognized duty, to listen patiently to what might be said to him upon any subject. . . . Akin to his disposition in this regard was his readiness to acknowledge error."[10]

In fact, far from exacting uniformity of opinion, Jackson so indulged disagreement that he exasperated his more radical followers, like Amos Kendall and Roger B. Taney. "If he be censurable on this score," wrote Kendall, "it is for too much forbearance." "Frank himself (perhaps almost to a fault in a public man)," observed Taney, "he loved frankness in others; and regarded opposition to his opinions, by one who held office under him, as evidence of firmness as well as of honesty of purpose."[11]

In his military campaigns he would consult his council of war, but never submit a question to vote. Similarly as President, he would open up problems to the full discussion of the Cabinet; but when the moment for action came, he always made up his own mind. "I have accustomed myself to receive with respect the opinions of others," he explained, "but always take the responsibility of deciding for myself." Once his mind was made up, no threats, no warnings of catastrophe, no dictates of prudence, could sway him. "I care nothing about clamors, sir, mark me! I do precisely what I think just and right."[12]

So superb a self-sufficiency could be effective only when

10. Thomas H. Benton, *Thirty Years' View* (New York, 1852–1854), I, 738; Van Buren, *Autobiography,* p. 312.

11. Amos Kendall, "Anecdotes of General Jackson," *Democratic Review,* XI (September 1842), 272; R. B. Taney, Bank War Ms. (Library of Congress).

12. Jackson's two remarks were quoted by J. A. Hamilton in a letter to Timothy Pickering, July 3, 1828, J. A. Hamilton, *Reminiscences* (New York, 1869), p. 77, and by N. P. Trist in a communication to James Parton, Parton, III, 605.

matched by an equally superb self-control. Again contrary to the Jackson myth, there was small basis for the picture of uncontrolled irascibility. Jackson, who knew his reputation, never hesitated to exploit it. "He would sometimes extemporize a fit of passion in order to overwhelm an adversary, when certain of being in the right," said one observer, "but his self-command was always perfect." His towering rages were actually ways of avoiding futile argument. To committees which called on him to protest his financial policy, he would fly into vehement denunciations of the moneyed monopoly. When they left in disgust, he would coolly light his pipe and, chuckling "They thought I was mad," remark blandly on the importance of never compromising vital issues; one always lost friends and never appeased enemies.

Once Van Buren, before he knew Jackson well, watched with disapproval while he stormed before a delegation. As soon as the door was closed behind them, Jackson commented mildly, "I saw that my remarks disturbed you." Van Buren admitted that they had. "No, my friend," his chief replied, "I have great respect for your judgment, but you do not understand these gentlemen as well as I do"; and the sequel vindicated Jackson. "This was but one of numerous instances," Van Buren wrote later, "in which I observed a similar contradiction between his apparent undue excitement and his real coolness and self-possession in which, I may say with truth, he was seldom if ever wanting." Amos Kendall reported flatly, "I never saw him in a passion." N. P. Trist, his private secretary, was equally emphatic: "I never witnessed any thing of the sort."[13]

13. The first quotation is from T. N. Parmalee, "Recollections of an Old Stager," *Harpers,* XLV (September 1872), 602; the anecdotes are from Wise, pp. 106–107, and Van Buren, *Political Parties,* p. 324; the last two quotations from Amos Kendall, *Autobiography,* William Stickney, ed., (Boston, 1872), p. 635, and Parton, III, 603.

There is abundant evidence of the calculation which lay beneath Jackson's famous rages. Cf. Wise's statement: "He knew that the world . . . counted him of a temperament weak, impassioned, impulsive, and inconsiderate in action; and he often turned this mistake as to character into a large capital of advantage. He was a consummate actor, never stepped without knowing and marking his ground, but knew that most men thought he was not a man of calculations. This enabled him to blind them by his affectation of passion and impulse." P. 106. George Bancroft described Jackson to Goldwin Smith

Jackson's intelligence expressed itself in judgment rather than in analysis. "He had vigorous thoughts," as Benton put it, "but not the faculty of arranging them in a regular composition." "Possessed of a mind that was ever dealing with the substance of things," said Van Buren, "he was not very careful in regard to the precise terms." "He had never studied the niceties of language," said Taney, "—and disliked what he was apt to regard as mere verbal criticisms." He certainly could never have written Benton's erudite discourses, or Van Buren's thoughtful recollections, or the masterly arguments of Taney, or the treatises of Edward Livingston, or the polemics of Amos Kendall. Yet he dominated them all.

In after years, the friends of Jackson wrestled with the problem of what gave his judgment a specific gravity which exposed their facile verbalizations or quick syllogisms and far outran their logical analysis. ("Beware of your metaphysics," Jackson would exclaim. ". . . Hair-splitting is dangerous business.") "The character of his mind," remarked Benton, "was that of judgment, with a rapid and almost intuitive perception, followed by an instant and decisive action." "General Jackson is the most rapid reasoner I have ever met with," declared Louis McLane. "He jumps to a conclusion before I can start on my premises." "He was indeed an extraordinary man," wrote the author James Kirke Paulding; "the only man I ever saw that excited my admiration to the pitch of wonder. To him knowledge seemed entirely unnecessary. He saw intuitively into everything, and reached a conclusion by a short cut while others were beating the bush for the game."[14]

One hot Sunday evening in July of 1858, while the Italian sun lingered over the housetops of Florence, two Americans discovered a mutual reverence for Jackson. Nathaniel Hawthorne had seen him but once, in 1833, when the old General visited

---

as "mild by nature and putting himself into a rage only when it would serve a purpose." Goldwin Smith, *Reminiscences,* Arnold Hautain, ed. (New York, 1910), p. 333. See also B. F. Perry, *Reminiscences of Public Men* (Philadelphia, 1883), p. 29; and Marquis James, *Andrew Jackson: Portrait of a President* (Indianapolis, 1937), pp. 366, 368.

14. The quotations are from Benton, I, 738; Van Buren, *Political Parties,* p. 313; Taney, Bank War Ms., p. 88; Parton, III, 610; Benton, I, 737; Kendall, *Autobiography,* p. 634; W. I. Paulding, *Literary Life of James K. Paulding* (New York, 1867), pp. 287–288.

Salem. The haunted young recluse had walked to the edge of town to catch a glimpse of the Old Hero. He never forgot the grim, majestic visage. Years later, when he saw Raphael's painting of Pope Julius II, "the best portrait in the whole world," his instant wish was that Raphael could have painted General Jackson.

Hiram Powers, the famous sculptor, had met Jackson and talked to him. "He thinks," Hawthorne reported, "that General Jackson was a man of the keenest and surest intuitions, in respect to men and measures, but with no power of reasoning out his conclusions, or of imparting them intellectually to other persons." Hawthorne mused over what others, Franklin Pierce and James Buchanan, had told him about Jackson. "Men who have known Jackson intimately, and in great affairs, would not agree as to this intellectual and argumentative deficiency, though they would fully allow this intuitive faculty." His conclusion was positive: "Surely he was a great man, and his native strength, as well of intellect as of character, compelled every man to be his tool that came within his reach; and the more cunning the individual might be, it served only to make him the sharper tool."[15]

Yet, as Jackson paused on the threshold of achievement in 1829, no one could have predicted that crisis would transform him into greatness. The challenge of events, the responsibilities of leadership, the stimulus of popular confidence, the intuitive grasp of the necessities of change: these shaped the man and drew out his finest possibilities. Like Washington, Lincoln, Wilson, Franklin Roosevelt, he gave small promise in his earlier career of the abilities he was to exhibit as chief magistrate. All were educated by the urgencies of the moment.[16]

15. Hawthorne thought that Powers' assertion would be inherently plausible, "were there not such strong evidence to the contrary. The highest, or perhaps any high administrative ability, is intuitive, and precedes argument, and rises above it. It is a revelation of the very thing to be done, and its propriety and necessity are felt so strongly that very likely it cannot be talked about; if the doer can likewise talk, it is an additional and gratuitous faculty, as little to be expected as that a poet should be able to write an explanatory criticism on his own poem." "French and Italian Note-books." *Writings of Nathaniel Hawthorne,* Manse Edition (Boston, 1900), XXII, 158–160.

16. Van Buren perhaps had Jackson in mind when he described the process: "that which similar crises in all countries and times, have brought

Jackson grew visibly from the day of his inauguration. His leadership gained steadily in confidence and imagination. He grew stronger after every contact with the people. In last analysis, there lay the secret of his strength: his deep natural understanding of the people. "They were his blood relations," said Van Buren, "—the only blood relations he had." He believed that "to labour for the good of the masses was a special mission assigned to him by his Creator and no man was ever better disposed to work in his vocation in season and out of season."[17] The people called him, and he came, like the great folk heroes, to lead them out of captivity and bondage.[18]

---

about, namely, the production of great men by great events, developing and calling into action upon a large scale intellects the power of which, but for their application to great transactions, might have remained unknown alike to their possessors and to the world." Van Buren, *Political Parties,* pp. 171–172.

17. Van Buren, *Autobiography,* p. 255.

18. Few modern historians hold to the Whig-Republican legend of Jackson in its literal form, but there is a visible tendency to revive it in somewhat more sophisticated version, led especially by Professor T. P. Abernethy in an article, "Andrew Jackson and the Rise of Southwestern Democracy," *American Historical Review,* XXXIII (October 1927), 64–77; in his excellent book, *From Frontier to Plantation in Tennessee* (Chapel Hill, 1932); and in his sketch of Jackson in Allen Johnson, Dumas Malone, and Harris E. Starr, eds., *Dictionary of American Biography,* 21 vols. (New York, 1928–1944), IX, 526–534.

Professor Abernethy's thesis seems to be that Jackson, not having been a great democratic leader in Tennessee politics, could not therefore have been a genuine champion of the people, but was an unprincipled opportunist, who happened through a set of accidents to head a democratic movement. Jackson was basically a conservative, Abernethy argues, but he and his backers "had no very strong convictions and were willing to make friends with the times. It is not the greatest men who go to the top in politics." (This aside is typical of the animus against Jackson which runs through Professor Abernethy's work.) "Not only was Jackson not a consistent politician, he was not even a real leader of democracy . . . he always believed in making the public serve the ends of the politicians. Democracy was good talk with which to win the favor of the people and thereby accomplish ulterior objectives. Jackson never really championed the cause of the people." *From Frontier to Plantation,* pp. 241, 248, 249; *passim,* especially Chap. 4. "No historian has ever accused Jackson, the great Democrat, of having had a political philosophy. It is hard to see that he even had any political principles. . . . He thought he was sincere when he spoke to the people, yet he never really championed their cause. He merely encouraged them to champion his." "Andrew Jackson and the Rise of Southwestern Democracy," pp. 76–77. "He had little understanding of the

The shouting crowd on Inauguration Day, Daniel Webster noted sarcastically, really seemed to think "the country is rescued from some dreadful danger."[19] Yet where was this danger? It was clear that Jackson had an impressive mandate, but it was not so clear what the mandate was for. Through the land, an excitement for change had welled up from profound frustration. But its concrete expressions were only slogans, epithets, meaningless phrases, the shout of crowds—not issues, programs, policies.

The new President's supporters in Congress had conspicuously failed to develop measures to meet the discontents which had toppled the previous administration. Their opposition to Adams and Clay had been confused and opportunistic, hiding a basic lack of ideas behind a smoke screen of parliamentary obstruction and campaign invective. The campaign had reflected its shallowness. Hardly an issue of policy figured in the canvass, and, when Jackson triumphed, no one could be certain that his administration would not duplicate that of Madison or Monroe or even of Adams.

As for the new President, he was not only tired, sick, and depressed by grief, but politically inexperienced. The problems he faced were new to him; and for a man who learned by dealing with actualities rather than by intellectual analysis this was a serious handicap. He had to feel his way and let things seep in before he

---

democratic movement which bears his name and he came to support it primarily because it supported him." *Dictionary of American Biography,* IX, 534.

The point about Professor Abernethy's thesis is that his conclusion is one to be established by evidence, not by deductive logic. A judgment on the character of Jackson's democracy must be founded on an examination of what Jackson did as President, and on nothing else; certainly not on an extrapolation made on the basis of his career before he became President.

No amount of inference based on what Jackson was like before 1828 can be a substitute for the facts after 1828. Yet Abernethy's own published work was concerned almost exclusively with Jackson in Tennessee. His bias is sufficiently betrayed by the odd and otherwise baffling proportions of his article in the *Dictionary of American Biography,* which devotes over two thirds of its space to Jackson before he became President. If Abernethy were to use the same method on Lincoln, or Wilson, or Franklin Roosevelt—that is, to dogmatize on their Presidencies on the basis of their pre-Presidential records—his results would be self-evidently absurd.

19. Webster to Mrs. Ezekiel Webster, March 4, 1829, Webster, I, 473.

could move with decision. In the meantime the demand for "reform" had to be met. The common man, too long thwarted by official indifference, had to be given a sense that the government was in truth the people's government. Jackson's answer was shrewd and swift: a redistribution of federal offices.

This measure served obvious political needs. It adapted to national purposes methods of political reward, long employed in some of the states, and became an invaluable means of unifying administration support. A party formed to aid special moneyed interests could depend on private contributions to pay the bills and keep the organization alive; but a party formed in the popular interest had no other resources save the offices at its disposal. "If you wish to keep up the party," a Pennsylvania politician told Van Buren, "you must induce them to beleive that it is their interest— Some few may adhere to the party from mere consciencious conviction of doing right but interest is a powerful stimulus to make them act energetically and efficiently."[20]

But, while helping to build the party, the spoils system also contributed to the main objective of helping restore faith in the government. In the eyes of the people, the bureaucracy had been corrupted by its vested interests in its own power. "Office is considered as a species of property," as Jackson told Congress, "and government rather as a means of promoting individual interests than as an instrument created solely for the service of the people." Jackson believed that official duties could be made "so plain and simple that men of intelligence may readily qualify themselves for their performance." His quick action on this principle meant that the government was no longer "an engine for the support of the few at the expense of the many."[21]

The doctrine of rotation in office was thus in large part conceived as a sincere measure of reform. Many professional reformers so regarded it. Robert Dale Owen hailed it enthusiastically in his radical New York sheet, the *Free Enquirer,* and Jeremy

20. David Petrikin to Van Buren, November 18, 1836, Van Buren Papers (Library of Congress).
21. James D. Richardson, comp., *A Compilation of the Messages and Papers of the Presidents, 1789–1907,* 10 vols. (Washington, 1908), II, 448–449.

Bentham, the great English reformer, confided to Jackson, as one liberal to another, that he had held the doctrine of rotation himself since 1821.[22]

In a larger context, which contemporary Americans could only have dimly apprehended, rotation in office possessed another significance. The history of governments has been characterized by the decay of old ruling classes and the rise of more vigorous and intelligent ones to replace them. This process had already begun in America. The "natural aristocracy" of Richard Hildreth—the class composed of merchant, banker, planter, lawyer, and clergyman—had started to decline after the War of 1812. The rise of the military hero, a new "natural" aristocrat, hastened the time for a general breaking-up of the old governing elite. In extreme cases one ruling order succeeds another by violent revolution, but a democracy which preserves sufficient equality of opportunity may escape so drastic a solution. The spoils system, whatever its faults, at least destroyed peaceably the monopoly of offices by a class which could not govern, and brought to power a fresh and alert group which had the energy to meet the needs of the day.

Modern research has shown that legend, invented and fostered for partisan purposes, has considerably exaggerated the extent of Jackson's actual removals. The most careful estimate is that between a fifth and a tenth of all federal officeholders were dismissed during Jackson's eight years, many for good reason. Frauds to the amount of $280,000 were discovered in the Treasury Department alone. Jackson ousted no greater a proportion of officeholders than Jefferson, though his administration certainly established the spoils system in national politics.[23]

Until recent years, the study of the spoils system has been marred by a tendency to substitute moral disapproval for an

22. *Free Enquirer,* January 2, 1830; Bentham to Jackson, April 26, 1830, Jeremy Bentham, *Works,* John Bowring, ed. (Edinburgh, 1843), XI, 40.

23. E. M. Eriksson, "The Federal Civil Service under President Jackson," *Mississippi Valley Historical Review,* XIII, 517–540. Petrikin's letter, cited above, blamed reduced Democratic majorities in Pennsylvania in part on "the course pursued by the Post office Department ever since Gen¹ Jackson was elected in refusing to remove postmasters who were and always have been opposed to the Democratic party." This complaint was not uncommon among Democratic politicians.

understanding of causes and necessities. There can be small doubt today that, whatever evils it brought into American life, its historical function was to narrow the gap between the people and the government—to expand popular participation in the workings of democracy. For Jackson it was an essential step in the gradual formulation of a program for democratic America. . . .

Jessie Benton knew she must keep still and not fidget or squirm, even when General Jackson twisted his fingers too tightly in her curls. The old man, who loved children, liked to have Benton bring his enchanting daughter to the White House. Jessie, clinging to her father's hand, trying to match his strides, would climb breathlessly up the long stairs to the upper room where, with sunshine flooding in through tall south windows, they would find the General in his big rocking chair close to the roaring wood fire. The child instinctively responded to the lonely old man's desire for "a bright unconscious affectionate little life near him," and would sit by his side while his hand rested on her head. Sometimes, in the heat of discussion, his long bony fingers took a grip that made Jessie look at her father but give no other sign. Soon Benton would contrive to send her off to play with the children of Andrew Jackson Donelson, the President's private secretary. Then the talk would resume. In the latter days of 1831 the discussions grew particularly long and tense.[24]

Jackson's grim calm during that year cloaked no basic wavering of purpose. With characteristic political tact he presented an irresolute and amenable face to the world in order to hold the party together.[25] Benton and Kendall were in his confidence, but very few others. His apparent moderation deceived not only Biddle but many of the Bank's enemies. James A. Hamilton considered making a hurried trip to London to discuss Jackson's vacillations with Van Buren; and William Dunlap, the artist, voiced the misgivings of many liberals in his remark to Fenimore Cooper that Jackson had "proved weaker than could have been anticipated; yet

24. Jessie Benton Frémont, *Souvenirs of My Time* (Boston, 1887), pp. 88–89.
25. The evidence for this view is set forth in Bassett, pp. 610–616.

those who hold under him will hold to him and strive to hold him up."[26]

In particular, Jackson's Cabinet misinterpreted his pose. Mc-Lane, Livingston, and Taney were all convinced that compromise was possible, greatly to the relief of the two and the despair of the third. Taney was coming to believe that he stood alone in the Cabinet and almost in the country in opposing recharter. In the meantime, the Bank's alacrity in opening new offices and making long-term loans, though its charter was soon to expire, seemed "conclusive evidence of its determination to fasten itself by means of its money so firmly on the country that it will be impossible . . . to shake it off without producing the most severe and extensive public suffering.—And this very attempt," he cried, "calls for prompt resistance—for future resistance will be in vain if the charter is renewed."[27]

But who would lead the resistance? He watched the debates drag on and the votes pile up through the spring of 1832 with mounting apprehension. In the late spring, having to attend the Maryland court of appeals, he decided to prepare a memorandum setting forth his conviction that recharter should be vetoed. He finished it the night before his departure and notified the President that the opinion would be delivered as soon as the bill was passed.

On July 3 Jackson received the bill. Hearing the news, Martin Van Buren, just back from England, went straight on to Washington, arriving at midnight. The General, still awake, stretched on a sickbed, pale and haggard and propped up by pillows, grasped his friend's hand. Passing his other hand through his snow-white hair, he said firmly but without passion, "The bank, Mr. Van Buren, is trying to kill me, *but I will kill it!*"[28]

A day or two later, Taney, busy in Annapolis, received word to hurry back to Washington. He found the President out of bed and eager for action. He had read Taney's memorandum with emphatic

26. Bassett, p. 612; Dunlap to Cooper, September 20, 1831, J. F. Cooper, *Correspondence,* J. F. Cooper, ed. (New Haven, 1922), I, 241.

27. Taney to Thomas Ellicott, December 15 and 23, 1831, Taney Papers (Library of Congress); Taney, Bank War Ms., p. 104.

28. Van Buren, *Autobiography,* p. 625; *Political Parties,* p. 314.

agreement and then had heard the arguments of the rest of the Cabinet. While disapproving the bill, they wanted him to place his rejection on grounds which would allow the question to be re-opened in the future. Jackson, unwilling to compromise, then turned to Amos Kendall for a first draft of the veto message. Andrew J. Donelson was now revising Kendall's draft in the room across the hall. Would Taney help? The lean, determined face of the Attorney General expressed no reservations.

It took three days to finish the document. The first day Taney and Donelson worked alone, except for Jackson and Ralph Earl, an artist who lived at the White House and used this room as a studio, painting away, oblivious of the tense consultations, the hasty scribbles, the words crossed out, the phrases laboriously worked over, the notes torn up and discarded. On the second day Levi Woodbury, having decided to change his stand, made an un-abashed appearance and assisted till the job was done. Jackson meanwhile passed in and out of the room, listening to the different parts, weighing the various suggestions, and directing what should be inserted or altered.[29]

The message, dated July 10, burst like a thunderclap over the nation. Its core was a ringing statement of Jackson's belief in the essential rights of the common man. "It is to be regretted, that the rich and powerful too often bend the acts of government to their selfish purposes," Jackson declared. "Distinctions in society will always exist under every just government. Equality of talents, of education, or of wealth can not be produced by human institutions. In the full enjoyment of the gifts of Heaven and the fruits of superior industry, economy, and virtue, every man is equally entitled to protection by law; but when the laws undertake to add to these natural and just advantages artificial distinctions . . . to make the rich richer and the potent more powerful, the humble members of society—the farmers, mechanics, and laborers—who have neither the time nor the means of securing like favors to themselves, have a right to complain of the injustice of their Government."[30]

29. Taney, Bank War Ms., pp. 118–126.
30. *Messages and Papers*, II, 590.

But the case against the Bank could not rest simply on generalities. Jackson's real opposition, of course, and that of Benton, Taney, and Kendall, arose from their hard-money views. Yet, a great part of their backing came from cheap-money men. Thus powerful hard-money arguments—the economic argument that the paper system caused periodic depressions, and the social argument that it built up an aristocracy—were unavailable because they were as fatal to the debtor and state banking positions as to the Bank itself.

The veto message was brilliantly successful in meeting this dilemma. It diverted attention from the basic contradiction by its passages of resounding and demagogic language; it played down the strictly economic analysis; and it particularly sought to lull Western fears by dwelling on the hardships worked by the long arm of the Bank in the Mississippi Valley. Its main emphasis fell, first, on the case against the Bank as unconstitutional, and then on the political argument that the Bank represented too great a centralization of power under private control. The stress on the "great evils to our country and its institutions [which] might flow from such a concentration of power in the hands of a few men irresponsible to the people" sounded good to the state banks and to the West, both of which had chafed long enough at the ascendancy of Chestnut Street.[31] The message thus thrust to the foreground the issues on which all enemies of the Bank could unite, while the special aims of the hard-money school remained safely under cover.[32]

The distinction between "the humble members of society" and "the rich and powerful" drew quick reactions from both classes. The common man through the land responded enthusiastically to

31. *Messages and Papers,* II, 581.
32. The Bank controversy elicited a few examples of what would be a natural modern argument: that the Bank was clothed with the public interest. Henry D. Gilpin, a former government director of the Bank and Attorney General under Van Buren, suggested somewhat this argument in 1836: "I am not sure that Dallas has put the argument [against the Bank] in its strongest form—that such an institution is essentially *public,* affecting the general value of property and exercising powers too broad to be regarded as private acts—and that whether public or private the chief legislative body have a right to rescind a franchise, as they have to take private property, when the public welfare requires it." Gilpin to Van Buren, September 14, 1836, Van Buren Papers.

his leader's appeal. "The veto works well everywhere," Jackson could report from the Hermitage in August; "it has put down the Bank instead of prostrating me."[33]

But men who believed that the political power of the business community should increase with its wealth were deeply alarmed. When Jackson said, "It is not conceivable how the present stockholders can have any claim to the special favor of the Government," did he mean that the common man had the same rights as the rich and wellborn to control of the state?[34] The Bank of the United States, according to the plan of Hamilton, would serve as the indispensable make-weight for property against the sway of numbers. Did not the veto message attack the very premises of Federalism, rejecting its axioms, destroying its keystone, and rallying the groups in society bent on its annihilation?

No wonder Nicholas Biddle roared to Henry Clay, "It has all the fury of a chained panther, biting the bars of his cage. It is really a manifesto of anarchy, such as Marat or Robespierre might have issued to the mob of the Faubourg St. Antoine." Or, as Alexander H. Everett wrote in Boston's conservative daily, the *Advertiser*, "For the first time, perhaps, in the history of civilized communities, the Chief Magistrate of a great nation . . . is found appealing to the worst passions of the uninformed part of the people, and endeavoring to stir up the poor against the rich." Webster, rising gravely in the Senate, summed up the indictment: "It manifestly seeks to influence the poor against the rich. It wantonly attacks whole classes of the people, for the purpose of turning against them the prejudices and resentments of other classes. It is a State paper which finds no topic too exciting for its use, no passion too inflammable for its address and its solicitation." For Webster, as for Jackson, it was becoming a battle between antagonistic philosophies of government: one declaring, like Webster at the Massachusetts convention, that property should control the state; the other denying that property had a superior claim to governmental privileges and benefits.[35]

33. Jackson to W. B. Lewis, August 18, 1832, Jackson-Lewis Letters (New York Public Library).

34. *Messages and Papers,* II, 577.

35. Biddle to Clay, August 1, 1832, Calvin Colton, ed., *Private Correspondence of Henry Clay* (New York, 1855), p. 341; A. H. Everett, *The*

The veto struck consternation through some parts of the Democratic party. . . . But the people had not spoken. Soon their time came: "The news from the voting States," Rufus Choate wrote to Edward Everett, "blows over us like a great cold storm."[36] The results rolled in: Jackson, 219, Clay, 49, John Floyd, 11, William Wirt, 7.[37] The bitterness with which conservatism faced the future flared up briefly in a post-election editorial in Joseph T. Buckingham's *Boston Courier.* "Yet there is one comfort left: God has promised that the days of the wicked shall be short; the wicked is old and feeble, and he may die before he can be elected. It is the duty of every good Christian to pray to our Maker to have pity on us."[38] . . .

Jackson's re-election and the popular acclaim following the nullification crisis only reinforced the administration's resolve to press the offensive against the American "nobility system." The first

---

Conduct of the Administration (Boston, 1831), pp. 60, 74–75; Webster in the Senate, July 11, 1832, *Register of Debates,* 22nd Congress, 1st Session, p. 1240.

36. Choate to Everett, November 10, 1832, Samuel G. Brown, *Life of Rufus Choate* (Boston, 1878), p. 61.

37. A later President's judgment on Jackson's opposition has bearing on both their experiences. "An overwhelming proportion of the material power of the Nation was against him. The great media for the dissemination of information and the molding of public opinion fought him. Haughty and sterile intellectualism opposed him. Musty reaction disapproved him. Hollow and outworn traditionalism shook a trembling finger at him. It seemed sometimes that all were against him—all but the people of the United States." Franklin D. Roosevelt, Jackson Day Address, January 8, 1936, Samuel I. Rosenman, ed. *Public Papers and Addresses of Franklin D. Roosevelt* (New York, 1938–   ), V, 40.

38. Reprinted in the *Washington Globe,* November 27, 1832. It continues in similar vein, declaring that the works of Paine "do not furnish Atheists with a single argument against the existence of a benign Providence, half so strong as the continuance of the misrule of Andrew Jackson. . . . We are constrained to acknowledge that the experiment of an absolutely liberal government has failed. . . . Heaven be praised that Massachusetts and Connecticut have escaped the moral and political contagion! As for the rest, they have proved themselves slaves, born to be commanded—they have put the whip into the hands of one who has shown every inclination to be absolute master, and it is some consolation to think that he will probably ere long lay it upon their backs till they howl again. . . . Who doubts that if all who are unable to read or write had been excluded from the polls, Andrew Jackson could not have been elected?"

necessity was to destroy its "head," the Bank. But the charter still had well over three years to run. The Bank was still backed by the national Republican party, most of the press, and many leading citizens. And the custody of the government deposits, the radicals feared, provided the Bank with campaign funds for recharter. Generous loans, subsidies, and retainers, strategically distributed, might substantially change public opinion before 1836. Moreover, the government deposits, by enabling the Bank to take most of the specie out of circulation in exchange for its bank notes, might place Biddle in a position, just before the election of 1836, to create a financial panic and insure the success of Bank candidates and the recharter of the Bank.[39]

The solution lay in withdrawing the deposits. This would cripple the Bank's attempt to convulse the money market and probably provoke it into an all-out fight against the only man who could whip it, thus foreclosing the issue once and for all. Jackson seems to have decided on this course shortly after his re-election.[40] It was his own plan, "conceived by him," as Benton later wrote, "carried out by him, defended by him, and its fate dependent upon him."[41]

. . .

July, as usual, was unbearable in Washington. Jackson, sick and weary, prepared to go to Ripraps in Virginia for a rest. . . . Frank Blair accompanied Jackson to the seaside, where the two households spent a pleasant month, the invigorating salt air restoring Jackson's appetite and improving his health. Letters bombarded the President, pleading with him not to disturb the deposits. What seemed an organized campaign only strengthened his purpose: "Mr. Blair, Providence may change me but it is not in

39. Evidence of the Bank's intention to use its funds for political activity was marshaled by Taney in his "Report on the Removal of the Public Deposites," *Register of Debates*, 23rd Congress, 1st Session, Appendix, pp. 66–67. For the fears of the radicals, see Kendall, *Autobiography*, p. 375; J. A. Hamilton to Jackson, February 28, 1833, J. S. Bassett, ed., *The Correspondence of Andrew Jackson*, 6 vols. (Washington, 1926–1933), V, 22–23; Taney's speech of August 6, 1834, *Washington Globe*, August 25, 1834; Benton's speech of July 18, 1835, *ibid.*, August 8, 1835; etc.

40. Marquis James effectively disposes of the story that Jackson believed the Bank insolvent. James, pp. 334–335 and n.

41. Benton, I, 374.

the power of man to do it."[42] In spare moments, he shaped his notes into a militant and uncompromising document. Returned to the White House late in August, he resolved to end the matter before Congress convened.

On September 10 he presented Kendall's report on the state banks to the Cabinet. Taney and Woodbury backed the proposal to discontinue placing funds with the Bank on October 1, while McLane, Cass, and Duane vigorously opposed it. Duane's assent as Secretary of the Treasury was necessary for the action. By September 14 Jackson, having tortuously overcome his scruples against discharging persons who disagreed with him, suggested to Duane that he resign; perhaps he might be named Minister to Russia. Duane refused. The next day Jackson handed Taney for revision the fiery paper he had dictated at Ripraps. On the eighteenth he read this paper to the Cabinet. Two days later the *Globe* announced the plan to cease deposits in the Bank after October 1. Duane continued in frightened obstinacy, agreeing to the removal of neither the deposits nor himself. "He is either the weakest mortal, or the most strange composition I have ever met with," Jackson wrote in exasperation.[43] The next five days exhausted even the President's patience. He dismissed Duane and appointed Taney to the place.[44] . . .

The new storm of denunciation made the attack on the veto seem a model of good temper. Biddle, convinced by midsummer that the deposits were doomed, began in August to fight back. Employing to the full his power over the state banks, he commenced to present their notes for redemption, reduce discounts and call in loans. While claiming to be simply winding up business in preparation for the expiration of the charter, he was in fact embarked on

42. Blair to Van Buren, November 13, 1859, Van Buren, *Autobiography*, p. 607.

43. Jackson to Van Buren, September 22, 1833, *Correspondence of Andrew Jackson*, V, 206.

44. Duane published in 1838 a plaintive defense of his odd behavior, called *Narrative and Correspondence Concerning the Removal of the Deposites*, and correctly described by the *New York Evening Post*, May 14, 1839, as a work of "feeble bitterness."

the campaign the radicals above all had feared: the deliberate creation of a panic in order to blackmail the government into rechartering the Bank. "Nothing but the evidence of suffering abroad will produce any effect in Congress," he wrote privately to a friend. ". . . if . . . the Bank permits itself to be frightened or coaxed into any relaxation of its present measures, the relief will itself be cited as evidence that the measures of the Govt. are not injurious or opressive, and the Bank will inevitably be prostrated." "My own course is decided," he informed another, "—all the other Banks and all the merchants may break, but the Bank of the United States shall not break."[45]

The strategy was at first brilliantly successful. The business community, already incensed by Jackson's measures, was easily persuaded that deflation was the inevitable consequence of removal. The contraction of loans by the Bank tightened credit all along the line. Businesses failed, men were thrown out of work, money was unobtainable. Memorials, petitions, letters, delegations, and protests of every kind deluged Congress. . . .

Delegations of businessmen, from New York, Baltimore, and Philadelphia, also beset the President. Jackson, disliking to argue with people who were either fools enough to believe Nicholas Biddle or knaves enough to work for him, would make his unshakable determination clear by launching into fearful tirades against the Bank. A deputation from New York found him writing at his desk, smoking fiercely away at his long pipe. He excused himself, finished the paper, and rose. "Now gentlemen, what is your pleasure with me?" James G. King, son of Rufus King, had hardly spoken a few sentences of a prepared address asking for relief when Jackson interrupted angrily: "Go to Nicholas Biddle. We have no money here, gentlemen. Biddle has all the money. He has millions of specie in his vaults, at this moment, lying idle, and yet you come to *me* to save you from breaking." And so on, with mounting vehemence, until the visitors departed. The man who had introduced them was overtaken by a messenger on the White House stairs and asked to return to the President's office. He found

45. Biddle to William Appleton, January 27, 1834, and to J. G. Watmough, February 8, 1834, R. C. McGrane, ed., *Correspondence of Nicholas Biddle* (Boston, 1919), pp. 219, 221.

Jackson chuckling over the interview: "Didn't I manage them well?"[46] . . .

But Biddle could not hope to fool the business community indefinitely. More and more merchants were coming to believe that he was carrying the money pressure farther than necessary, and few would agree that it was worth breaking "all the other Banks and all the merchants" to restore Nicholas Biddle to power. . . .

Biddle acknowledged the answer himself on September 16 when he gave the lie direct to the case for curtailment by suddenly entering on a policy of expansion. After reducing its loans by well over eighteen million dollars from August 1, 1833, to November 1, 1834, under the plea of winding up its affairs, the Bank in the next five months *increased* its loans by almost fourteen and a half million. On June 1, 1835, the loans were almost what they were when Biddle's campaign began in August, 1833, and the note circulation was actually greater than ever before.[47] The panic was over, and the Bank had not recovered the deposits.

Somewhere along the way, Biddle had lost his grip on reality. Ambition, vanity, and love of power had crossed the thin line to megalomania. So little had he understood the American people that he ordered the circulation of thirty thousand copies of the Bank veto as a campaign document for Henry Clay. He completely misconceived the grounds of the Jacksonian attack; and, when the President stated them, Biddle brushed the explanation aside as mere demagogy. As late as the summer of 1833, he still believed that Jackson's secret purpose was to found a new National Bank of his own.[48] . . .

The determination which enabled Jackson to resist the hysteria of panic came basically from the possession of an alternative policy of his own. Madison had surrendered to a corresponding, though less intense, pressure in 1816 because he had no constructive program to offer. But, for Jackson, the emotions and ideas which

46. Parton, III, 549–550.
47. *Washington Globe*, April 13 and June 10, 1835.
48. R. C. H. Catterall, *The Second Bank of the United States* (Chicago, 1903), p. 241; Biddle to J. S. Barbour, July 11, 1833, Biddle, *Correspondence*, p. 210.

underlay the hard-money case against the Bank were crystallizing into a coherent and concrete set of measures, designed to capture the government for "the humble members of society," as Hamilton's system had captured it for "the rich and powerful."

The Jeffersonian tradition provided the main inspiration for this program. The Virginia condemnation of paper money, pronounced by Jefferson, formulated profoundly by Taylor, kept pure and uncompromising by Macon and Randolph, had passed on as a vital ideological legacy to Jackson, Benton, Van Buren, Polk, Cambreleng. Yet it was handed down as a series of keen but despairing criticisms delivered in the shadow of an invincible industrialism. The creative statesmen of the Jackson administration now proposed to transform it into a positive governmental policy.

The Bank war played an indispensable role in the precipitation of hard-money ideas. It dramatized currency questions in a way which captured the imagination of the people and excited their desire for further action on the financial front. It enlisted the enthusiasm of intellectuals, stimulating them to further analysis, widening the range and competence of economic theory. It tightened class lines, and the new bitterness of feeling sharpened the intellectual weapons.

Above all, the Bank war triumphantly established Jackson in the confidence of the people. Their faith in him had survived ordeals and won vindication: thereafter, when faced by a choice between Jackson and a cherished policy, most of them would choose Jackson. The effect of this mandate was particularly to sell the West on an intricate economic program, which many Westerners did not understand and which ran counter to their preconceptions.

The uncertainty about the West had postponed the avowal of the hard-money system.[49] The veto message, written by three men of known hard-money convictions, Jackson, Taney, and Kendall,

---

49. Orestes A. Brownson later declared that he had been urged in 1831 by "men high in the confidence of the party . . . to support the administration of that day, on the ground that it was opposed to all corporate banking, whether state or national." This was, of course, long before any such purpose was avowed as party policy. *Boston Reformer*, August 4, 1837.

suppressed mention of the doctrine, as if by main force. But the election of 1832 increased Jackson's confidence. He could have lost the entire West and still have broken even with Clay, but he carried the whole West except for Kentucky.[50] He now felt certain of vigorous national support, and also of probable Western support, even for his economic ideas. . . .

He thus was emboldened to come out publicly for the hard-money policy, expressing himself first in his interview with the Philadelphia delegation a few days before his Second Inaugural. His objective, he said, was gradually to reduce the circulation of paper, by forbidding deposit banks to issue small notes and by refusing such notes in payment for taxes, until all notes under twenty dollars would be eliminated and "thus a metallic currency be ensured for all the common purposes of life, while the use of bank notes would be confined to those engaged in commerce."[51] . . .

The Bank war compelled people to speculate once again about the conflict of classes. "There are but two parties," exclaimed Thomas Hart Benton, giving the period its keynote; "there never has been but two parties . . . founded in the radical question, whether PEOPLE, OR PROPERTY, shall govern? Democracy implies a government by the people. . . . Aristocracy implies a government of the rich. . . . and in these words are contained the sum of party distinction."[52]

The paper banking system was considered to play a leading role in this everlasting struggle. Men living by the issue and circulation of paper money produced nothing; they added nothing to the national income; yet, they flourished and grew wealthy. Their prosperity, it was argued, must be stolen from the proceeds of productive labor—in other words, from the honest but defenseless "humble members of society." . . .

The system was further important in the strategy of the warfare. Taney described the big Bank as "the centre, and the citadel of the moneyed power." "A national bank," declared the Massachusetts

50. The "West" here includes Alabama, Mississippi, Louisiana, Kentucky, Tennessee, Ohio, Indiana, Illinois, and Missouri. Jackson had only to carry one Western state to get a majority of the electoral votes.
51. *Niles' Weekly Register*, March 1, 1834.
52. *Niles' Weekly Register*, August 29, 1835.

Democratic convention of 1837, "is the bulwark of the aristocracy; its outpost, and its rallying point. It is the bond of union
for those who hold that Government should rest on property."[53]
To a lesser degree all banks acted as strongholds of conservatism.
They provided the funds and often the initiative for combat. Their
lawyers, lobbyists, and newspapers were eternally active. Politicians would gather in their boardrooms and consult their presidents and accept gifts of stock. More than any other kind of
corporate enterprise, banks boldly intervened in politics when they
felt their interests menaced.

The hard-money policy attacked both the techniques of plunder
and the general strategy of warfare. By doing away with paper
money, it proposed to restrict the steady transfer of wealth from
the farmer and laborer to the business community. By limiting
banks to commercial credit and denying them control over the
currency, it proposed to lessen their influence and power. By
reducing the proportion of paper money, it proposed to moderate
the business cycle, and order the economy to the advantage of the
worker rather than the speculator. It was a coherent policy, based
on the best economic thought of the day, and formulated on a
higher intellectual level than the alternatives of the opposition.
. . .

Andrew Jackson ably summed up its broad aims. "The planter,
the farmer, the mechanic, and the laborer," he wrote, "all know
that their success depends upon their own industry and economy,
and that they must not expect to become suddenly rich by the
fruits of their toil." These classes "form the great body of the people of the United States; they are the bone and sinew of the
country." Yet "they are in constant danger of losing their fair
influence in the Government." Why? "The mischief springs from
the power which the moneyed interest derives from a paper
currency, which they are able to control, from the multitude of
corporations with exclusive privileges which they have succeeded
in obtaining in the different States." His warning to his people was
solemn. "Unless you become more watchful . . . you will in the
end find that the most important powers of Government have been

---

53. *Washington Globe,* August 25, 1834, October 27, 1837.

given or bartered away, and the control over your dearest interests
has passed into the hands of these corporations."[54] . . .

But the administration's campaign came too late. The wise coun-
sels of the hard-money advocates were drowned out by the roar of
the nation's greatest boom in years. The Bank of the United States
alone enlarged its loans an average of $2.5 million a month and its
paper circulation by a total of $10 million between December,
1834, and July, 1835.[55] Smaller banks rushed to follow, increasing the amount of paper money from $82 million on January 1,
1835, to $108 million, a year later, and $120 million by December
1, 1836.[56] . . .

A basic cause of the inflation was land speculation, and the
administration had already moved to plug up this great hole in the
national economy. . . . Benton introduced a resolution requiring
that the public lands be paid for in specie. Webster, with his usual
policy of supporting sound money except when concrete measures
were proposed which might secure it, led the attack on this
measure, and a combination of Whigs and conservative Democrats
killed it in the Senate. But after adjournment Jackson had Benton
draw up an executive order embodying his idea, and the famous
Specie Circular was issued. . . .

Jackson thus had to overrule Congress to sustain the hard-
money policy. But the Specie Circular furnished the only tense
financial issue in the last years of his administration. After the
panic session the great scenes of battle began to shift to the states.
Here, in places inaccessible to the long arm and grim energy of
General Jackson, little bands of devoted Jacksonians fought to
stem the rush for bank and corporate charters, unfolding the
potentialities of the Jacksonian program, enriching the techniques,
and amplifying the intellectual resources.

Above all, these local battles called forth the common people in
cities, towns, and country—the poor day laborer, the industrious

54. *Messages and Papers,* III, 305–306.
55. *Washington Globe,* June 10, 1835, May 12, 1836.
56. Levi Woodbury, "Report from the Secretary of the Treasury,"
December 6, 1836, *Register of Debates,* 24th Congress, 2nd Session,
Appendix, p. 80.

mechanic, the hardhanded farmer—the "humble members of society" everywhere. They listened for hours on hot summer days to dry expositions of financial policy. They crowded in bare and unheated halls on cold winter nights to hear about the evils of banking. They read, and thumbed, and passed along tracts and speeches attacking the paper system. They saw the dizzy climb of prices, wages lagging behind, raged silently at discounted bank notes, and wondered at the behavior of Democratic politicians pledged against voting for incorporations. They talked among themselves, with shrewdness and good sense and alarm. . . . Their discontent was real and widespread. . . .

The tradition of Jefferson and Jackson might recede, but it could never disappear. It was bound to endure in America so long as liberal capitalistic society endured, for it was the creation of the internal necessities of such a society. American democracy has come to accept the struggle among competing groups for the control of the state as a positive virtue—indeed, as the only foundation for liberty. The business community has been ordinarily the most powerful of these groups, and liberalism in America has been ordinarily the movement on the part of the other sections of society to restrain the power of the business community. This was the tradition of Jefferson and Jackson, and it has been the basic meaning of American liberalism.

BRAY HAMMOND

✪

The Assault on the Federal Bank

During the half-century that ended with General Jackson's election, America underwent changes perhaps the most radical and sweeping it has ever undergone in so short a time. It passed the climacteric separating a modern industrial economy from an older one of handicraft; it passed from colonial weakness through bare independence to actual power and from an unjostled rural culture to the complexities of populousness, sectionalism, urban slums, mechanized industry, and monetary credit. Men who had spent their childhood in a thin line of seaboard colonies, close even in their little cities to the edge of the westward continental wilderness, spent their late years in a tamed and wealthy land spread already to the Missouri and about to extend beyond it. They lived to ride on railways and steamships, to use the products of steam-driven machinery, to dwell in metropolitan centers, and to feel within their grasp and the grasp of their sons more potential and accessible wealth than had ever before excited the enterprise of man. . . .

The changes in social outlook were profound. Steam was generating conceptions of life, liberty, and the pursuit of happiness that were quite alien to Thomas Jefferson's; and the newcomers pushing into the country from Europe had more impatient economic motives than their eighteenth-century predecessors. People were led as they had not been before by visions of money-making.

Selections from chapters 12, 13, and 14 in Bray Hammond, *Banks and Politics in America from the Revolution to the Civil War* (copyright © 1957 by Princeton University Press; Princeton Paperback, 1967). Reprinted by permission of Princeton University Press.

Liberty became transformed into *laissez faire*. A violent, aggressive, economic individualism became established. The democracy became greedy, intolerant, imperialistic, and lawless. It opened economic advantages to those who had not previously had them; yet it allowed wealth to be concentrated in new hands only somewhat more numerous than before, less responsible, and less disciplined. There were unenterprising and unpropertied thousands who missed entirely the economic opportunities with which America was thick. There was poverty in the Eastern cities and poverty on the frontier. Those who failed to hold their own in the struggle were set down as unfit.

Wealth was won and lost, lost and won. Patient accumulation was condemned. People believed it was not what they saved but what they made that counted. Jay Cooke, one of America's future millionaires, who was scarcely born poor on a farm but primitively at least, in a frontier settlement, was already on his way to fortune in a private banking firm before the age of twenty and writing home about his work with enthusiasm. This was in the winter of 1839–1840. "My bosses are making money fast," he said. "This business is always good, and those who follow it in time become rich. . . . Among our customers are men of every age and every position in society, from the hoary miser to the dashing buck who lives upon his thousands. Through all grades I see the same all-pervading, all-engrossing anxiety to grow rich." Something of the same sort, to be sure, was taking place in Western Europe and especially in Great Britain. Half the people and most of the money for America's transformation came from there. But though industrial and technological revolution occurred also in the Old World, in the New, where vast resources awaited exploitation, it produced a dazzling, democratic expansion experienced nowhere else. The situation was such that the rallying cry, "*Laissez nous faire!*" expressed the views of Americans perfectly, when translated.

Socially, the Jacksonian revolution signified that a nation of democrats was tired of being governed, however well, by gentlemen from Virginia and Massachusetts. As Professor Sumner observed, what seems to have enchanted people with General Jackson when he became a candidate for President was not any principles or policies he advocated but his breaches of decorum,

real or alleged.[1] Economically, the revolution signified that a
nation of potential money-makers could not abide traditionary,
conservative limitations on business enterprise, particularly by
capitalists in Philadelphia. The Jacksonian revolution was a consequence of the Industrial Revolution and of a farm-born people's
realization that now anyone in America could get rich and through
his own efforts, if he had a fair chance. A conception of earned
wealth arose which rendered the self-made man as superior
morally to the hereditary well-to-do as the agrarian had been. It
was like the conception which led Theodoric the Great to boast
that he held Italy solely by right of conquest and without the
shadow of legal, that is, hereditary, right. The humbly born and
rugged individualists who were gaining fortunes by their own toil
and sweat, or wits, were still simple Americans, Jeffersonian, anti-
monopolistic, antigovernmental, but fraught with the spirit of
enterprise and fired with a sense of what soon would be called
manifest destiny. They envied the social and economic advantages
of the established urban capitalists, mercantile and financial; and
they fought these aristocrats with far more zeal and ingenuity than
the agrarians ever had. They resented the federal Bank's interference with expansion of the monetary supply. They found it
bestriding the path of enterprise, and with Apollyon's brag but
Christian's better luck they were resolved to spill its soul. They
democratized business under a great show of agrarian idealism and
made the Age of Jackson a festival of *laissez faire* prelusive to the
Age of Grant and the robber barons.

In their attack on the Bank of the United States, the Jacksonians still employed the vocabulary of their agrarian back-
grounds. The phraseology of idealism was adapted to money-
making, the creed of an earlier generation becoming the cant of its
successor. Their terms of abuse were "oppression," "tyranny,"
"monied power," "aristocracy," "wealth," "privilege," "monopoly"; their terms of praise were "the humble," "the poor," "the
simple," "the honest and industrious." Though their cause was a
sophisticated one of enterpriser against capitalist, of banker

1. Ellis P. Oberholtzer, *Jay Cooke, Financier of the Civil War* (Philadelphia, 1907), I, 57–58; William G. Sumner, *Andrew Jackson* (Boston,
1882), p. 179.

against regulation, and of Wall Street against Chestnut, the language was the same as if they were all back on the farm. Neither the President, nor his advisers, nor their followers saw any discrepancy between the concept of freedom in an age of agrarianism and the concept of freedom in one of enterprise. Only the poets and philosophers were really aware that a discrepancy existed and though troubled by it their vision was far from clear. Notwithstanding their language, therefore, the Jacksonians' destruction of the Bank of the United States was in no sense a blow at capitalism or property or the "money power." It was a blow at an older set of capitalists by a newer, more numerous set. It was incident to the democratization of business, the diffusion of enterprise among the mass of people, and the transfer of economic primacy from an old and conservative merchant class to a newer, more aggressive, and more numerous body of businessmen and speculators of all sorts.

The Jacksonians were unconventional and skillful in politics. In their assault on the Bank they united five important elements, which, incongruities notwithstanding, comprised an effective combination. These were Wall Street's jealousy of Chestnut Street, the businessman's dislike of the federal Bank's restraint upon bank credit, the politician's resentment at the Bank's interference with states' rights, popular identification of the Bank with the aristocracy of business, and the direction of agrarian antipathy away from banks in general to the federal Bank in particular. Destruction of the Bank ended federal regulation of bank credit and shifted the money center of the country from Chestnut Street to Wall Street. It left the poor agrarian as poor as he had been before and it left the money power possessed of more money and more power than ever. . . .

Andrew Jackson himself had been lawyer, legislator, jurist, merchant, and land speculator, but principally planter and soldier. His origin was humble and agrarian. He was a self-made man. He belonged to an aristocracy of a frontier sort peculiar to the Southwest of his day—landed, proud, individualistic, slave-owning, and more bound by the cruder conventions than the politer ones. Cockfighting, betting, horse-racing, and the punctilio of the duel seem to have satisfied its cultural needs. It was without the education and discipline of the older aristocracies of the seaboard. It possessed more of the aristocrat's assertive and obnoxious vices than his gentler, liberal virtues and stood on property and pretension rather than birth and breeding. In a quarrel General Jackson would resort to the field of honor if his enemy were a "gentleman" but merely beat him with a stick on sight if he were not. Such distinctions seem to have been lost on Albert Gallatin, an aristocrat of a different water, in whose fastidious judgment President Jackson was "a pugnacious animal."[2]

Yet the distinction and courtesy of the General's manners took by surprise those who knew him first as President; he was by then unwell, grieving over the death of his wife, and softened besides by what age will sometimes do to men. He was not now the brawler in taverns and at racetracks. "I was agreeably disappointed and pleased," wrote William Lyon Mackenzie of Upper Canada in 1829—a man of considerable violence himself in word and deed— "to find in General Jackson great gentleness and benevolence of manner, accompanied by that good natured affability of address which will enable persons who wait upon him to feel at ease in his presence. . . ." When he chose, however, the General still could storm outrageously enough. He could simulate bursts of passion that terrified strangers, who shrank from having the President of the United States burst a blood vessel on their account, even though they were not fond of him. But his tongue seldom slipped. No one profited from blunders of his. What mistakes he made arose from a childlike trust in his friends and not from carelessness with his adversaries.[3]

He was exceptionally susceptible to the flattery and suggestion of his friends. This did not impair his maintaining a forceful, determined leadership. He listened to his advisers individually and chose his plan of action himself. His native views were agrarian and Jeffersonian, though of Jefferson himself he could entertain very low opinions, and no one—not Alexander Hamilton himself —ever went further from the constitutional principles of Jefferson

2. Marquis James, *Life of Andrew Jackson* (Indianapolis, 1938), p. 109; Henry Adams, *Life of Albert Gallatin* (Philadelphia, 1879), p. 651.

3. William L. Mackenzie, *Sketches of Canada and the United States* (London, 1833), pp. 46–47.

than Jackson did in his nullification proclamation of December, 1832. With him, moreover, as with other self-made men of his time, agrarian and Jeffersonian views faded into *laissez faire*. He was a rugged individualist in all directions. He was no friend to the shiftless and indigent who got into debt and then could not get out. He paid his own debts, no matter how hard he found it to do so, and he expected others to pay theirs.

"Andrew Jackson was on the side of the capitalists," writes Mr. Marquis James of his earlier career. "His first case in Nashville in 1788 had landed him as champion of the creditors against the debtors. Jackson desired wealth." He had been opposed to Western relief measures taken on behalf of debtors in the ten years preceding his election to the Presidency. They were wicked, pernicious, profligate, and unconstitutional. Opinions like this put him logically on the side of the Bank of the United States, which was the pivotal creditor, and opposed him to the banks made of paper, such as the Bank of the Commonwealth of Kentucky, over which his Kitchen adviser, Francis Preston Blair, had presided. But solecisms embarrassed the General very little. On the frontier more than elsewhere, the modification of an agrarian economy into an industrial and financial one was such, in William Lyon Mackenzie's words, as to "make speculation as extensive as life, and transform a Jeffersonian democracy into a nation of gamesters and our land into one great gaming house where all are forced to play, while but few can understand the game." General Jackson's prejudices were stronger than his convictions, and he was himself among the least consistent and stable of the Jacksonians. "Not only was Jackson not a consistent politician," says Professor Thomas P. Abernethy, "he was not even a real leader of democracy. He had no part whatever in the promotion of the liberal movement which was progressing in his own state. . . . He was a self-made man . . . he always believed in making the public serve the ends of the politician. Democracy was good talk with which to win the favor of the people and thereby accomplish ulterior objectives. Jackson never really championed the cause of the people; he only invited them to champion his. He was not consciously hypocritical in this. It was merely the usual way of doing business in these primitive and ingenuous times." Of his

election to the Presidency Professor Richard Hofstadter writes that
it was not "a mandate for economic reform; no financial changes,
no crusades against the national Bank, were promised. . . . Up
to the time of his inauguration Jackson had contributed neither a
thought nor a deed to the democratic movement, and he was
elected without a platform."[4]

What counts is that Jackson was popular. He was a picturesque
folk character, and it does his memory an injustice to make him
out a statesman. "All the remodelling and recoloring of Andrew
Jackson," says Professor Abernethy, "has not created a character
half so fascinating as he was in reality." To the dissatisfied,
whether through distress or ambition, Andrew Jackson offered a
distinct and attractive change from the old school of leaders the
country had had—and not the least by his want of real ideas. He
became the champion of the common man, even though the latter
might be no longer either frontiersman or farmer but speculator,
capitalist, or entrepreneur of a new, democratic sort, who in every
village and township was beginning to profit by the Industrial
Revolution, the growth of population, and the expanding supply of
bank credit. This new common man was manufacturer, banker,
builder, carrier, and promoter. He belonged to the "active and
enterprising," in the luminous contrast put by Churchill C. Cambreleng, as against the "wealthier classes." And his conflict was
not the traditionary one between the static rich and the static poor
but a dynamic, revolutionary one between those who were already
rich and those who sought to become rich.[5]

General Jackson was an excellent leader in the revolt of enterprise against the regulation of credit by the federal Bank. Though
the inferior of his associates in knowledge, he was extraordinarily
effective in combat. And as a popular leader he combined the
simple agrarian principles of political economy absorbed at his
mother's knee with the most up-to-date doctrine of *laissez faire*.
Along with several of the best constitutional authorities of his

4. James, p. 89; William L. Mackenzie, *Lives and Opinions of B. F.
Butler and Jesse Hoyt* (Boston, 1845), p. 105 n.; Thomas P. Abernethy,
From Frontier to Plantation in Tennessee (Chapel Hill, 1932), pp. 248–249;
Richard Hofstadter, *The American Political Tradition* (New York, 1948), p.
54.

5. Abernethy, p. 124; 22nd Congress, 1st Session, HR 460, p. 333.

day—but not Mr. Taney—General Jackson believed that the notes issued by state banks were unconstitutional. In 1820 he wrote to his friend Major Lewis: "You know my opinion as to the banks, that is, that the constitution of our state as well as the Constitution of the United States prohibited the establishment of banks in any state. Sir, the tenth section of the first article of the federal Constitution is positive and explicit, and when you read the debates in the convention you will find it was introduced to prevent a state legislature from passing such bills." Seventeen years later, in 1837, he wrote to Senator Benton: "My position now is and has ever been since I have been able to form an opinion on this subject that Congress has no power to charter a Bank and that the states are prohibited from issuing bills of credit or granting a charter by which such bills can be issued by any corporation or order." Yet in effect he did as much as could be done to augment the issue of state bank notes and was proud of what he did. Most statesmen would feel some embarrassment in such a performance.[6]

The Jacksonians were anything but rash. Once decided that they should fight the Bank rather than wed with it, they developed their attack patiently, experimentally, shrewdly, probing the aristocratic victim and teasing public interest into action. The President himself took no unnecessary chances, but those he had to take he took without fear. He was a man of "sagacious temerity," in the words of one of his contemporaries. His attack on the Bank was like his careful slaying of Charles Dickinson in a duel thirty years before. His opponent had been formidable—much younger than he and an expert marksman, which he himself was not. Each was to have one shot. Jackson and his second had gone over the prospects carefully and decided it would be best to wait for Dickinson to fire first. For though Jackson would probably be hit, "he counted on the resource of his will to sustain him until he could aim deliberately and shoot to kill, if it were the last act of his life." So he awaited his adversary's fire and, as he had expected, he was hit. But his coat, buttoned loosely over his breast, as was his wont, had presented a deceptive silhouette, and the ball had missed his heart. He con-

6. New York Public Library, *Bulletin*, IV (1900), 190; J. S. Bassett, ed., *The Correspondence of Andrew Jackson*, 6 vols. (Washington, 1926–1933), IV, 446; J. S. Bassett, *Life of Andrew Jackson* (New York, 1931), II, 590.

cealed his hurt and concentrated on his helpless enemy, whose life
he now could take. "He stood glowering at him for an instant, and
then his long pistol arm came slowly to a horizontal position." He
aimed carefully and pulled the trigger. But the hammer stopped at
half-cock. The seconds consulted while the principals stood, and
Jackson was allowed to try again. Once more he took deliberate
aim, his victim waiting in evident horror, and fired. Dickinson fell,
mortally hurt. "I should have hit him," Jackson asserted later, "if
he had shot me through the brain." The same mystical willpower,
the same canny and studious appraisal of probabilities and of
relative advantages and disadvantages, weighed in the conflict with
the Bank. The President tantalized the frank and impatient Mr.
Biddle, he waited for him to make the appropriate mistakes, and
then with care and effectiveness he struck. His adversaries' weak-
nesses were no less at his command than his own skill.[7] . . .

The first Jacksonian feints at the Bank, as already said, implied
less desire to destroy it than to fetch it within the party pale as
spoils of victory. . . . But this course was soon superseded by the
more ambitious plan to replace the Bank with something entirely
new and not in Philadelphia. The President himself always denied
that he had ever entertained the idea of continuing the Bank. "The
charge made," he said later, "of my being friendly to the Bank of
the United States until I found it could not be used for my political
purposes, when I turned against it, is one of the foulest and basest
calumnies ever uttered. . . . I have always been opposed to it
upon constitutional grounds as well as expediency and policy." He
also affirmed that he had wished to speak out against it so early as
in his Inaugural but had been dissuaded: everyone knew, he said,
that he always had been opposed to the Bank of the United States,
"nay all banks." In May and October following his inauguration in
March, 1829, he was in fact already in correspondence with Senator
Felix Grundy about a wholly new "national bank" to replace the
existing federal Bank.[8]

7. Charles J. Ingersoll, *Historical Sketch of the Second War between
Great Britain and United States* (Philadelphia, 1849), p. 264; James, pp.
116–118; Bassett, pp. 63–64.

8. *Correspondence of Andrew Jackson*, IV, 37, 83–84, 445; V, 236; R. C.
H. Catterall, *The Second Bank of the United States* (Chicago, 1903), pp.
182–185.

This does not mean that the General went into the White House girded up to exterminate the federal Bank. The evidence, the circumstances, the personalities, and the relevant interest suggest something far less simple. The General, I think, had entered the White House with nothing more definite than, as he said, a traditionary aversion to all banks and constitutional scruples about them. His feelings had not kept him from dealing with banks, however, or in particular with the Nashville office of the federal Bank, where he had his account. He may nevertheless have looked forward to preventing a renewal of the federal charter, which would expire within his administration if he were to serve two terms. Before any such program became formulated, however, certain of his subordinates were moving in on the federal Bank as into all departments of the federal government. This and presumably nothing more was what Isaac Hill and Secretary Ingham purposed in opening their initial skirmish with the Bank's president.

When these routine steps in the party interest were begun Mr. Van Buren was still in Albany, fostering his Safety Fund bank bill; but after the bill was enacted and he had joined General Jackson in Washington, Mr. Van Buren must have had no difficulty in supplanting the Treasury's unimaginative scheme with his own more radical one. He could simply suggest to the President a procedure for bringing to an end the offensive and unconstitutional Bank in Philadelphia. No emphasis whatever need be given the benefits to New York. The course Mr. Van Buren wanted seems to have been agreed upon at Richmond in October, 1829, and to have made destruction of the federal Bank, "as at present constituted," the definite purpose of the President and his intimates.

The Richmond meeting is the one of which reports, confirmed by Senator Felix Grundy's correspondence with the President, were made to Nicholas Biddle from various quarters that its purpose was to commit the party to attack the Bank. Major Lewis alone seems to have dissented from its decision and to have continued cultivating the Bank in good faith; and, though Secretary Ingham, as a self-made businessman, may have relished laying down the rules for the aristocratic banker Nicholas Biddle, still, being a Pennsylvanian himself, he may have shrunk from proceeding too far against Pennsylvania's principal institution.

The plan to end the Bank called for care and caution. There was not now the popular hatred of it that there had been five years before. From General Jackson's inauguration in March, 1829, the charter had almost seven years to run. At the moment the Jacksonians had to recognize that the Bank's standing in public esteem was high; it was as good as it ever had been, or better. Five years had elapsed since the Supreme Court had last denied the right of an individual state to interfere with it, and prosperity had lessened the occasion for interference. The Bank was resented by the state banks, but nothing more had occurred to arouse ill will. If the Bank were to be done away with, a case against it must be worked up.

Nicholas Biddle, meanwhile, though without very explicit assurances from the administration of its good will, had been led to hope for the best. Major Lewis, October 16, 1829, only a week or so before the Richmond meeting, had written him from the White House to acknowledge a conciliatory letter about political influences on branch office appointments. The President was gratified, the Major said, and requested him to say that he had too much confidence in Mr. Biddle to believe for a moment that he would knowingly tolerate the conduct in the branch offices of which the Jacksonians complained. "The President thinks," he said, "as you do, that the Bank of the United States should recognize *no* party; and that in all its operations it should have an eye *single* to the interest of the stockholders and the good of the country. . . ." A few days later, October 21, 1829, one of the Bank's directors, from Philadelphia, Matthew L. Bevan, wrote to Mr. Biddle as follows after calling on the President in Washington: ". . . I cannot withhold a moment the pleasure it gives me in saying the result of my visit is most satisfactory, inasmuch as the President expressed himself in the most clear and decided manner friendly to the Bank—'that it was a blessing to the country administered as it was, diffusing a healthful circulation, sustaining the general credit without partiality or political bias'—that he entertained a high regard for its excellent President (I use his own words), who with the Board of the parent Bank possessed his entire confidence. . . ."[9]

9. Biddle Papers (Library of Congress), 21, Folio 4219 (also in R. C. McGrane, ed., *Correspondence of Nicholas Biddle* [Boston, 1919], pp. 79–80, 81–82).

A few days later, October 26, 1829, Samuel Jaudon, the Bank's cashier, wrote Mr. Biddle that he had called on the President, who had said, *inter alia,* "that in reference to yourself particularly he had the most unbounded confidence in the purity of your intentions; that the support which you had given to the financial operations of the Government was of the most gratifying as well as effectual kind. . . . Throughout our interview, which lasted for an hour, the tone and manner of the President were of the most mild and friendly character. . . ." Major Lewis, November 9, 1829, wrote a fellow-Jacksonian in Philadelphia: "Say to Mr. Biddle the President is much gratified with the report I have made him upon the subject of his Bank; all things with regard to it will be well."[10]

About this time Mr. Biddle sent Major Lewis a plan for retirement of the public debt, respecting which the Major sent him word, November 11, 1829: "I will submit it to the General. I think we will find the *old fellow* will do justice to the Bank in his message for the handsome manner in which it assisted the Government in paying the last instalment of the national debt."[11]

About a week later Mr. Biddle was himself in Washington and had a cordial interview with the President. According to an undated, informal memorandum in Biddle's papers, the President thanked him for his plan of paying off the national debt and told him he would have no difficulty in recommending it to Congress. "But," the President had said, according to the memorandum, "I think it right to be perfectly frank with you—I do not think that the power of Congress extends to charter a Bank out of the ten mile square.[12] I do not dislike your Bank any more than all banks. But ever since I read the history of the South Sea Bubble I have been afraid of banks. I have read the opinion of John Marshall, who I believe was a great and pure mind—and could not agree with him. . . . I feel very sensibly the services rendered by the Bank at the last payment of the national debt and shall take an opportunity of declaring it publicly in my message to Congress."

10. Biddle Papers, 21, Folios 4232–4233 (also in Biddle, *Correspondence*, p. 84).

11. Biddle Papers, 21, Folio 4249, in Biddle's own hand as an extract from correspondence of W. B. Lewis with Henry Toland (also in Biddle, *Correspondence*, p. 85).

12. That is, the federal District of Columbia, then ten miles square, in which the city of Washington is situated.

Mr. Biddle told him that he was "very much gratified at this frank explanation" and that "we shall all be proud of any kind mention in the message—for we should feel like soldiers after an action commended by their General"; to which the President replied, "Sir, it would be only an act of justice to mention it."[13]

However, a week later, Nicholas Biddle was warned by Alexander Hamilton, Jr., November 27, 1829, that the President would speak against the Bank in his message: "I have long had an anxious solicitude for the permanency of the Bank of the United States," he wrote, "and it is consequently a source of deep regret that I understood the renewal of its charter is to be unfavourably noticed in the President's message." Mr. Biddle refused to believe the warning. He replied the next day: "The rumor to which you allude," he said, "I have not heard from any other quarter, and I believe it is entirely without foundation. My reason for thinking so is that during a recent visit to Washington from which I returned on Thursday last, I had much conversation of a very full and frank character with the President about the Bank, in all which he never intimated any such purpose. On the contrary he spoke in terms the most kind and gratifying towards the institution—expressed his thanks for the services it had rendered the Government since his connection with it, and I look to the message with expectations of the most satisfactory kind."[14]

He also wrote in his draft of a letter to Hamilton four days later that "the administration of the Bank is on the best footing with the President and his particular friends," but he scratched out those words to say instead—alluding to a certain Jacksonian editor—that "abuse of the Bank does him no service in the opinion of the President and his best friends."[15] In this comfortable mood, Mr. Biddle was confronted almost immediately by the unexpected words of the President's message to Congress. The Bank's charter,

13. Biddle Papers, 21, Folio 4248 (also in Biddle, *Correspondence*, pp. 93–94); Bassett, II, 599–600.
14. Biddle Papers, 3 President's Letter Books (1829), p. 98. Alexander Hamilton, Jr., was a supporter of John C. Calhoun—his brother James A. Hamilton, a supporter of Andrew Jackson. But it is a reasonable conjecture that the first brother got from the second the news of which he warned Nicholas Biddle.
15. Biddle Papers, 21, Folio 4298.

the President said, would expire in 1836 and it was not too soon to begin considering if it should be renewed. "Both the constitutionality and the expediency of the law creating this Bank are well questioned by a large portion of our fellow citizens; and it must be admitted by all that it has failed in the great end of establishing a uniform and sound currency."[16]

That the constitutionality and expediency of the Bank were questioned is one thing—that they were "well questioned" is another. Thirty-eight years had elapsed since establishment of the first Bank, and it or its successor had served the administrations of all six of Jackson's predecessors. One of its original opponents, Thomas Jefferson, had as President acknowledged its constitutionality by acquiescence, and another, James Madison—the foremost authority on the Constitution—had specifically abandoned his former objections to the Bank, had recommended re-establishment, and had approved the act effecting it. The Supreme Court had twice affirmed the Bank's constitutionality. Indeed, after 1791 nobody of comparable authority with its original opponents— Jefferson and Madison—ever attacked the Bank on constitutional grounds.

The President's second assertion—that the Bank had failed to establish a sound and uniform currency—was preposterous. When Mr. Gallatin asked him what he meant, he got no intelligible reply. Half a century later Professor Sumner wrote that the currency had never before been so good as when President Jackson spoke, and that it had never been so good since. "The proceedings," he wrote, "of which the paragraph in the message of 1829 was the first warning, threw the currency and banking of the country into confusion and uncertainty . . . and they have never yet recovered. . . ." Subsequent studies have confirmed Professor Sumner's judgment. "Probably never since 1789," writes Professor Walter B. Smith, "had the United States had a dollar which was sounder or more stable" than in the period—1826 to 1832—of General Jackson's assertion.[17]

16. Biddle Papers, 21, Folios 4308, 4311; James D. Richardson, comp., *Messages and Papers of the Presidents* (New York, 1897–1927), III, 1025.
17. Sumner, pp. 281–282; Walter B. Smith, *Economic Aspects of the Second Bank of the United States* (Cambridge, Mass., 1953), p. 76.

Besides slurring the Bank, in one part of the message, the President commended it in another, as he had told Mr. Biddle he would. "The payment on account of public debt made on the 1st of July last was $8,715,462.87," he said. And he continued in words obviously prepared by the Treasury: "It was apprehended that the sudden withdrawal of so large a sum from the banks in which it was deposited, at a time of unusual pressure in the money market, might cause much injury to the interests dependent on bank accommodations. But this evil was wholly averted by an early anticipation of it at the Treasury, aided by the judicious arrangements of the officers of the Bank of the United States." This fulfilled the President's promise, and was probably all that Nicholas Biddle expected.[18] The part that he had not expected came later in the message.[19] . . .

In both houses of Congress the President's questions about the Bank were referred to committees, and both committees upheld the Bank forcefully. . . . The House committee, whose chairman was George McDuffie of South Carolina, produced a lengthier and more comprehensive report. . . . They stated on the basis of clear evidence that the Bank had furnished a circulating medium more uniform than specie, "a currency of absolutely uniform value in all places."[20] . . .

Meanwhile the evidences of official policy were conflicting and perplexing. Most of the official Cabinet opposed an attack on the Bank. Working relations with the Treasury continued normal and

18. *Messages and Papers*, III, 1014.
19. James A. Hamilton says that he was called on to help President Jackson with this message and that in the draft already written the Bank "was attacked at great length in a loose, newspaper, slashing style." He says he advised that the subject be omitted, but the President declared himself to be "pledged against the Bank." He says the President told him a little later that in attacking the Bank he disliked to act contrary to the opinion of a majority of his Cabinet but could not shirk his duty. At the same time, Hamilton says he was asked to work out the details of Jackson's "proposed National Bank," which was to be "attached" to the Treasury and to have the "Customhouse a branch." Hamilton, *Reminiscences*, p. 151.
20. M. St. Clair Clarke and D. A. Hall, *Legislative and Documentary History of the Second Bank of the United States* (Washington, 1832), pp. 745–749.

Mr. Biddle was himself renominated government director by the President. Major Lewis of the Kitchen Cabinet kept the door open, exchanged friendly letters, and proposed Jackson supporters for branch appointments, Judge Overton, "a particular friend of the President," among them. "The President is well," he said in closing such a letter, May 3, 1830, "and desires me to present his respects to you." But the same day, May 3, 1830, the President himself sent Colonel James A. Hamilton in New York a copy of the McDuffie report on the Bank with these words: "I presume it to be a joint effort and the best that can be made in its support, and *it is feeble.* This is intended, no doubt, as the first shot; it will pass without moving me." A month later, June 3, 1830, he wrote Colonel Hamilton again, calling the Bank three times a "hydra of corruption"; it is "dangerous to our liberties by its corrupting influences everywhere and not the least in the Congress of the Union"; it has "demoralizing effects upon our citizens. . . ." And later that same month, June 26, 1830, he wrote to Major Lewis a complaint that Duff Green could not be trusted with the attack on the Bank.[21] "The truth is, he has professed to me to be heart and soul against the Bank," but Calhoun "controls him as the shew-man does his puppets, and we must get another organ to announce the policy. . . ."[22]

A month before, however, May 25, Major Lewis had again written Mr. Biddle, marking his letter "confidential":

Before closing this letter permit me to say one word in reference to a subject mentioned in your last letter to me—I mean the information you received of the President's having declared that if Congress should pass a law renewing the charter of the United States Bank, he would put his veto on it. I told you in Philadelphia when you first mentioned the thing to me, that there must be some mistake, because the report was at variance with what *I* had heard him say upon the subject. In conversing with him a few days ago upon the subject, he still entertained the opinion that a *National* Bank might be established

21. Biddle, *Correspondence*, p. 99; J. A. Hamilton, *Reminiscences* (New York, 1869), pp. 164, 167; *Correspondence of Andrew Jackson*, IV, 156.
22. Duff Green was Vice-President Calhoun's devoted supporter. His daughter married Calhoun's son. Calhoun was Van Buren's rival for the Presidency, succeeding Jackson's.

that would be preferable to the present United States Bank; but that, if Congress thought differently and it was deemed necessary to have such a Bank as the present, with certain modifications, he should not object to it. If the President finds that his scheme is not likely to take, I do not believe he will be opposed altogether to the present Bank.[23]

Two months later Mr. Biddle received a letter from Josiah Nichol, July 20, 1830, president of the Nashville office and a friend of President Jackson, reporting conversations with the latter, who had just been for some two days a guest in his home and of whom he said:

He appears to be well satisfied with the facilities that the Bank have given to government and individuals in transferring their funds from one point to another and acknowledges that a Bank such as the present only can do so. He appears to be generally pleased with the management of the Bank of the United States and branches—and particularly so with this office. I have taken considerable pains and gave him all the information I consistently could on banking subjects—and believe have convinced him that the present Bank and branches could not be dispensed with without manifest injury to the country and particularly so to this western country, as no other currency could be substituted. . . . The only objection he appears to have to the present Bank is that a great part of the stock is held by foreigners, consequently the interest is taken from the country. He is well satisfied that politics have no influence in the Bank or in the choice of directors, and I am well convinced that he will not interfere with Congress on the subject of renewing the charter of the Bank—although on this subject he keeps his opinion to himself. He speaks of you in the most exalted terms and says there is no gentleman that can be found would manage the Bank better or do the Bank and country more justice.[24]

So while the General privately breathed animosity for the hydra of corruption, Mr. Biddle was let think by the General's friends that all was well. . . .

In his second annual message, December, 1830, the President

23. Biddle Papers, 22, Folio 4624 (also in Biddle, *Correspondence*, pp. 103–104).
24. Biddle Papers, 23, Folio 4721 (also in Biddle, *Correspondence*, pp. 106–107).

disparaged the Bank somewhat more harshly, saying that nothing had occurred that lessened "the dangers which many of our citizens apprehend from that institution as at present organized." He asked if it would not be possible to have a bank in its place that should be a branch of the Treasury, "based on the public and individual deposits, without power to make loans or purchase property," and that should remit the funds of the government, its expenses to be met by the sale of exchange. "Not being a corporate body, having no stockholders, debtors, or property, and but few officers, it would not be obnoxious to the constitutional objections which are urged against the present bank." The President also expressed the belief, in a passage which indirectly acknowledges the federal Bank's regulatory function, that "the states would be strengthened by having in their hands the means of furnishing the local paper currency through their own banks, while the Bank of the United States, though issuing no paper, would check the issues of the state banks by taking their notes in deposit and for exchange only so long as they continue to be redeemed with specie." Presumably the proposed Bank would have no liabilities, and would be no more than a name over a door in the Treasury. It sounds much like the hollow political affairs, set up in several Western states, that exemplified banking at about its worst. It also sounds like the proposals of the Boston promoter and political boss David Henshaw, published three months later. Thus to avoid the federal government's continuing to violate the Constitution through the National Bank, the states were to continue violating it through the banks chartered by them to issue notes.[25]

Baffled by the Jacksonian behavior, Mr. Biddle continued month after month plucking petals from daisies. . . . He was left in uncertainty in part because though General Jackson's more intimate advisers were committed against the Bank, some were unready, and several official advisers were not committed at all. Mr. Calhoun, the Vice-President, had first to be removed from Mr. Van Buren's path to the Presidency, and the Bank must wait its

25. *Messages and Papers*, III, 1091–1092; David Henshaw, *Remarks upon the Bank of the United States* (Boston, 1831), pp. 38 ff.; Hamilton, pp. 167–168.

turn to have its head taken off. And just then, as it happened, attention became diverted from the Bank still more by the ladies of official Washington, who refused to recognize one of their number, Peggy Eaton, the Secretary of War's wife, whom they considered a hussy. This was in defiance of the President, who gallantly and venerably championed her. He had known her long. She was a witty, pretty, saucy creature; he had been touched years before by the way she sang hymns of an evening to her aged mother, and her new husband was an old and dear friend of his. The affair seems for months to have absorbed more of the President's attention than he gave to business of state. At length Mr. Van Buren resolved the problem by his proposal that the Cabinet be wholly reconstituted. This was done, and by accident the change in favor of Mrs. Eaton produced a membership better disposed also to the Bank, including particularly a new Secretary of State, Edward Livingston of New Orleans, and a new Secretary of the Treasury, Louis McLane of Delaware. Both were in favor of continuing the Bank and let the President know it, frankly and earnestly.[26]

This seems not to have annoyed the President, whose wish now was that the question of the Bank be deferred till after next year's election. For if it came up at once, the charter would pass Congress, and he would be confronted with the choice of approving or disapproving it. Approval would offend his party in some states, including New York; disapproval would offend his party in others, including Pennsylvania. If the matter could be postponed till after 1832, the election would be in less jeopardy.

On the Bank's side of the question, there was no want of time, in a sense, because the present charter would not expire till 1836, four years after next year's election. Had the President been well disposed, the question of recharter could certainly have been postponed; had the President been in doubt, the question might still have been postponed. Actually there seems now to have been no doubt in his mind about the Bank but only about the way to kill it off. . . .

At the same time, the opponents of President Jackson had coalesced in a new party, the National Republicans, and nominated

26. James Parton, *Life of Andrew Jackson,* 3 vols. (Boston, 1883), III, 184; *Correspondence of Andrew Jackson,* III, 218.

Henry Clay for President and John Sergeant, counsel for the Bank and one of Biddle's closest advisers, for Vice-President. This was later the Whig party. Its leaders were almost importunate that the Bank apply at once for recharter, not because they loved it so much but because they believed the President would be fatally embarrassed if he were confronted with a new charter before election and had to choose between approval of it and veto. John Sergeant and Daniel Webster were both convinced of this. So was Henry Clay. So were many others. It was not Nicholas Biddle's idea, but he did fall in with it—less perhaps because he believed it would work than because he had found the arrangement with the President would not. Accordingly, January 6, 1832, a month after the message had reawakened his misgivings, he asked that the Bank's application for recharter be laid before Congress; which was done.

This decision to put the matter before Congress was come to thoughtfully and with the concurrence of able politicians, though not the ablest. The Bank had every right to apply directly to Congress but had sought the administration's approval first as a matter of common sense and courtesy. For three years the administration had been blowing hot and cold by way of answer. Charles Jared Ingersoll, while he was still a friend of the Bank, which he later sided against, said that Secretary Livingston acknowledged to him that the President's various messages in effect invited reference of the question to Congress for action. However the request to Congress has generally been called a mistake. It was one, certainly, if to resist Andrew Jackson were sacrilege. And it was one, certainly, in the sense that it failed to achieve recharter. But no one supposes that the Bank would have been rechartered had the question been left to the President's convenience. He was determined to kill the Bank; behind him were his select advisers and lieutenants—Amos Kendall, Roger Taney, Churchill Cambreleng, Thomas Hart Benton, and most inscrutable of all, Martin Van Buren—who were determined to kill it. And behind them were the state banks and state politicians determined to kill it. All that Mr. Biddle could do was to make the end come a little harder or a little less hard, a little sooner or a little later.[27]

27. Biddle, *Correspondence*, p. 178.

This is not to say positively that the influence of McLane, Livingston, and Lewis—especially in the absence of Van Buren at the Court of St. James—was negligible, and that it must have failed even had Biddle refrained from asking Congress for recharter. Yet it seems to me that this was practically the case. I find Jackson so much committed by his own prejudices to the program of Taney, Kendall, and Cambreleng that he could not have been persuaded in any probable circumstances by McLane, Livingston, and Lewis; and I think he listened to the latter partly out of politeness to old friends but mainly for the tactical purpose of confusing and deceiving the enemy. He was in combat. . . .

The tariff and the Clayton report out of the way, Congress passed the new charter early in July, 1832. The President, July 10, vetoed it.

The message accompanying the veto is a famous state paper. It is legalistic, demagogic, and full of sham. Its economic reasoning was said by Professor Catterall, over fifty years ago, to be beneath contempt. Its level is now no higher. The message was prepared by Amos Kendall, who made the first draft, and by Roger Taney, who put it in final form, with the assistance of the President's secretary, Andrew Donelson. Taney wrote later: "I passed three days in this employment, the President frequently coming in, listening to the reading of different portions of it from time to time as it was drawn up and to the observations and suggestions of Mr. Donelson and myself, and giving his own directions as to what should be inserted or omitted." This procedure doubtless produced the conflicts and inconsistencies in the message, Taney from his long interest in banks having very different ideas from Jackson's on the subject. The part of the message which dealt with the constitutionality of the Bank reaffirmed the Jacksonian tenderness for states' rights and anxiety at the aggrandizement of federal powers. The part which dealt with economic matters was an unctuous mixture of agrarianism and *laissez faire*. The message asserted that the federal government's "true strength lies in leaving individuals and states as much as possible to themselves." It conformed to Amos Kendall's axiom that the world is governed too much. It ignored the public nature of the Bank and repudiated its regulatory responsibilities: all that monetary regulation required was a mint and an occasional act of Congress. The message rested heavily on an identification of the Bank with the rich, by whom it was used to oppress the poor.[28]

"It is to be regretted that the rich and powerful too often bend the acts of government to their selfish purposes," the President said. "Many of our rich men have not been content with equal protection and equal benefits but have besought us to make them richer by act of Congress." The government should not be prostituted "to the advancement of the few at the expense of the many." The charter was objectionable not only because it favored the rich but also because it stood in the way of the better proposition offered by citizens "whose aggregate wealth is believed to be equal to all the private stock in the existing bank." The question, apparently, was not one of wealth but of whose wealth. That a bank "competent to all the duties which may be required by the government" might be so organized as to avoid constitutional objections, the President did "not entertain a doubt"; and had he been called on to furnish a better project, "the duty would have been cheerfully performed." This implies that he had to be called on—though he himself had raised the issue and it had been a burning one for many months. The President's correspondence indicates that he had no project of his own; and of those advertised by Jacksonian politicians in Boston and New York, he had condemned none, and one he mentioned with favor in the veto message.

It is typical of the legalistic bias of the message that the alleged enrichment of the rich was ascribed wholly to the value of the charter and not at all to the Bank's operations. There would be a premium on the shares of stock, and this premium would in some metaphysical fashion be money transferred by act of Congress to rich men in Philadelphia from poor men everywhere else. "The powers, privileges, and favors bestowed" upon the Bank, "by increasing the value of the stock far above its par value operated as a gratuity of many millions to the stockholders." This "gratu-

28. Taney Papers, Bank War Ms., p. 126 (also in Carl B. Swisher, *Roger B. Taney* [New York, 1935], p. 194); *Messages and Papers,* III, 1139, 1153.

ity," "present," "bounty," or other equivalent comes up paragraph after paragraph. Presumably the stock of a Jacksonian bank would not rise to a premium. "It appears that more than a fourth part of the stock is held by foreigners and the residue is held by a few hundred of our own citizens, chiefly of the richest class"—and it was to them that the charter would "make a present of some millions of dollars." That a fifth of the shares were owned by the United States government was not mentioned.

It was frequently implied in the message that foreign investments in America were objectionable. The Jacksonians, however, did not discourage foreign borrowing as a matter of general policy. With the possible exception of President Jackson himself, they knew as well as anyone that a new country eagerly bent on a rapid exploitation of its resources procures abroad all the capital it can. Their objecting to the Bank's foreign shareholders could only have been intended to impress the ignorant, who were numerous. To this end, the message made its way solemnly into the absurd. If the Bank came to be mainly owned abroad, it was said, and if the owners were of a country with which war arose, what would be the condition of the United States? "Of the course which would be pursued by a bank almost wholly owned by the subjects of a foreign power and managed by those whose interests if not affections would run in the same direction there can be no doubt. . . . Controlling our currency, receiving our public moneys, and holding thousands of our citizens in dependence, it would be more formidable and dangerous than the naval and military power of the enemy." The Bank, that is, though situated across the ocean from its "owners" and in the jurisdiction of a government possessing police powers of its own, was pictured as able nevertheless to defy that government. Yet it was recognized that the charter denied foreign shareholders any part in control of the Bank; for paragraphs earlier in the message, the argument had been that since foreign shareholders had no vote, any increase in their holdings would have the effect of throwing control of the Bank into the laps of a diminishing proportion of domestic shareholders. The message had things both ways. The foreign stockholders were on the one hand a menace because they might control the Bank; they were also a menace because they could not.

The professed belief of President Jackson was that banking created fictitious capital in the place of specie; yet the President was made to contend that foreign capital was not only dangerous but superfluous. For domestic capital was "so abundant . . . that competition in subscribing for the stock of local banks has recently led almost to riots." Indeed, he declared, "subscriptions for $200,000,000 could be readily obtained." He was doubtless right; but they could be obtained only in the fictitious capital that in other paragraphs incensed him. By the hard-money standards he really cherished, not one tenth of $200 million existed in the country altogether. But this fact did not impress the legalistic Mr. Taney, nor, through the veil of Mr. Taney's cant, did it impress the General.

There was the same casuistry in identifying the Bank with the rich as with foreigners. Of its total capital of $35 million, the government owned $7 million and foreign shareholders $8 million, which left $20 million to be owned by Americans. Though a substantial part of this was held by stockholders in Philadelphia, the shares were widely distributed and actively traded. The stockholders at any given moment, including the permanent and impermanent, represented a great deal of wealth but by no means *the* wealth or *the* rich. There were many wealthy men who owned little or none. Relatively little was owned in New York, though by now there was probably more wealth there than in Philadelphia. Prime, Ward, and King, the wealthiest firm in New York or the whole country, owned none. The attack on the Bank was not an attack on the rich men of the country but on some rich men and in the interest of some other rich men. These were Mr. Taney's "poor and oppressed."[29] . . .

The veto message was prodigiously popular. Its critics replied to it feebly. They could not reply effectively because they could get down to no fundamental disagreement with the materialistic, *laissez nous faire,* everybody-get-rich philosophy of the message. The purposes and services of the Bank were forgotten even by its friends in a childish outburst of resentment at Jackson's interfer-

29. Baring Papers (National Archives, Ottawa), Office Correspondence, Prime, Ward, and King to Baring Brothers, December 7, 1832.

ence. Henry Clay and Daniel Webster had never appreciated or
understood the Bank except as a source of fees or as a fine, big
bone to fight the other party over; and for them the issue now was
simply one between ins and outs. Nicholas Biddle did not forget
the Bank's purposes and services, but he did forget that they alone
were the grounds for a defense of the Bank—whether successful or
not. He, with the others, in effect, let the administration choose
grounds and procedures that gave Andrew Jackson every advantage in combat. They took the defensive on his terms. "It is
difficult," said the *Washington Globe,* July 12, 1832, "to describe
in adequate language the sublimity of the moral spectacle now
presented to the American people in the person of Andrew Jackson." The General's political opponents were so sodden in the
same earthy claptrap as the Jacksonians themselves that they could
not give the American people a penetrating view of the "moral
spectacle" presented to them. But a quiet gentleman in Concord,
Ralph Waldo Emerson, saw the matter more clearly. "We shall all
feel dirty," he feared, "if Jackson is re-elected."[30] . . .

The new business world . . . was dominated by self-made men
born on farms and reared in the spirit of agrarian democracy.
These men exulted in their humble origins and acquisitive achievements. The spirit of enterprise was fierce in them. Their ideal was
laissez faire. Their employment of power and resources to serve
material human needs altered the people's ways of living. Their
business success alienated them insensibly from their origins,
however, and from uncontaminated Jeffersonians. It was the despair of the poets and transcendentalists.

The Jacksonian revolution was largely the conquest of the
economy by these self-made men; and a prominent political crisis
—the Jacksonian attack on the Bank of the United States—was
produced by their intolerance of restraint upon their use of bank
credit. The ambitious, farm-born entrepreneur, envious of the rich
and set to become rich, wanted credit for his enterprises; his banks
wanted to provide it. But the "aristocratic" federal Bank situated
in conservative Philadelphia restricted bank lending. The restraint
was resented especially in New York, otherwise Philadelphia's

30. Ralph Waldo Emerson, *Journals* (Boston, 1909–1914), II, 528.

superior rival, and in Boston and Baltimore. Taking advantage of the traditional agrarian aversion to banks and of President Jackson's particularly, the entrepreneurial rebels attacked what they called the monopoly and the tyranny of the federal Bank, ended its existence, neutralized the federal government's constitutional responsibility for the currency, made banking a business free to all, and thereby insured to enterprise an abundance of banks and of bank credit.

Their rebellion was a popular and democratic one but not agrarian. It accomplished the antithesis of agrarian aims. It was led by men whose skill in propaganda, in cant, and in demagogy was supported by envy and an uncritical belief that the divine blessing was on their efforts. "There is perhaps no business," said Roger B. Taney, Andrew Jackson's devoted aide, "which yields a profit as certain and liberal as the business of banking and exchange; and it is proper that it should be open, as far as practicable, to the most free competition and its advantages shared by all classes of society"—sentiments strangely incompatible with those of Thomas Jefferson, of John Taylor of Carolina, and of Andrew Jackson himself when expressing his own convictions.

✪

Jacksonian Democracy as the Rise of Liberal Capitalism

Could it really be urged that the framers of the constitution intended that our Government should become a government of brokers? If so, then the profits of this national brokers' shop must inure to the benefit of the whole and not to a few privileged monied capitalists to the utter rejection of the many.   ANDREW JACKSON

The making of a democratic leader is not a simple process. Because Andrew Jackson came into prominence on the Tennessee frontier, he has often been set down as typical of the democratic frontiersman; but many patent facts about his life fit poorly with the stereotype. From the beginning of his career in Tennessee he considered himself to be and was accepted as an aristocrat, and his tastes, manners, and style of life were shaped accordingly. True, he could not spell, he lacked education and culture, but so did most of those who passed as aristocrats in the old Southwest during the 1790's and for long afterward; even many Virginians of the passing generation—George Washington among them—spelled no better. Since Virginians and Carolinans of the upper crust seldom migrated, the Southwestern aristocracy came mainly from middle- or lower-class migrants who had prospered and acquired a certain half-shod elegance. Jackson, the mid-Tennessee nabob, was typical, not of the Southwest's coonskin Democrats, but of its peculiar blend of pioneer and aristocrat.

Jackson was born in 1767 on a little farm in the Carolinas some months after the death of his father. He enlisted in the Revolution at thirteen, was captured and mutilated by British troops at fourteen, and lost his entire family in the war when one brother was killed, another succumbed to smallpox in prison, and his mother was carried off by "prison fever" while nursing captured American militiamen. From his family he inherited a farm-size plot of land in North Carolina, from the Revolution a savage and implacable patriotism. For six months Jackson was apprenticed to a saddler. Then, although his own schooling had been slight and irregular, he turned for a brief spell to schoolteaching. When a relative in Ireland left him a legacy of over three hundred pounds, he moved to Charleston, where, still in his teens, he aped the manners of the seaboard gentry and developed a taste for gambling, horses, and cockfighting. When he was not playing cards or casting dice for the rent with his landlord, Jackson studied law. At twenty, knowing little about jurisprudence but a great deal about making his own way, he was admitted to the bar of North Carolina. A year later, tradition says, he turned up in Jonesboro, Tennessee, owning two horses, a pack of foxhounds, and a Negro girl.

Before long Jackson made what he intended to be a brief visit to the growing settlement of Nashville. The one established lawyer in the vicinity was retained by a syndicate of debtors, leaving creditors legally helpless. Jackson went to work for the creditors, collected handsome fees, and earned the gratitude and friendship of local merchants and money-lenders. From a fellow Carolina law student he also accepted an appointment as public solicitor. He soon fell in with the machine of William Blount, a powerful territorial land speculator and political patron, and began to consolidate his position among the budding aristocrats, the owners of slaves and horses, the holders of offices and titles. With his salary and fees he began to buy land and Negroes.

Thus far Jackson's story was by no means unusual, for the one-generation aristocrat was a common product of the emerging

South:[1] Because of the ease and rapidity with which the shrewd and enterprising farmer might become a leader of the community, and hence a gentleman, during the decades when the cotton economy was expanding into the uplands, the upper classes of the Southwest came to combine the qualities of the frontier rough-necks and the landed gentry. The sportsmanlike, lawless, indi-vidualistic, quick-tempered, brawling nature of the first was soon sublimated into the courtly, sentimental, unreflective, touchy spirit of the second. As slaveholding, horsemanship, patriarchal digni-ties, money, and the deference of the community deepened the ex-frontiersman's sense of pride, the habit of command was added and the transformation was complete. The difference between the frontiersman's readiness to fight and the planter's readiness to defend his "honor" is not so much a difference of temperament as of method, and there is no better exemplar of the fact than Jackson. It is not recorded that the master of the Hermitage, a justice in the state courts, and a Major General of the militia, ever engaged in a brawl—although one encounter with the Bentons has so been called—or had a wrestling match such as a commoner like Abraham Lincoln enjoyed on the Illinois frontier. Nor did it occur to Jackson to use his fists, although it is true that he threatened at least one social inferior with a caning. Insulted by anyone who technically qualified as a gentleman, he resorted to the code duello; his quarrels are classic in the history of that institution in the South. Charles Dickinson insulted Jackson over a horse race in 1806, and went to his grave for it; and Jackson carried from the encounter a bullet close to his heart. The same violent, self-asser-tive subjectivism of the duelist can be found in Old Hickory's conduct as a public man. "I have an opinion of my own on all subjects," he wrote in 1821, "and when that opinion is formed I persue it *publickly*, regardless of who goes with me." Historians have never been certain how much his policies were motivated by public considerations and how much by private animosities.

Yet in his calmer moods Jackson's manner ripened quickly into gentleness and gravity. Measured against the picture of the "cotton

1. There is a superb account of these emergent aristocrats in W. J. Cash's *The Mind of the South* (New York, 1941), pp. 14–17.

snob" painted by more than one sympathetic observer of the Old South, where, as F. L. Olmsted put it, "the farce of the vulgar rich" was played over and over again, Jackson was a man of gentility and integrity. In 1824 Daniel Webster could say of him: "General Jackson's manners are more presidential than those of any of the candidates." Mrs. Trollope, who admitted finding precious few gentlemen in America, saw him on his way to Washington in 1829 and reported that he "wore his hair carelessly but not ungracefully arranged, and in spite of his harsh, gaunt features looked like a gentleman and a soldier." With the common citizen he had a patient and gracious air.

The frontier, democratic in spirit and in forms of government, was nevertheless not given to leveling equalitarianism. The ideal of frontier society, as Frederick Jackson Turner has remarked, was the self-made man. And the self-made man generally received a measure of casual deference from the coonskin element, which itself was constantly generating new candidates for the local aristocracies. Keen class antagonisms were not typical of frontier politics, and class struggles did not flourish in a state like Tennessee until the frontier stage was about over.[2] The task of fighting the Indians gave all classes a common bond and produced popular heroes among the upper ranks. The cotton economy, as it spread, also brought its own insurance against bitter antagonisms, for the presence of a submerged class of slaves gave the humbler whites a sense of status and all whites a community of interest. Frontiersmen may have resented alien Eastern aristocrats—as Jackson did himself—but felt otherwise about those bred in their own community, as they thought, out of competitive skill rather than privilege. Even in those states and territories where suffrage was broadly exercised, men who owned and speculated in land and had money in the bank were often accepted as natural leaders, and political offices fell to them like ripe fruit. Such beneficiaries of

2. Thomas Perkins Abernethy points out that in Tennessee during the 1790's "no strong and universal antagonism existed . . . between the rich and the poor. In fact, political office was rarely sought even on the frontier by any but the natural leaders of society, and they secured the suffrage of their neighbors by reason of their prestige, without resorting to electioneering methods."

popular confidence developed a stronger faith in the wisdom and justice of popular decisions than did the gentlemen of the older seaboard states, where class lines were no longer fluid and social struggles had venerable histories. A man like Jackson who had been on the conservative side of economic issues in Tennessee could become the leader of a national democratic movement without feeling guilty of any inconsistency. When we find a planter aristocrat of this breed expressing absolute confidence in popular judgment, it is unfair to dismiss him as a demagogue. He became a favorite of the people, and might easily come to believe that the people chose well.

Offices, chiefly appointive, came quickly and easily to Jackson in the territory and youthful state of Tennessee. He was a solicitor at twenty-two, United States Attorney at twenty-three, a Congressman at twenty-nine, a United States Senator at thirty, and justice of the supreme court of Tennessee at thirty-one—all this without particularly strong political ambitions, for he applied himself casually to all these offices except the judgeship and resigned them readily after brief tenure. He accepted them, it seems clear, more as symbols of status than as means of advancement. Jackson's persistent land speculations, business ventures, and military operations suggest that he aspired more urgently to have wealth and military glory than political power.

It was, in fact, his achievements as a fighter of Indians and Englishmen that brought Jackson his national popularity.

Jackson's victory in January, 1815, over the British forces besieging New Orleans, the crowning triumph of his military career, made him a national hero almost overnight. Americans had already developed their passion for victorious generals in politics. The Hero of New Orleans was instantly acclaimed as another Washington, and in 1817 the first campaign biography appeared. But Jackson soon experienced severe political criticism for the conduct of his postwar campaigns in Florida, and he feared the effect of political prominence on his domestic happiness; at first he was slow to rise to the bait of Presidential ambition. "I am wearied with public life," he wrote President Monroe in 1821. "I have been accused of acts I never committed, of crimes I never thought of." When a New York newspaper editor commented on the ambition of his friends to put him in the White House, the General grew impatient. "No sir," he exclaimed. "I know what I am fit for. I can command a body of men in a rough way: but I am not fit to be President."

II

The rise of Andrew Jackson marked a new turn in the development of American political institutions. During the period from 1812 to 1828 the two-party system disappeared and personal, local, and sectional conflicts replaced broad differences over public policy as the central fact in national politics. As the Presidency declined from its heights under the leadership of Washington and Jefferson, the contest for the Presidential seat resolved into a scramble of local and sectional princelings for the position of heir apparent. The Virginia dynasty's practice of elevating the forthcoming President through the Vice-Presidency or Cabinet seemed to have become a set pattern. Presidential nominations, made by party caucuses in Congress, were remote from the popular will, and since the elections of 1816 and 1820 were virtually uncontested, nomination by "King Caucus" was equivalent to being chosen President. Since the days of Jefferson there had been no major turnover in the staff of officeholders, whose members were becoming encrusted in their posts.

However, the people, the propertyless masses, were beginning, at first quietly and almost unobtrusively, to enter politics. Between 1812 and 1821 six Western states entered the Union with constitutions providing for universal white manhood suffrage or a close approximation, and between 1810 and 1821 four of the older states substantially dropped property qualifications for voters.[3] As poor farmers and workers gained the ballot, there developed a type of politician that had existed only in embryo in the Jeffersonian

3. In 1824, the first election on which we have statistics, there were only 355,000 voters, chiefly because the triumph of a particular candidate—e.g., Jackson in Tennessee and Pennsylvania, Adams in Massachusetts, Crawford in Virginia—was so taken for granted in most states that voters lost interest. By 1828, when interest was greatly heightened, 1,155,000 voted. Between 1828 and 1848 the vote trebled, although the population did not quite double.

period—the technician of mass leadership, the caterer to mass sentiment; it was a coterie of such men in all parts of the country that converged upon the prominent figure of Jackson between 1815 and 1824. Generally subordinated in the political corporations and remote from the choicest spoils, these leaders encouraged the common feeling that popular will should control the choice of public officers and the formation of public policy. They directed popular resentment of closed political corporations against the caucus system, which they branded as a flagrant usurpation of the rights of the people, and spread the conviction that politics and administration must be taken from the hands of a social elite or a body of bureaucratic specialists and opened to mass participation. Success through politics, it was implied, must become a legitimate aspiration of the many.[4] Jackson expressed the philosophy of this movement in his first annual message to Congress, December, 1829, when he confidently asserted:

The duties of all public offices are, or at least admit of being made, so plain and simple that men of intelligence may readily qualify themselves for their performance, and I can not but believe that more is lost by the long continuance of men in office than is generally to be gained by their experience. . . . In a country where offices are created solely for the benefit of the people no one man has any more intrinsic right to official station than another.

Rotation in office, he concluded, constituted a "leading principle in the Republican creed."

The trend toward popular activity in politics was heightened by the Panic of 1819, which set class against class for the first time since the Jeffersonian era. A result of rapid expansion, speculation, and wildcat banking, the panic and ensuing depression fell heavily upon all parts of the country, but especially upon the South and West, where men had thrown all their resources into reckless buying of land. The banks, which had grossly overextended themselves,

4. Jackson wrote to an editor of the *Richmond Enquirer* in 1829: "The road to office and preferment, being accessible alike to the rich and poor, the farmer and the printer, honesty, probity, and capability constituting the sole and exclusive test will, I am persuaded, have the happiest tendency to preserve, unimpaired, freedom of action."

were forced to press their debtors to the wall, and through the process of foreclosure the National Bank particularly became a great absentee owner of Western and Southern property. "All the flourishing cities of the West," complained Thomas Hart Benton, "are mortgaged to this money power. They may be devoured by it at any moment. They are in the jaws of the monster!" This alien power was resented with particular intensity in the West, where, as the *New York American* put it, "a wild son of Tennessee who has been with Jackson could ill brook that his bit of land, perhaps his rifle, should be torn from him by a neighboring shopkeeper, that the proceeds may travel eastward, where the 'sceptre' of money has fixed itself." The panic brought a cruel awakening for thousands who had hoped to become rich. John C. Calhoun, talking with John Quincy Adams in the spring of 1820, observed that the last two years had produced "an immense revolution of fortunes in every part of the Union, enormous multitudes in deep distress, and a general mass of disaffection to the Government not concentrated in any particular direction, but ready to seize upon any event and looking out anywhere for a leader."

Calhoun's "general mass of disaffection" was not sufficiently concentrated to prevent the re-election, unopposed, of President Monroe in 1820 in the absence of a national opposition party; but it soon transformed politics in many states. Debtors rushed into politics to defend themselves, and secured moratoriums and relief laws from the legislatures of several Western states. State legislatures, under pressure from local banking interests, waged tax wars against the Bank of the United States. A popular demand arose for laws to prevent imprisonment for debt, for a national bankruptcy law, and for new tariff and public-land policies. For the first time many Americans thought of politics as having an intimate relation to their welfare. Against this background Jackson's star rose. But, curiously, the beneficiary of this movement not only failed to encourage it, but even disapproved. The story of his evolution as a national democratic leader is a strange paradox.

North Carolina, the scene of Jackson's childhood, had been a Jeffersonian stronghold, and Jackson was nurtured on Jeffersonian ideas. In 1796 and 1800 the young Tennessean voted for the sage of Monticello. Except for his nationalism, Jackson's politics chiefly resembled agrarian Republicanism of the old school, which was opposed to banks, public debts, paper money, high tariffs, and federal internal improvements. When the Burr trial and Jefferson's pacificism disillusioned him with Jefferson, Jackson did not become a convert to Federalism but rather adhered to the Randolph-Macon school of intransigent Republicans.

Jackson's personal affairs shed much light on his ambiguous political evolution from 1796 to 1828. An event of 1796 that had a disastrous effect on his fortunes may have sown in him the seeds of that keen dislike of the Eastern money power and "paper system" which flowered during his Presidency. Jackson had gone to Philadelphia to sell several thousand acres of land to a rich merchant and speculator, David Allison; he accepted notes from Allison, which he endorsed and promptly used to pay for supplies he planned to use in opening a general-merchandise store in Nashville. Allison failed, and defaulted on his notes; Jackson became liable. In order to pay the notes as they fell due, he was forced to retrench, give up the estate on which he lived, move to a smaller one built of logs, and sell many of his slaves. Subsequently his store enterprise turned out badly and he was obliged to sell out to his partners. Jackson seems never to have whined about his misfortune, but he lived for nineteen years in its shadow, remaining in debt from 1796 to 1815, when at last his military pay and allowances brought him into the clear. In the fall of 1815 he had a cash balance of over twenty-two thousand dollars at the Nashville bank, was again heavily committed in land speculations, and was building the fine new estate that has become famous as the Hermitage. Just at this time, when he was so vulnerable, the Panic of 1819 struck.

The general distress of Tennessee debtors led, as in many other places, to a movement for relief. Felix Grundy, elected to the state Senate on a "relief" platform, brought forth a proposal to establish a state loan office to help debtors out of the state treasury.[5]

5. Grundy's history makes it clear that he represented what may be called entrepreneurial rather than lower-class radicalism. In 1818 he was a leader in a movement to bring a branch of the Second United States Bank to Nashville.

Creditors who refused to accept notes of the loan bank in payment of debts would have their collections suspended for two years. Jackson's own obligations forced him to press his debtors hard, and he instituted a single lawsuit against 129 of them at once. One of the few men in Middle Tennessee to stand against Grundy's relief program, he sent a protest to the state legislature, which was rejected on the ground that its language was disrespectful. Having learned from the Allison episode to feel for the luckless entrepreneur, Jackson was now learning to see things from the standpoint of the local moneyed class. The emergence of class conflict in Tennessee found him squarely on the side of the haves. In 1821, when General William Carroll ran for the Governorship of the state on a democratic economic program, Jackson supported Carroll's opponent, Colonel Edward Ward, a wealthy planter who had joined Jackson in fighting Grundy's scheme. Carroll was elected, and proceeded to put through a program of tax revision and constitutional and humanitarian reform, which has many elements of what historians call "Jacksonian" democracy. At the moment when Jackson was pitting himself against Carroll in Tennessee, his friends were bringing him forward as a Presidential candidate. None of this prevented Grundy and Carroll from later joining the Jackson bandwagon.

Had Jackson's record on popular economic reform been a matter of primary importance, he might never have been President. But by 1824, when he first accepted a Presidential nomination, prosperity had returned, hostility to banks and creditors had abated, and breaking up established political machines seemed more important to the parvenu politician and the common citizen. As chief "issues" of the campaign the caucus system shared honors with the defense of New Orleans.[6] An outsider to the Congressional machines, a man of humble birth whose popularity was based on military achievement and whose attitude toward economic questions was unknown and of little interest to the average voter, Jackson had a considerable edge with the new electorate.

The consequences of the campaign of 1824 settled all doubt in

6. Actually only one of the four candidates, William H. Crawford, was nominated by the customary Congressional caucus; the others were nominated by state legislatures.

Jackson's mind about the Presidency. Far stronger in the popular vote than any of his three rivals, John Quincy Adams, Clay, and Crawford, he still fell short of the necessary majority in the Electoral College, and the election was thrown into the House of Representatives. There the position of Clay became decisive, and Clay threw his support to Adams. Subsequently, when President Adams named Clay his Secretary of State, a bitter cry went up from the Jackson following. Jackson himself was easily persuaded that Clay and Adams had been guilty of a "corrupt bargain" and determined to retake from Adams what he felt was rightfully his. The campaign of 1828 began almost immediately with Adams' administration. For four years the President, a man of monumental rectitude but a career politician of the dying order par excellence, was hounded by the corrupt-bargain charge and subjected by the Jackson professionals to a skillful campaign of vilification, which culminated in the election of 1828. In Jackson's second Presidential campaign the Bank was hardly mentioned. The tariff was played for what it was worth where men cared especially about it; but a series of demagogic charges about Adams' alleged monarchist, aristocratic, and bureaucratic prejudices served the Jackson managers for issues. Jackson got 647,000 votes, Adams 508,000.

The election of 1828 was not an uprising of the West against the East nor a triumph of the frontier: outside of New England and its colonized areas in the West, Federalist Delaware, New Jersey, and Maryland, Jackson swept the country. Nor was his election a mandate for economic reform; no financial changes, no crusades against the National Bank, were promised. The main themes of Jacksonian democracy thus far were militant nationalism and equal access to office. Jackson's election was more a result than a cause of the rise of democracy, and the "revolution of 1828" more an overturn of personnel than of ideas or programs. Up to the time of his inauguration Jackson had contributed neither a thought nor a deed to the democratic movement, and he was elected without a platform. So far as he can be said to have had a popular mandate, it was to be different from what the people imagined Adams had been and to give expression to their unformulated wishes and aspirations. This mandate Jackson was prepared to obey. Democrat and aristocrat, failure and success, debtor and creditor, he had had a varied and uneven history, which made it possible for him to see public questions from more than one perspective. He was a simple, emotional, and unreflective man with a strong sense of loyalty to personal friends and political supporters; he swung to the democratic camp when the democratic camp swung to him.

III

For those who have lived through the era of Franklin D. Roosevelt it is natural to see in Jacksonian democracy an earlier version of the New Deal, for the two periods have many superficial points in common. The Jacksonian movement and the New Deal were both struggles of large sections of the community against a business elite and its allies. There is a suggestive analogy between Nicholas Biddle's political associates and the "economic royalists" of the Liberty League, and, on the other side, between the two dynamic landed aristocrats who led the popular parties. Roosevelt himself did not fail to see the resemblance and exploit it.

But the two movements differed in a critical respect: the New Deal was frankly based upon the premise that economic expansion had come to an end and economic opportunities were disappearing; it attempted to cope with the situation by establishing governmental ascendancy over the affairs of business. The Jacksonian movement grew out of expanding opportunities and a common desire to enlarge these opportunities still further by removing restrictions and privileges that had their origin in acts of government; thus with some qualifications, it was essentially a movement of *laissez faire,* an attempt to divorce government and business. It is commonly recognized in American historical folklore that the Jackson movement was a phase in the expansion of democracy, but it is too little appreciated that it was also a phase in the expansion of liberated capitalism. While in the New Deal the democratic reformers were driven to challenge many assumptions of traditional American capitalism, in the Jacksonian period the democratic upsurge was closely linked to the ambitions of the small capitalist.

To understand Jacksonian democracy it is necessary to re-create the social complexion of the United States in the 1830's. Although industrialism had begun to take root, this was still a nation of farms and small towns, which in 1830 found only one of every fifteen citizens living in cities of over eight thousand. Outside the South, a sweeping majority of the people were independent property-owners. Factories had been growing in some areas, but industry was not yet concentrated in the factory system; much production was carried out in little units in which the employer was like a master craftsman supervising his apprentices. The development of transportation made it possible to extend trade over large areas, which resulted in a delay in collections and increased the dependence of business upon banks for credit facilities. The merchant capitalist found it easier to get the necessary credits than humbler masters and minor entrepreneurs, but the hope of growing more prosperous remained intensely alive in the breast of the small manufacturer and the skilled craftsman.

The flowering of manufacturing in the East, the rapid settlement of the West, gave to the spirit of enterprise a large measure of fulfillment. The typical American was an expectant capitalist, a hardworking, ambitious person for whom enterprise was a kind of religion, and everywhere he found conditions that encouraged him to extend himself. Francis J. Grund, an immigrant who described American social conditions in 1836, reported:

> Business is the very soul of an American: he pursues it, not as a means of procuring for himself and his family the necessary comforts of life, but as the fountain of all human felicity. . . . It is as if all America were but one gigantic workshop, over the entrance of which there is the blazing inscription, "No admission here, except on business."

More than one type of American, caught up in this surge of ambition, had reason to be dissatisfied with the United States Bank. Some farmers were more interested in the speculative values of their lands than in their agricultural yield. Operators of wildcat banks in the South and West and speculators who depended upon wildcat loans shared the farmers' dislike of Biddle's Bank for restraining credit inflation. In the East some of the heads of strong, sound state banks were jealous of the privileged position of the

National Bank—particularly the bankers of New York City, who resented the financial supremacy that the Bank brought to Philadelphia.[7] In Eastern cities the Bank was also widely disliked by workers, craftsmen, shopkeepers, and small business people. Labor was hard hit by the rising cost of living, and in many cases the workmen's agitation was directed not so much against their immediate employers as against the credit and currency system. Small business and workingmen felt that banks restricted competition and prevented new men from entering upon the avenues of enterprise.[8]

The prevalent method of granting corporation charters in the states was a source of enormous resentment. The states did not have general laws governing incorporation.[9] Since banks and other profit-making businesses that wished to incorporate had to apply to state legislatures for individual acts of incorporation, the way was left open for favoritism and corruption. Very often the corporation charters granted by the legislatures were, or were construed to be, monopolies. Men whose capital or influence was too small to gain charters from the lawmakers were barred from such profitable and strategic lines of corporate enterprise as banks, bridges, railroads, turnpikes, and ferries. The practice was looked upon as an artificial closure of opportunity: laborers often blamed it for the high price of necessities.[10] The practice of

7. State-bank men were prominent in Jackson's councils. Roger Brooke Taney had been a lawyer for and stockholder in the Union Bank of Maryland. Two key members of the Kitchen Cabinet, Amos Kendall and Francis Preston Blair, were recruits from the famous relief war in Kentucky, and the former had been president of the Commonwealth Bank of Kentucky.

8. Workingmen had a special grievance against banks. Employers often paid them in the notes of distant or suspected banks, which circulated below par value. They were thus defrauded of a portion of their pay. Although the United States Bank was not responsible for such practices, it had to share in the general odium that attached to banks. "I was not long in discovering," remembered the Whig politician Thurlow Weed, "that it was easy to enlist the laboring classes against a 'monster bank' or 'monied aristocracy.' . . . The bank issue 'hung like a millstone' about our necks."

9. There were exceptions. New York in 1811 and Connecticut in 1817 adopted laws permitting general incorporation for certain types of manufacturing enterprises.

10. "We cannot pass the bounds of the city," complained one of the left-wing Jacksonian leaders in New York, "without paying tribute to monopoly;

granting economic privileges was also considered a threat to popular government. Jackson, explaining in one of his Presidential messages why "the planter, the farmer, the mechanic, and the laborer" were "in constant danger of losing their fair interest in the Government," had a standard answer: "The mischief springs from the power which the moneyed interest derives from a paper currency, which they are able to control, from the multitude of corporations with exclusive privileges which they have succeeded in obtaining in the different States."

Among all the exclusive privileged monopolies in the country the Bank of the United States was the largest, the best known, and the most powerful. It became a symbol for all the others, and the burden of many grievances for which it was not really responsible fell upon it. As a national institution it was doubly vulnerable: it was blamed by Western inflationists for deflationary policies and by Eastern hard-money men for inflation. One certain accomplishment of Jackson's war on the Bank was to discharge the aggressions of citizens who felt injured by economic privilege.

Jackson himself was by no means unfamiliar with the entrepreneurial impulse that gave Jacksonian democracy so much of its freshness and vitality. An enterpriser of middling success, he could spontaneously see things from the standpoint of the typical American who was eager for advancement in the democratic game of competition—the master mechanic who aspired to open his own shop, the planter or farmer who speculated in land, the lawyer who hoped to be a judge, the local politician who wanted to go to Congress, the grocer who would be a merchant. He had entered the scramble himself in a variety of lines, as a professional man, a merchant, a land speculator, a planter, an officeholder, and a military chieftain. He understood the old Jeffersonian's bias against overgrown government machinery, the Westerner's resentment of the entrenched East, the new politician's dislike of the old bureaucracy, and the aspiring citizen's hatred of privilege. Years

---

our bread, our meat, our vegetables, our fuel, all, all pay tribute to monopolists." William Leggett of the *New York Post* declared: "Not a road can be opened, not a bridge can be built, not a canal can be dug, but a charter of exclusive privileges must be granted for the purpose. . . . The bargaining and trucking away chartered privileges is the whole business of our lawmakers."

before his Presidency, he recalled, when a few Tennesseans proposed in 1817 to bring a branch of the Bank to Nashville, he had opposed it on the ground that the Bank "would drain the state of its specie to the amount of its profits for the support and prosperity of other places, and the Lords, Dukes, and Ladies of foreign countries who held the greater part of its stock—no individual but one in our state owning any of its stock." In 1827, when a branch of the Bank was finally created at Nashville, and its agent, General Thomas Cadwalader, coyly hinted to Jackson that its patronage could be turned over to the Jackson party, he was rebuffed.

Looking at the Bank from the White House, Jackson saw an instrument of great privilege and power ruled by a man of uncommon force and intelligence. As a fiscal agency it was comparable in magnitude to the government itself. It issued about one fourth of the country's bank paper; because of its power over the discounts of innumerable smaller banks, especially in the West and South, it was the only central instrument in the United States that could affect the volume of credit. A private agency performing a major public function, it was yet substantially free of government control.[11] As Hezekiah Niles put it, the Bank had "more power than we would grant to any set of men unless responsible to the people." Nicholas Biddle, boasting of the forbearance with which he ran the Bank, once stated in a Congressional investigation that there were "very few banks which might not have been destroyed by an exertion of the powers of the Bank." "As to mere power," he wrote to Thomas Cooper in 1837, "I have been for years in the daily exercise of more personal authority than any President habitually enjoys." Understandably the Bank's critics regarded it as a potential menace to democratic institutions.

As an economic instrument, there was a great deal to be said for the Bank. Under Biddle it had done a creditable job in stabilizing the currency and holding in check inflationary pressure from the wildcatters. Before Jackson's election Biddle had also been concerned to keep the Bank out of partisan politics and, as he wrote

11. Five of its twenty-five directors were appointed by the federal government. Nicholas Biddle, who actually ran the Bank without interference, was one of the government directors; before the Bank controversy began, his appointment had been renewed by Jackson himself.

Webster, "bring it down to its true business character as a Counting House." But the Bank inspired too many animosities to stay out of political life. After 1829 it had large loans outstanding to a great number of prominent politicians and influential newspaper editors, and Biddle was well aware how great its power would be if it should be employed directly in corruption. "I can remove all the constitutional scruples in the District of Columbia," he arrogantly informed a correspondent in 1833. "Half a dozen Presidencies—a dozen Cashierships—fifty Clerkships—a hundred Directorships—to worthy friends who have no character and no money."

Since the Bank's charter was to expire in 1836, and since a second term for Jackson was probable, it seemed necessary that a renewal of the charter be secured under Jackson. Biddle attempted at first to be conciliatory, made earnest efforts to answer Jackson's grievances against the Bank, appointed Jacksonian politicians to several branch directorships, and sent the President a not ungenerous proposal for assistance in discharging the government's indebtedness in return for recharter. Yet in the fall or winter of 1829–1830, when Biddle and Jackson had an amicable interview, the General frankly said: "I do not dislike your Bank any more than all banks. But ever since I read the history of the South Sea bubble I have been afraid of banks." By December, 1830, when Jackson questioned the Bank's expediency and constitutionality, it was clear that he would not consent to renew its life. Biddle, reluctantly, uncertainly, and under prodding from Whig politicians, decided in the summer of 1832 to ask Congress for recharter before the Presidential election. "The bank," said Jackson to Van Buren, "is trying to kill me, *but I will kill it!*" To the frontier duelist the issue had instantly become personal.

Jackson lost no time in returning the recharter bill to Congress with his famous veto message,[12] described by Biddle as "a manifesto of anarchy, such as Marat and Robespierre might have issued to the mob." The body of the message was an argument against the Bank's constitutionality. The social indictment of the Bank was inclusive: it was a monopoly, a grant of exclusive

12. The message was composed with the assistance of Amos Kendall, Andrew J. Donelson, Roger B. Taney, and Levi Woodbury.

privilege; the whole American people were excluded from competition in the sale of the privilege, and the government thus received less than it was worth; a fourth of the Bank's stock was held by foreigners, the rest by "a few hundred of our citizens, chiefly of the richest class"; it was a menace to the country's liberty and independence. At the end the President launched into a forthright statement of the social philosophy of the Jacksonian movement:

It is to be regretted that the rich and powerful too often bend the acts of government to their selfish purposes. Distinctions in society will always exist under every just government. Equality of talents, of education, or of wealth cannot be produced by human institutions. In the full enjoyment of the gifts of Heaven and the fruits of superior industry, economy, and virtue, every man is equally entitled to protection by law; but when the laws undertake to add to these natural and just advantages artificial distinctions, to grant titles, gratuities, and exclusive privileges, to make the rich richer and the potent more powerful, the humble members of society—the farmers, mechanics, and laborers—who have neither the time nor the means of securing like favors to themselves, have a right to complain of the injustice of their Government. There are no necessary evils in government. Its evils exist only in its abuses. If it would confine itself to equal protection, and, as Heaven does its rains, shower its favors alike on the high and the low, the rich and the poor, it would be an unqualified blessing.

Certainly this is not the philosophy of a radical leveling movement that proposes to uproot property or to reconstruct society along drastically different lines. It proceeds upon no Utopian premises—full equality is impossible, "distinctions will always exist," and reward should rightly go to "superior industry, economy, and virtue." What is demanded is only the classic bourgeois ideal, equality before the law, the restriction of government to equal protection of its citizens. This is the philosophy of a rising middle class; its aim is not to throttle but to liberate business, to open every possible pathway for the creative enterprise of the people. Although the Jacksonian leaders were more aggressive than the Jeffersonians in their crusades against monopoly and "the paper system," it is evident that the core of their philosophy was the same: both aimed to take the grip of government-granted privileges off the natural economic order.[13] It was no coincidence that Jacksonians like William Leggett and Thomas Hart Benton still venerated John Taylor, a thinker of what Jackson affectionately called "the old republican school."

IV

Pursuing the Bank war to its conclusion, Jackson found defeat in victory. Re-elected overwhelmingly on the Bank issue in 1832, he soon removed all United States funds from the Bank. Biddle, in the course of a fight to get the federal deposits back, brought about a short-lived but severe depression through restriction of credit, which ended only when the business community itself rebelled. No sooner did this artificial depression end than an inflationary movement began. The federal deposits that Jackson had taken from Biddle were made available to several dozen state banks; these promptly used their new resources to start a credit boom, which broke disastrously in 1837. This had been no part of Jackson's original intention, nor that of his hard-money followers. "I did not join in putting down the Bank of the United States," complained Thomas Hart Benton, "to put up a wilderness of local banks." By destroying Biddle's Bank Jackson had taken away the only effective restraint on the wildcatters, and by distributing the

13. This was the position not only of the regular Jacksonians but also of the more "radical" Locofoco school. For example, William Leggett, who was considered to be a hound of anarchy by New York conservatives, believed implicitly in free trade and was extremely solicitous of the rights of property when divorced from special privilege. He looked upon a general law of incorporation as "the very measure to enable poor men to compete with rich." "My creed," said Isaac Smith, a prominent Locofoco candidate, "is to leave commercial men to manage their own affairs." And Martin Van Buren: "I have ever advocated . . . limiting the interference of the Government in the business concerns of the People to cases of actual necessity, and [have been] an enemy to monopoly in any form." "The people, the democracy," asserted Ely Moore, the New York labor leader, "contend for no measure that does not hold out to individual enterprise proper motives for exertion." William Gouge, the most popular economic writer of the period, declared that his hard-money policy would mold a society in which "the operation of the natural and just causes of wealth and poverty will no longer be inverted, but . . . each cause will operate in its natural and just order, and produce its natural and just effect—wealth becoming the reward of industry, frugality, skill, prudence, and enterprise, and poverty the punishment of few except the indolent and prodigal."

deposits had enlarged the capital in the hands of inflationists. He was opposed to both privilege and inflation, but in warring on one he had succeeded only in releasing the other. In killing the Bank he had strangled a potential threat to democratic government, but at an unnecessarily high cost. He had caused Biddle to create one depression and the pet banks to aggravate a second, and he had left the nation committed to a currency and credit system even more inadequate than the one he had inherited.

Biddle, from 1823, when he took control of the Bank, to 1833, when removal of the deposits provoked him to outrageous retaliation, had followed a policy of gradual, controlled credit expansion, which was well adapted to the needs of the growing American economy. Had Jackson not yielded to archaic hard-money theories on one hand and the pressure of interested inflationary groups on the other,[14] it might have been possible—and it would have been far wiser—for him to have made a deal with Biddle, trading recharter of the Bank for more adequate government control of the Bank's affairs. it would have been possible to safeguard democratic institutions without such financial havoc but the Jacksonians were caught between their hostility to the Bank and their unwillingness to supplant it with adequate federal control of credit. The popular hatred of privilege and the dominant *laissez-faire* ideology made an unhappy combination.

The Bank war flared up, died, and was forgotten, its permanent results negative rather than positive. But the struggle against corporate privileges which it symbolized was waged on a much wider front. In the states this struggle bore fruit in a series of general incorporation acts, beginning with Connecticut's in 1837, and spreading to the other states in the two decades before the

14. There was a division of purpose among those who supported the Bank war. The hard-money theorists wanted to reduce all banks to the functions of discount and deposit and deny them the right to issue currency notes; they believed that overissue of bank notes was an essential cause of booms and depressions. The inflationary groups, including many state banks, objected to the Bank of the United States because it restrained note issues. Caught between these two forces, Jackson pursued an inconsistent policy. Deposit of federal funds with state banks pleased the inflationists. The Specie Circular and the Independent Treasury policy adopted under Jackson's successor, Van Buren, was more consonant with the views of the hard-money faction.

Civil War. By opening the process of incorporation to all comers who could meet state requirements, legislators progressively sundered the concept of the corporate form of business from its association with monopoly privilege and for many decades made it an element in the growth of free enterprise—a contribution to the development of American business that can hardly be overestimated. The same was done for banking. In 1838 New York, the center of the Locofoco agitation against bank monopolies, passed a free banking law that permitted banking associations to operate under general rules without applying for specific acts of incorporation. A precedent for similar laws in other states, it has been described by one authority, Bray Hammond, as "the most important event in American banking history."

While the state legislatures were writing Jacksonian ideals into the law of corporations, a Jacksonian Supreme Court under Chief Justice Taney was reading them into the clauses of the Constitution. Taney, appointed by Jackson in 1836, sat on the Court until his death in 1864, and during his long tenure the Court propagated the Jacksonian view of business without privilege. Professor Benjamin F. Wright, in his study of *The Contract Clause of the Constitution,* has pointed out that as a result of the Court's work under Taney the contract clause "was a more secure and broader base for the defense of property rights in 1864 than it had been in 1835." Taney's most startling case, as symbolic of the fight against privilege in the juridical sphere as the Bank war had been in politics, was the Charles River Bridge case. The majority decision, prepared by Taney, which represented a long forward step in detaching from the corporation the stigma of monopoly, stands as a classic statement of the Jacksonian faith.

The Charles River Bridge had been erected in the 1780's by Harvard College and prominent Bostonians under a Massachusetts charter. As the population of Boston and Cambridge grew, business flourished, traffic mounted, and the par value of the bridge's stock shot upward. A share bought in 1805 at $444 was worth $2,080 in 1814. Since a new bridge was badly needed, the state legislature in 1828 chartered another, the Warren Bridge, to be built very close to the original, and to be free after sufficient tolls were collected to pay for its construction. Anxious to prevent a development that would destroy the value of their stock, the proprietors of the older bridge attempted to restrain the new builders from erecting the Warren Bridge. When Taney began sitting as Chief Justice in 1837, the issue was still pending before the Supreme Court. The case clearly involved a conflict between vested rights on one side and new entrepreneurs and the rest of the community on the other. Four distinguished Massachusetts lawyers, including Daniel Webster, represented the promoters of the Charles River Bridge. They argued that the legislative grant to the original bridge company was a contract, and that implicit in such a ferry or bridge franchise was a promise on the part of the state not to break the contract by granting another competing franchise that would lower the value of the original.

The Court decided for the new bridge, five to two. Since the two dissenting Justices, Story and Thompson, were holdovers from the pre-Jackson period and the five majority Judges were all Jackson appointees, the decision may accurately be called a Jacksonian document. Story's dissent, which expressed horror at "speculative niceties or novelties" and invoked the interests of "every stockholder in every public enterprise of this sort throughout the country," was reasoned in the language of entrenched capital, of monopoly investors who abhorred risk. Taney's majority decision was a plea for the public interest, for technological progress and fresh enterprise.[15]

The object of all government, Taney asserted, is to promote the happiness and prosperity of the community, and it could never be assumed that a government intended to curtail its own powers in this respect. "And in a country like ours, free, active, and enterprising, continually advancing in numbers and wealth," new channels of communication and travel are continually found necessary; an abandonment of the state's power to facilitate new developments should not be construed from contracts that do not contain an explicit statement of such intent.

What would happen, Taney asked, if the idea of an implied monopoly in charters should be sustained by the Court? What

15. Taney's moderate and balanced view of state policy toward corporations is most clearly brought out by his deft decision in Bank of Augusta *v.* Earle (1839). For this and his continuing friendliness to the nonmonopoly corporation, see Carl Brent Swisher's *Roger B. Taney* (New York, 1935), Chap. 18.

would become of the numerous railroads established on the same line of travel with old turnpike companies? He thought he knew: if these old corporations were given an "undefined property in a line of travelling," they would awaken from their sleep and call upon the Court to put down new improvements to protect their vested interests. The "millions of property" that had been invested in railroads and canals upon lines of travel once occupied by turnpike corporations would be endangered. Until obsolete claims were settled, the community would be deprived of the benefits of invention enjoyed by every other part of the civilized world. The rights of property, Taney conceded, should be "sacredly guarded," but "we must not forget that the community also have rights, and that the happiness and well being of every citizen depends upon their faithful preservation."

To the Whig press and conservative lawyers like Kent and Story this opinion appeared as another "manifesto of anarchy," comparable to Jackson's Bank veto message. In fact, as Charles Warren observes in his history of the Court, it gave encouragement to "all businessmen who contemplated investments of capital in new corporate enterprise and who were relieved against claims of monopoly concealed in ambiguous clauses of old charters."

In the Congressional session of 1823–1824, at the beginning of the Jackson era, Daniel Webster had observed: "Society is full of excitement: competition comes in place of monopoly; and intelligence and industry ask only for fair play and an open field." No friend of Jacksonian democracy expressed more accurately than this opponent the historic significance of the Jackson movement. With Old Hickory's election a fluid economic and social system broke the bonds of a fixed and stratified political order. Originally a fight against political privilege, the Jacksonian movement had broadened into a fight against economic privilege, rallying to its support a host of "rural capitalists and village entrepreneurs." When Jackson left office he was the hero of the lower and middling elements of American society, who believed in expanding opportunity through equal rights, and by the time of his death in 1845 the "excitement" Webster had noticed had left a deep and lasting mark upon the nation. "This," exulted Calvin Colton, "is a country of self-made men, than which there can be no better in any state of society."

MARVIN MEYERS

✪

The Jacksonian Persuasion[1]

An artful editor of the works of eminent Jacksonians might
arrange one volume to portray the revolt of the urban masses
against a business aristocracy; a second in which simple farming
folk rise against the chicanery of capitalist slickers; a third volume
tense with the struggle of the fresh forest democracy for liberation
from an effete East; and still another book of men on the make
invading the entrenched positions of chartered monopoly. With no
undue demand upon editorial resourcefulness, the Jacksonian
series might turn next to the party machine, managing a newly
made mass electorate through the exploitation of some of the
preceding themes. The terminal volume might well rest in the
shadow of Jefferson: the patriotic friends of wise and frugal
government, equal rights and equal laws, strict construction and
dispersed power, resisting the eternally scheming tory, monocrat,
and rag-baron.[2]

1. In this article I mean to suggest a rather free and wide-ranging
commentary resting immediately upon a limited selection of documents.
Precise references and quotations are designed to be illustrative or suggestive, not conclusive evidence for my interpretations of Jacksonian democracy. Some of the necessary elaborations, refinements, and documentary
supports will I hope be found in my larger study of the Jacksonian ethos,
now in progress, from which these notes have been drawn.
2. The historical interpretations of Jacksonian democracy are not, of
course, so flat and monolithic as I make them out here. I have abstracted
what seem to me central thesis-lines and deployed them for my own purposes. The variety of interpretations may be represented by such works as

From *American Quarterly,* Vol. V (Spring 1953), pp. 3–15. Copyright,
1953, Trustees of the University of Pennsylvania.

This partial list of possible uses of Jacksonian thought does not quite suggest that Jacksonian democracy may mean all things to all men. Some omissions have been made with a point: for example, it is not suggested that any plausible editorial selection could identify Jacksonian democracy with the rise of abolitionism; or (in an exclusive sense) with the temperance movement, school reform, religious enthusiasm, or theological liberalism; or (in any sense) with Utopian community building. Yet the variety of meanings which can command some documentary support is too wide for easy assimilation in a coherent interpretation of Jacksonian democracy. Here there is, I think, a fair field for the critical examination of the major contending theses and, of greater importance, for a fresh reading of the most obvious Jacksonian sources.

The present approach takes its departure from the debunking theses of recent writers like Dorfman and Abernethy, who in their separate ways have corrected a number of major and minor errors by an exemplary regard for original sources viewed carefully in historical context. Yet their very suspicions of such things as campaign appeals and public messages lead them to discount as meaningless a large part of the sustenance of the Jacksonian public, in order to pursue the "real thing"—i.e., the objective import of legal and institutional changes. If, for example, in Dorfman's terms, the major economic consequences of Jacksonian reform politics in New York were to establish free banking and incorporation laws and constitutional limits upon credit undertakings of the state—then what is the meaning of the highly charged polemical jargon, the vague class appeals, the invocation of grand principles?

Arthur M. Schlesinger, Jr., *The Age of Jackson* (Boston, 1945); Joseph Dorfman, *The Economic Mind in American Civilization,* Vol. II (New York, 1946); Frederick Jackson Turner, *The United States, 1830–1850* (New York, 1935); Alexis de Tocqueville, *Democracy in America,* 2 vols. (New York, 1948. Bradley edition); M. Ostrogorski, *Democracy and the Party System in the United States* (New York, 1926); Thomas P. Abernethy, *From Frontier to Plantation in Tennessee* (Chapel Hill, 1932); Louis Hartz, *Economic Policy and Democratic Thought* (Cambridge, 1948); and the excellent chapter III in Richard Hofstadter, *The American Political Tradition* (New York, 1948), together with the bibliographical essay in *ibid.*, pp. 353–357.

Why, in short, did the language go so far beyond the practical object?

Simply to say "propaganda" does not tell why a particular lingo makes good propaganda and another kind does not. Nor is there obvious reason for regarding the traffic in "propaganda" as less significant intrinsically than the traffic in harder goods. And so these notes return to a staple of pre- or nonrevisionist historians, the popular political discourse, in an attempt to identify the social values expressed or implied by opinion leaders of the Jacksonian persuasion.

The difficulties in such an enterprise are no doubt abundant and serious: the subject matter is in its nature elusive; the temptation is powerful indeed—as the debunking writers have been quick to note—to select passages from selected spokesmen, with considerable neglect of textual and situational context, in order to find some grand motif establishing the spirit of Jacksonian democracy; and always one faces the relatively easy out of fabricating some systematic theory of Jacksonian Democrats from fragmentary words and acts, with results which tend to be laborious, intellectually arid, and unrevealing of the qualities of the Jacksonian movement.

There is nevertheless a commanding case for examining the sort of values offered to and preferred by the Jacksonian public; the popular political statement would seem a prime example of such communication; and the first spokesman must be Andrew Jackson. His Presidential papers taken in all their dimensions, theory, policy, and rhetoric, and searched for certain constant, elementary moral postures, provide a revealing and somewhat unexpected commentary upon the character of Jacksonian democracy.

THE OLD HERO AND THE RESTORATION

Andrew Jackson, most students agree, rose to national leadership on the strength of reputed personal qualities: the blunt, tough, courageous "Old Hero" of New Orleans—honest and plain "Old Hickory." "Old" refers to age, of course, but perhaps more to "old-style." Again, not so much to old-style ideas as to the old *ways* of our fathers. He could be—and was in a boy's capacity—a fit

companion for the Revolutionary heroes. Jackson never figured as
the speculative statesman. In his own estimate and the public's, he
was executor of a republican tradition which required not elabora-
tion or revision but right action, taken from a firm moral stance.

It is no novelty to say that the world revealed in Andrew
Jackson's public statements appears, like the public image of the
man, strikingly personal and dramatic, built upon the great
struggle of people *vs.* aristocracy for mastery of the Republic. In
relation to such issues as the Bank war, the view offers a sharp
pattern: on one side, the great body of citizens, demanding only an
equal chance; on the other, their temptors and adversaries, the
small greedy aristocracy, full of tricks and frauds, absorbing power
and privilege. Yet the grand conflict, as it emerges from Jackson's
public statements, has its ambiguities—*viz.,* the variant interpretations of Jacksonian democracy. Within the gross polemical image
of social drama much remains for further explication and explanation.

On the side of virtue, in Jackson's world, one finds the plain
republican—direct descendant of Jefferson's yeoman hero—along
with Poor Richard and such other, lesser friends. The presence of
the sturdy, independent citizen-toiler has been no secret to historians—yet some interesting possibilities have been missed. In
creating the character and role of the plain republican Jackson has
provided, I think, an important clue for the interpretation of
Jacksonian values.

"Keep clear of Banks and indebtedness," Jackson wrote to his
adopted son after settling the boy's debts, "and you live a freeman,
and die in independence and leave your family so . . . and
remember, my son, . . . that we should always live within our
means, and not on those of others."[3] Read this little paternal
homily against the familiar public statements. Can it be that
Jacksonian democracy appeals not to some workingman's yearning
for a brave new world; not to the possibilities of a fresh creation at
the Western limits of civilization; not to the ambitions of a rising
laissez-faire capitalism—not to any of these so much as to a

---

3. Quoted in J. S. Bassett, *The Life of Andrew Jackson,* II (New York,
1916), 707–708.

restoration of old virtues and a (perhaps imaginary) old republican way of life?

It will be my contention that the Jacksonian appeal evokes the
image of a calm and stable order of republican simplicity, content
with the modest rewards of useful toil; and menacing the rustic
peace, an alien spirit of risk and novelty, greed and extravagance,
rapid motion and complex dealings. In short, we may discover in
the political discourse of Jacksonian democracy a powerful strain
of restorationism, a stiffening of republican backs *against* the busy
tinkerings, the restless projects of innovation and reform—against
qualities so often set down as defining characteristics of Jacksonian America.

Of course this is not to say that the Jacksonians—master
politicos and responsible rulers—designed to whisk away the given
world, nor that their public actions yielded such a result. In
practice they met issues as they came out of the play of current
politics, adapting skillfully to the requirements of local conditions,
special interests, and party rule. If the plain-republican theme is
a substantial component of the Jacksonian persuasion, it need not
dictate the precise policy line or control the objective consequences
of party action in order to qualify as significant. The degree of
coincidence or divergence is another (most important) question
which cannot be approached until one knows what appeared in
that dimension of political life which consists in the effective
communication of value-charged language.

THE REAL PEOPLE

Jackson's contemporary rivals damned him for appealing to class
against class; some modern writers praise him for it. Beyond
question, his public statements address a society divided into
classes invidiously distinguished and profoundly antagonistic. But
to understand the meaning of such cleavage and clash, one must
see them within a controlling context. There is for Jackson a whole
body, the sovereign people, beset with aristocratic sores.

The relentless and apparently irresistible use of "the people" in
Jacksonian rhetoric is reflected in the diary of a wealthy New York
City Whig, Philip Hone, who daily grinds the phrase through his

teeth; or, with accumulated effect, in the growling humor of a Whig delegate to the New York Constitutional Convention of 1846—"The love of the people, the dear people was all that the gentlemen said influenced them. How very considerate. The love of the people—the dear people—was generally on men's tongues when they wanted to gain some particular end of their own. . . ."[4]

In the opposition view Jackson—and Jacksonians generally— were the worst sort of demagogues who could appropriate with galling effectiveness both the dignity of the sovereign people and the passion of embattled classes. That is just the point for Jackson: nasty imputations about demagoguery aside, there are the whole people and the alien aristocracy, and the political advantages which result from the use of this distinction further confirm its validity. Jackson's notion of the-class-of-the-people is grounded first in the political order, more precisely in the republican order. From this fixed base, and with this fixed idea of the double character of the people, Jackson's representation of the group composition of society may be analyzed first in the standard terms of Jacksonian scholarship, and then, by what seems to me a necessary extension, in the context of the restoration theme.

In the most inclusive and high-toned usage, the people would comprise "all classes of the community" and "all portions of the Union." From their midst arises a general "will of the American people" which is something considerably more than a fluctuating majority vote (though the vote for Jackson is acknowledged as a fair index). There are interests of a class and sectional character, legitimate and often illegitimate; but also a pervasive common interest (which corresponds neatly with the main items of the Democratic platform). The general will is originally pure— ("Never for a moment believe that the great body of the citizens of any State or States can deliberately intend to do wrong . . ."); liable to temporary error through weakness—(corruptionists will sometimes succeed in "sinister appeals to selfish feelings" and to "personal ambition"); and in the end, straight and true—("but in a community so enlightened and patriotic as the people of the

4. Allan Nevins, ed., *The Diary of Philip Hone, 1828–1851,* 2 vols. (New York: Dodd, Mead, 1927), *passim. Report of the Debates . . . of the Convention for the Revision of the Constitution of the State of New-York. 1846* (Albany, 1846), p. 179.

United States argument will soon make them sensible of their errors").[5]

A brief, sharp exemplification of this view occurs in Jackson's argument for direct election of the President. The extent of American territory—Madison's chief reliance for controlling the threat of majority faction—suggests to Jackson the dangerous prospect of sectional parties, which in turn will present sectional candidates and, in the zeal for party and selfish objects, "generate influences unmindful of the general good." Evil comes from the official apparatus, the mechanical contrivances of the complex electoral system. However, "the great body of the people" armed with a direct Presidential vote which can express the general "will" must always defeat "antirepublican" tendencies and secure the common good.[6]

These "antirepublican" forces are identified as the "intriguers and politicians" and their tools, who thrive on political consolidation, chartered privilege, and speculative gain. Jackson sums up in relation to the Bank war:

The bank is, in fact, but one of the fruits of a system at war with the genius of all our institutions—a system founded upon a political creed the fundamental principle of which is a distrust of the popular will as a safe regulator of political power, and whose ultimate object and inevitable result, should it prevail, is the consolidation of all power in our system in one central government. Lavish public disbursements and corporations with exclusive privileges would be its substitutes for the original and as yet sound checks and balances of the Constitution —the means by whose silent and secret operation a control would be exercised by the few over the political conduct of the many by first acquiring that control over the labor and earnings of the great body of the people. Wherever this spirit has effected an alliance with political power, tyranny and despotism have been the fruit.[7]

In these rough outlines there is enough to reconstruct what there is of a Jacksonian theory concerning the people and the classes. I

---

5. James D. Richardson, comp., *Messages and Papers of the Presidents, 1789–1897* (Washington, D.C., 1896), III, 5, 296, 118–119, 296.

6. *Ibid.*, pp. 147–148, 176–177.

7. *Ibid.*, p. 165.

doubt that the job is worth doing in any elaborate way. The Jacksonian persuasion is both more and much less than a theoretic structure; and Jackson's "people" are not reducible to a lump-quantity in a formal democratic scheme. What is missing is a sense of the nurture, character, and worth of the people as they are represented in Jackson's public papers. In Jackson's revealing phrase, there are still *"the real people"* to be considered.

When Jackson speaks of the people—the real people—he regularly specifies: planters and farmers, mechanics and laborers, "the bone and sinew of the country." Thus a composite class of industrious folk is marked off within society. It appears to be a narrower group than "the sovereign people" of democratic doctrine—though it would surely encompass the mass of enumerated inhabitants of the Jacksonian era. Historians who identify the favored Jacksonian class simply as the common man tell too little. Others, who make the separation upon wage-earner lines, or by rich/poor, town/country, East/West, or North/South, accept what seem to me variable secondary traits. Jackson's real people are essentially those four specified occupational groups, whose "success depends upon their own industry and economy," who know "that they must not expect to become suddenly rich by the fruits of their toil." The lines are fixed by the moral aspects of occupation.[8]

Morals, habits, character are key terms in Jackson's discussion of the people—and almost every other subject. Major policies, for instance, are warranted by their capacity to "preserve the morals of the people," or "to revive and perpetuate those habits of economy and simplicity which are so congenial to the character of republicans." And so with the differentiation of classes according to worth: the American "laboring classes" are "so proudly distinguished" from their foreign counterparts by their "independent spirit, their love of liberty, their intelligence, and their high tone of moral character." At a still higher level within the bloc of favored classes, those who work the land—"the first and most important occupation of man"—contribute to society "that enduring wealth which is composed of flocks and herds and

8. *Ibid.*, p. 305.

cultivated farms" and themselves constitute "a hardy race of free citizens."[9]

The positive definition of the real people significantly excludes pursuits which are primarily promotional, financial, or commercial. This does not mean that Jackson raises a class war against mere occupational categories. (He was himself lawyer, office-holder, land-speculator, and merchant at various times.) The point seems to be that virtue naturally attaches to, and in fact takes much of its definition from, callings which involve some immediate engagement in the production of goods. Vice enters most readily through the excluded pursuits, though it may infect all classes and "withdraw their attention from the sober pursuits of honest industry." As indicated before, vice is to be understood largely in terms of certain occupational ways, the morals, habits, and character imputed to the trades which seek wealth without labor, employing the stratagems of speculative maneuver, privilege-grabbing, and monetary manipulation.[10]

Like the Jeffersonians, Jackson regularly identifies the class enemy as the money power, the moneyed aristocracy, etc. There is in this undoubtedly some direct appeal against the rich. The mere words call up the income line as an immediate source of invidious distinction. Yet I would maintain that this is a secondary usage. First, Jackson's bone-and-sinew occupational classes clearly allow for a considerable income range—it would be fair to say that upper-upper and lower-lower could enter only exceptionally, while there would be a heavy concentration at the middling-independent point. Income as such does not become a ground for class preference in the usual terms of differential economic or power interest. Instead, Jackson links income with good and evil ways. The real people cannot expect sudden riches from their honest, useful work. And surplus wealth would in any case prove a temptation to the antirepublican habits of idleness and extravagance, as well as an engine of corruption. Briefly, a stable income of middling proportions is generally associated with the occupations, and with the habits, morals, and character of the real people.[11]

9. *Ibid.*, pp. 19, 67–69, 166, 162.
10. *Ibid.*, p. 302.
11. *Ibid.*, p. 305.

More important, however, is the meaning given to phrases like "money power"—and note that Jackson typically uses this expression and not "the rich." The term occurs invariably in discussions of corporations and, particularly, of banking corporations; it signifies the *paper* money power, the *corporate* money power—i.e., concentrations of wealth arising suddenly from financial manipulation and special privilege, ill-gotten gains. If the suggestion persists in Jackson's public statements that such is the common road to wealth—and certainly the only quick way—then it is still the mode and tempo of acquisition and not the fact of possession which is made to damn the rich before Jackson's public.

Further, the money power—as I have defined it—is damned precisely as a *power,* a user of ill-gotten gains to corrupt and dominate the plain republican order. Any concentration of wealth may be a potential source of evil; but the real danger arises when the concentration falls into hands which require grants of special privilege for economic success. So a wealthy planter (and Jackson was this, too) should need no editorial or legislative hired hands; a wealthy banker cannot do without them.

Thus Jackson's representation of the real people in the plain republican order supplies at least tentative ground for an interpretation of Jacksonian democracy as, in vital respects, an appeal to an idealized ancestral way. Beneath the gross polemical image of people *vs.* aristocracy, though not at all in conflict with it, one finds the steady note of praise for simplicity and stability, self-reliance and independence, economy and useful toil, honesty and plain dealing. These ways are in themselves good, and take on the highest value when they breed a hardy race of free citizens, the plain republicans of America.[12]

12. The familiar identification of Jacksonian democracy and its favored folk with the West has its points, but not when it blends into the image of the Wild West. Jackson shows little sympathy for the rural adventurer, the marginal mover and jumper. Nor does the moral restoration projected in his public papers bear any resemblance to American primitivism in the Davey Crockett mode. Neither the forest shadows, nor the half-man, half-alligator tone, nor a wild-woods democracy lies at the heart of the Jacksonian persuasion. Rather, it sees a countryside of flocks and herds and cultivated farms, worked in seasonal rhythm and linked in republican community.

HARD COIN AND THE WEB OF CREDIT

As a national political phenomenon, Jacksonian democracy drew heavily upon the Bank war for its strength and its distinctive character. The basic position Andrew Jackson established for the Democratic party in relation to money and banking continued to operate as a source of political strength through the eighteen-forties. So powerful, in fact, was the Jacksonian appeal that large sections of the rival Whig party finally capitulated on this issue explicitly for the purpose of saving the party's life. First, shrewd Whig party managers like Weed of New York, and later the generality of Whig spokesmen were forced to plead in effect: a correct (Old Whig) position on banking is incompatible with political survival in America.

The standard outlines of Jackson's case against banking and currency abuses have already been sketched above. Within the matrix of his Bank war, the crucial class split is discovered and the general principles of Jacksonian democracy take shape. However, the Bank war—viewed as a struggle for possession of men's minds and loyalties—does not simply offer a self-evident display of its own meaning. Out of the polemical language there emerges a basic moral posture much like the one which fixes Jackson's representation of the republican order.

Jackson's appeal for economic reform projects, at bottom, a dismantling operation: to pull down the menacing constructions of federal and corporate power, and restore the wholesome rule of "public opinion and the interests of trade." This has the sound of *laissez faire,* it is *laissez faire* with a difference suggested by the previous discussion of the real people and their natural, legitimate economic interests. Poor Richard and economic man may be given a common enemy with the plain republican; surmounting serious difficulties, the forest democrat, poor man, and workingman might be recruited for the same cause. Indeed the sweeping effect of Jackson's negative case may be explained in part by his touching off a common hatred of an all-purpose villain. Yet if the dismantling operation gives promise of catching several particular enemies in the broad aristocracy trap, does it not promise still more winningly a *dismantling,* and a restoration of pure and simple ways?

Tocqueville, though he reaches an opposite conclusion, suggests very effectively this unmaking spirit:

The bank is a great establishment, which has an independent existence; and the people, accustomed to make and unmake whatsoever they please, are startled to meet with this obstacle to their authority. In the midst of the perpetual fluctuation of society, the community is irritated by so permanent an institution and is led to attack it, in order to see whether it can be shaken, like everything else.[13]

But what is it about the great establishment which provokes hostility and a passion for dismantling? How can the permanence of the Bank, set over against the perpetual fluctuation of society, explain the ceaseless Jacksonian complaint against the tendency of the Bank to introduce perpetual fluctuation in the economic affairs of society? There is, I think, another and better explanation of the symbolic import of the Bank war.

The Bank of the United States, veritable incarnation of evil in Jackson's argument, assumes the shape of "the monster," which is to say, the unnatural creature of greed for wealth and power. Its managers, supporters, and beneficiaries form the first rank of the aristocracy, i.e., the artificial product of legislative prestidigitation. The monster thrives in a medium of paper money, the mere specter of palpable value. The bank system suspends the real world of solid goods, honestly exchanged, upon a mysterious, swaying web of speculative credit. The natural distributive mechanism, which proportions rewards to "industry, economy, and virtue," is fixed to pay off the insider and the gambler.

To knock down this institution, then, and with it a false, rotten, insubstantial world, becomes the compelling object of Jackson's case. He removed the public deposits, so he said, "to preserve the morals of the people, the freedom of the press, and the purity of the elective franchise." Final victory over the Bank and its paper spawn "will form an era in the history of our country which will be dwelt upon with delight by every true friend of its liberty and independence," not least because the dismantling operation will

13. Tocqueville, *Democracy in America,* I, 178–179.

"do more to revive and perpetuate those habits of economy and simplicity which are so congenial to the character of republicans than all the legislation which has yet been attempted."[14]

The Jacksonian appeal for a dismantling operation and the restoration of old republican ways flows easily into the course of the hard-coin argument. Hard coin, I have already suggested, stands for palpable value as against the spectral issue of the printing press. In plainer terms, Jackson argues before the Congress: "The great desideratum in modern times is an efficient check upon the power of banks, preventing that excessive issue of paper whence arise those fluctuations in the standard of value which render uncertain the rewards of labor." Addressing a later Congress, Jackson pursues the point: Bank paper lacks the stability provided by hard coin; thus circulation varies with the tide of bank issue; thus the value of property and the whole price level are at the mercy of these banking institutions; thus the laboring classes especially, and the real people generally, are victimized, while the few conniving speculators add to their riches.[15]

A related appeal to the attractions of stability, of sure rewards and steady values and hard coins, can be found in Jackson's warnings against the accumulation and distribution of the revenue surplus: an overflowing federal Treasury, spilling into the states, would produce ruinous expansions and contractions of credit, arbitrary fluctuations in the price of property, "rash speculation, idleness, extravagance, and a deterioration of morals." But above all it is the banks and their paper system which "engender a spirit of speculation injurious to the habits and character of the people," which turn even good men from "the sober pursuits of honest industry." To restore hard coin is to restore the ways of the plain republican order. Dismantling of the unnatural and unjust bank and paper system is the necessary first step.

THE SUM OF GOOD GOVERNMENT

The one essential credential of public or private worth—whether of individual, or class, or trade—is conveyed by Jackson through

14. *Messages and Papers,* III, 19, 166.
15. *Ibid.,* pp. 164, 247–248.

the term "republican"; that which is antirepublican is the heart of evil. With all valuations referred to the republican standard, and that standard apparently a category of politics, one might expect some final revelation of the Jacksonian persuasion in Jackson's representation of the good state. The truth is, on my reading, somewhat different: Jackson rather defines republican by ways of living and working, than refers those ways to republicanism in the strict political sense. The good Republic he projects—and remembers from the Revolutionary days of '76 and 1800—is on the political side the ornament, the glory, and the final security of the worthy community, not its creator.

Jackson's sketch of a political system congenial to old republican ways uses nothing beyond the memorable summation in Jefferson's First Inaugural Address: "a wise and frugal government, which shall restrain men from injuring one another, shall leave them otherwise free to regulate their own pursuits of industry and improvement, and shall not take from the mouth of labor the bread it has earned. This is the sum of good government, and this is necessary to close the circle of our felicities." The literal Jacksonian translation prescribes: the Constitution strictly construed; strict observance of the "fundamental and sacred" rules of simplicity and economy; separation of the political power from the conduct of economic affairs.[16]

His political appeal both parallels and supports the general themes discussed in previous sections. This is no government of projects and ambitions. It does its simple, largely negative business in a simple, self-denying way. Firm and strong, it trims drastically the apparatus of power. The hardy race of independent republicans, engaged in plain and useful toil, require no more than a stable government of equal laws to secure them in their equal rights. In Jacksonian discourse, government becomes a fighting issue only when it grows too fat and meddlesome. Again, the Republic is defined and judged positively by its republicans and only negatively by its government.

The Bank war once more provides the crucial case. Jackson mobilized the powers of government for what was essentially a

16. *Ibid.,* pp. 18, 108, 161–162.

dismantling operation. His cure avoids with terror any transference of the powers of the Bank to another agency: to give to the President the currency controls and the power over individuals now held by the Bank "would be as objectionable and as dangerous as to leave it as it is." Control of banks and currency—apart from the strictly constitutional functions of coinage and regulation of value—should be "entirely separated from the political power of the country." Any device is wicked and dangerous which would "concentrate the whole moneyed power of the Republic in any form whatsoever." We must, above all, ignore petty, expediential considerations, and "look to the honor and preservation of the republican system."[17]

PARADOX

And so the circuit of Jackson's public appeal may be closed. Plain, honest man; simple, stable economy; wise and frugal government. It reads less as the herald of modern times and a grand project of reform than as a reaction against the spirit and body of the changing world. Jacksonian democracy, viewed through Jackson's public statements, wants to undo far more than it wishes to do; and not for the purpose of a fresh creation, but for the restoration of an old republican idyll. The tremendous popularity of Andrew Jackson and his undoubted public influence suggest that this theme can be ignored only at great peril in any general interpretation of Jacksonian democracy. We must prepare for a paradox: the movement which in many ways cleared the path for the triumph of *laissez-faire* capitalism and its culture in America, and the public which in its daily life acted out that victory, held nevertheless in their conscience an image of a chaste republican order, resisting the seductions of risk and novelty, greed and extravagance, rapid motion and complex dealings.

17. *Ibid.*, pp. 7, 18, 111.

✪

Andrew Jackson, Symbol for an Age

NATURE

Foreign commentators, speaking within the context of a type of European romanticism, called Jackson "one of nature's noblemen."[1] Usually in this sense, nature was used abstractly. As a normative idea, it was negative, meant to deny certain vices of European civilization rather than to affirm nature in the concrete. In the United States, however, nature was not simply an abstraction. The categories for a philosophy of nature were to a large extent imported from Europe; the substance was indigenous.[2]

A rudely fashioned notebook still exists in which the historian George Bancroft, in his crabbed and nearly unreadable hand, made random notes on the life of Andrew Jackson. There is a rough chronology to these notes, which are generally the staccato fragments of half-formulated thoughts. On one page, however, the hesitant character of the writing disappears for one brief phrase. In bold, large letters, across half a page Bancroft wrote, "from 17[?]8 to 1812 He grew as the forest trees grow."[3]

1. Francis J. Grund, *Aristocracy in America,* 2 vols. (London, 1839), II, 306.
2. Jacksonian philosophy is here exhibiting a trait that characterizes much of American thought: reacting to native stresses and strains, the American thinker reaches out to the older and denser culture of Europe for suitable concepts, but in transmission the ideas of Europe become altered to fit American needs and American conditions.
3. George Bancroft, Manuscript Notebook, Jackson Papers (New York Public Library), p. [13]. Thomas Hart Benton, after reading Parton's *Life*

Abridged from *Andrew Jackson: Symbol for an Age* (*1815–1845*) by John William Ward. Copyright 1955 by John William Ward. Reprinted by permission of Oxford University Press, Inc.

Both the image and the dates of Bancroft's phrase are significant. The year 1812 marks the emergence of Andrew Jackson on the national scene. Bancroft is suggesting that Jackson's early preparation for the successful role he was to fill on the national stage was analogous to the natural growth of the forest. Another Jacksonian had suggested the same thought when he said of Jackson, "he grew up in the wilds of the West, but he was the noblest tree in the forest."[4] Senator Hugh Lawson White, while still an ardent Jacksonian, drew the lesson more clearly. In accounting for the comprehensiveness of Jackson's mind, White derived it from the fact that Jackson had been "educated in Nature's school."[5]

These appraisals of Jackson suggest more than the eighteenth-century belief that all men are endowed with certain natural powers. They imply a dynamic relation between physical nature and human character. Such an attitude possesses enormous implications. Because of the geographical situation of the United States it lends itself to national pride and the rejection of Europe, not simply because Europe is not-America (although this gives the idea its emotional appeal), but because Europe is not-nature. It also lends itself to a preference for the natural over the artificial, the intuitive over the logical, with all the ramifications inherent in such a point of view. But before developing and demonstrating the presence of concepts that derive from a certain attitude toward nature, it will be useful to define with greater precision what was generally meant by "nature." . . .

The problem here is one that was introduced by Nathaniel

---

of Jackson, had suggested that a "democratic" biography needed to be written and suggested that Bancroft was the man for the job. Bancroft's notes may be the rudimentary beginnings of a life of Jackson or, more probably, the preparation for Bancroft's funeral oration on the occasion of Jackson's death. The notebook is homemade and consists of lined paper, stitched along the left-hand edge. There is no interior evidence for a precise attribution.

4. Speech of Francis Boylies, the *Western Sun and General Advertiser,* September 20, 1828.

5. *Richmond Enquirer,* January 18, 1827. For further expressions of the same sentiment, see Nathaniel B. Felton, *Addresses of Messrs. Hill, Thornton, Felton and Harper, January 8, 1828* (Concord, N.H., 1828), pp. 42–43; *Jackson Wreath,* p. 56; *Argus of Western America,* February 6, 1828; *Richmond Enquirer,* January 3, 1828; *Illinois Gazette,* January 15, 1825.

Claiborne's use of the word "cultivated" in describing the special worth of the yeomen who conquered the British at New Orleans. Claiborne's choice of language is singularly useful in getting at the problem. "Cultivated," as a figure of speech applied to the mind or character, is derived from the language of agriculture; in either its literal or its figurative sense, the significance is that something artificial has been introduced into the natural order, that man has interposed in some way to improve the processes of nature.[6] Followed to its logical conclusion, cultivation should be greater to the degree that it departs from nature. This is not, of course, what Claiborne is saying. The British, unlike the Americans, have been recruited from the streets of cities, whereas the Americans are "freeholders," with the implication of being close to the land and nature.[7] It is an *extreme* departure from nature that makes the British "dissipated and corrupt" as opposed to "cultivated."

Implicit in Claiborne's remarks is an attitude toward the development of society. It is that history is the record of progression from "nature" to 'civilization," either extreme of which is undesirable; one might chart this progression in Claiborne's own terms, as the movement from the soil to the city. In Claiborne's view of the War of 1812, Europe, represented by the British troops, has already passed into the extreme phase of civilization which is corruption and degeneracy; whereas America is still on the upward slope of the curve and is in the area which is nourished by *both* nature and civilization. This attitude was so widespread that it informed Charles A. Goodrich's *History of the United States.* Goodrich's *History* was the most widely used textbook in America's secondary schools before the Civil War.[8] In it he wrote: "A marked distinction undoubtedly exists between the inhabitants of

6. The OED attributes the first use of the word to Joseph Glanvill (*Scepsis Scientifica,* p. 81) in 1665. In the literal sense of improving the soil, the OED attributes the word to the period 1620–1655, so it seems that the figurative usage was adopted almost as soon as the word appeared. However, the word "cultive," meaning roughly "to air the ground," dates from 1483, and Hobbes speaks of children's education in *Leviathan* as "a culture of their minds."

7. Chester E. Eisinger, "The Freehold Concept in Eighteenth Century American Letters," *William and Mary Quarterly,* 3d Ser., IV (January 1947), 42–59.

8. Agnew D. Roorbach, *The Development of Social Studies in American Secondary Education Before 1861* (Philadelphia, 1937), pp. 113–114.

the commercial and maritime towns and the villages of the country. The former, in a more considerable degree, as to luxury and vice, resemble the great towns of Europe. Those of the country, who lead an agricultural life, preserve much of the simplicity, with something of the roughness of former days; but they enjoy all that happiness which proceeds from the exercise of the social virtues in their primitive purity."[9]

The attitude of Claiborne and others can be demonstrated further by reference to two addresses by Andrew Jackson to his troops. In the first Jackson is addressing his Tennessee troops after their victory over the Creek Indians at Horseshoe Bend. After recounting the particulars of the victory, Jackson remarks that the Indians too had anticipated victory. But, he goes on to say,

They knew not what brave men could effect. . . . Barbarians they were ignorant of the influence of civilization and government over the human powers. . . . The fiends of Tallapoosa will no longer murder our Women and Children. . . . They have disappeared from the face of the earth. In their places a new generation will arise who will know their duties better. The weapons of warfare will be exchanged for the utensils of husbandry; and the wilderness which now withers in sterility and seems to mourn the disolation [*sic*] which overspreads it, will blossom as the rose, and become the nursery of the arts.[10]

In his affirmation of civilization in this quotation, Jackson, as Claiborne does in his use of the word, "cultivated," seeks an image of man's intervention in the natural order. The second address is the one to the embodied militia before the Battle of New Orleans . . . In that address, Jackson congratulates the "inhabitants of an opulent and commercial town [who] have by a spontaneous effort, shaken off the habits which are created by wealth."

In these two addresses, Jackson is praising his troops. In one, he lauds them as civilized men; in the other, as men able to resist the debilitating effects of civilization. It would seem that Jackson is violating the canons of logic in saying that civilization is both good and bad. If, however, one reads Jackson's addresses in the light of

9. Charles A. Goodrich, *A History of the United States of America* (New York, 1829), p. 399.
10. J. S. Bassett, ed., *The Correspondence of Andrew Jackson,* 6 vols. (Washington, D.C., 1926–1933), I, 494–495.

a rejection of two extremes, the logic is impeccable. A letter Jackson wrote to Governor Blount, of Tennessee, after the first taking of Pensacola leads to the suggestion that the latter is the case. "The good order and conduct of my troops whilst in Pensacola [wrote Jackson], has convinced the Spaniards of our friendship, and our prowess, and has drawn from the citizens an expression, that our Chactaws are more civilized than the British."[11] Compare this sentiment with that of a writer in 1815 giving an imaginative account of the Creek campaign. The British tell the Red-Sticks, the warring Creek Indians, that after victory they can rape the American women, to which an Indian chief replies, "We red people whom you Christians call savages, that know nothing about your Christian God, do not force the women of any nation or people, but when we take prisoners in battle, the laws of female virtue and chastity are sacred to us; and even the beasts in the field and the cattle on a thousand hills teach us better human modesty than this."[12] In these two statements the Indians are affirmed and the British derogated by their opposites; in other words, the Indians are good because they are more civilized than the British, the British are bad because they are more savage than the Indians. The optimum condition then becomes an admixture of the best of each state. Who better symbolizes this midway point than a man who defeated both the Indians and the British? George M. Dallas, Vice-President of the United States, in his eulogy on the death of Jackson, pointed to Jackson's midway position in the cultural spectrum, the extremes of which are the savagery of unqualified nature and the degeneracy of overdeveloped civilization: "The *sagacity* of General Jackson was the admiration of the sophist, and the wonder of the savage; it unravelled the meshes of both, without the slightest seeming effort."[13] . . .

Looking back over the career of Andrew Jackson, one can

11. *National Intelligencer,* December 24, 1814; [Rev. Samuel Williams], *Sketches of the War Between the United States and the British Isles Intended as a Faithful History* (Rutland, Vt., 1815), p. 454.

12. Jesse Denson, *The Chronicles of Andrew: Containing an Accurate and Brief Account of General Jackson's Victories in the South, Over the Creeks. Also His Victory over the British at New Orleans, With a Biographical Sketch of His Life* (Lexington, Ky., 1815), pp. 22–23.

13. George M. Dallas, "Eulogy Delivered at Philadelphia, June 26, 1845," *Monument,* p. 55.

sympathize with his opponents in their fury at the widespread image of Jackson as a farmer. He was, as a modern student of Jackson has observed, what we should now call a member of the *rentier* class.[14] His personal tastes might favor French hand-printed wallpaper for the hallway of the Hermitage and express themselves in orders for fifteen hundred dollars worth of cut glass for his personal use,[15] but when Jackson arrived in Washington his opponents expected to see a savage armed with a tomahawk and with a scalping knife in his teeth. "Many here [in Washington, Jackson wrote to a friend] . . . had expected, I understand, to see a most uncivilized, unchristian man."[16] Unsympathetic observers sneeringly referred to Jackson's pre-inauguration headquarters at Gadsby's hotel as "the Wigwam."[17]

Andrew Jackson's opponents saw his relation to nature as that of the savage; Jackson's name was synonymous with barbarism.[18] Jackson's friends and political managers preferred to stress his relation to nature in more honorific terms. Thus, Jackson referred to himself in his correspondence as "a plain cultivator of the soil" and expressed the desire to remain on "my own farm."[19] A Democratic meeting in Philadelphia in 1823 referred to Jackson as the "American Cincinnatus" retired on his farm, "cultivating with his own hand the soil that he defended from the grasp of a foreign foe."[20] The Cincinnatus theme was echoed throughout the land,

14. Arthur M. Schlesinger, Jr., "The Pattern of Democratic Change in the United States: Andrew Jackson and Franklin D. Roosevelt," *The Democratic Process: Lectures on the American Liberal Tradition* (New London, Conn., 1948), pp. 3–16.

15. *Register of Pennsylvania,* IV (August 1829), 80.

16. Andrew Jackson to General Francis Preston, January 27, 1824, Avery O. Craven, ed., *Huntington Library Bulletin,* No. 3 (February 1933), 124–125.

17. [Margaret Bayard Smith], *The First Forty Years of Washington Society,* Gaillard Hunt, ed. (New York, 1906), p. 283.

18. Mitford M. Mathews, *A Dictionary of Americanisms on Historical Principles* (Chicago, 1951), I, 896, gives an example of just such usage. The following sentence was recorded in *American Speech,* XVIII (1842), 126: "Away with the wild Kentuckian. . . . Take this barbarian from my sight! This Jacksonist—away!"

19. Andrew Jackson to Samuel Swartwout, December 14, 1824, Henry F. DuPuy, ed., "Some Letters of Andrew Jackson," *American Antiquarian Society Proceedings,* N.S., XXXI (1921), 76, 78, and cf. 86.

20. *Columbian Observer,* quoted in *National Intelligencer,* November 14, 1823. The introduction of the Cincinnatus theme here might logically raise

and the Pittsburgh Committee of Correspondence, friendly to Jackson's election, invoking Washington as well as Cincinnatus, beseeched the nation to "call him from the plough to direct the destinies of his country."[21] Amos Kendall, when he had occasion to refer to Jackson's military exploits, liked to call him the farmer-soldier.[22] Supporters toasted Jackson as the "Farmer of Tennessee."[23] John Henry Eaton, writing under the pseudonym of

---

an objection in the mind of the reader. One of the points of this chapter is that the United States rejected Europe by stressing the superiority of nature over civilization, that is America over Europe. The Roman imagery in which the period of this study is saturated seems, however, to imply an obeisance to European tradition rather than an alienation from it. I suggest, however, that Americans were so fond of classical imagery because they imagined themselves to constitute a return to the uncorrupted state of the past, before the fall, so to speak, while contemporary Europe seemed a corruption of the virtues of *its own* past. The significant point, particularly in regard to the image of Cincinnatus, is that the classical world was thought to draw its vigor from its historical position, from being the earliest stage of civilization, that is from its recent (and with Cincinnatus still continuing) contact with nature. Thus, a contemporary periodical, in a panegyric on "The Life of the Husbandman," compared the American farmer to the Romans because "the ancient Romans venerated the plough, and at the earliest purest time of the Republic, the greatest praise which could be given to an illustrious character was a judicious and industrious husbandman." (*The Rough Hewer,* I [March 26, 1840], 43.) Now it might have been logically possible for Americans in their rejection of Europe as degenerate to have become antiquarians and to have exemplified Europe's present fall from grace by reference to the golden past; whatever the logical possibilities, it was psychologically improbable. A dramatist, using the Battle of New Orleans as his theme, stated the matter succinctly when he put in the mouth of General Coffee the words: "Our western wilds preserve the ancient glory." C. E. Grice, *The Battle of New Orleans, or Glory, Love, and Loyalty; An Historical and National Drama in Five Acts* (Georgetown, 1816), pp. 44–45. If nature nourished the classical past, there was no need to seek out the past; it was only necessary to recognize the source of its greatness. Nature was plentifully at hand.

This is a suggestion which I have not had time to explore to my own satisfaction and I offer it tentatively. It does fit the cyclical course of history which lies back of Thomas Cole's famous series of paintings "The Course of Empire," done in this period. It is undeniably present in the words of the playwright quoted above. In any event, the image of Cincinnatus, which introduced this digression, is intimately associated with the power of nature. Cincinnatus comes down to us out of the shadowy past of 458 B.C. as Roman, yes, but plowman first.

21. *Knoxville Register,* February 6, 1824.
22. *Argus of Western America,* July 9, 1828.
23. *Ibid.,* September 17, 1828.

"Wyoming," concluded his series of letters in behalf of Jackson's candidacy in 1824 by saying if he had consulted Jackson's personal happiness he would have preferred "that he should remain upon his farm and at his plough."[24] It was made clear by reference to his neat and prosperous acres that Jackson was a good farmer.[25] When he died a eulogist summed it up: "He wielded the axe, guided the plough, and made, with his own hands, the most of his farming utensils—as nature had made him a farmer and a mechanic, besides making him a statesman and soldier."[26]

Despite the fact that Andrew Jackson was no "farmer," that he did not work his land "with his own hand," and that as the owner of the Hermitage he hardly qualified as a "plain cultivator of the soil," he was so presented to the American people. Friendly portrayals pictured Jackson at his plow and stressed the fact that he worked his farm himself. Adverse comments attempted to push Jackson out beyond the pale of civilization into the chaotic regions of unorganized nature. Both versions embodied a rejection by the American mind of the extreme of nature which was savagery, but the image of Jackson apparently accepted by the majority of the people just as carefully rejected a complete acceptance of the advanced stages of civilization. This ambivalent attitude was possible as long as the United States fronted free land so that its progress in civilization was constantly regenerated by contact with nature. The solution of a periodic return to nature was an uneasy one, however, since it had an obvious temporal limit. What was more important, the ideal of the admixture of nature and civilization was a static one. It could be achieved only in the pioneer stage when the wildness of nature had been subdued but the enervating influence of civilization had not yet been felt. As America moved toward a denser civilization, the conflict in logic implicit in the two ideas made ideological adjustment to a new social stage difficult.

24. [John Henry Eaton], *The Letters of Wyoming, to the People of the United States on the Presidential Election and in favor of Andrew Jackson* (Philadelphia, 1824), p. 103. These letters first appeared individually in the *Columbian Observer*.

25. *New-Hampshire Patriot and State Gazette,* February 12, 1827.

26. Samuel A. Cartwright, "Eulogy Delivered at Natchez, Miss., July 12, 1845," B[enjamin] M. Dusenbery, comp., *Monument to the Memory of General Andrew Jackson: Containing Twenty-five Eulogies and Sermons Delivered on the Occasion of His Death* (Philadelphia, 1848), p. 302.

Jacksonian democratic thought, built upon a philosophy of nature in the concrete, was oriented toward a period in American social development that was slipping away at the very moment of its formulation.

One of the many indexes to the difference between Jeffersonian and Jacksonian democracy is to observe the shift in mental attitude that supported each. The shift may be one of emphasis, as all shifts in intellectual history are, but it is fair to say that where the Jeffersonians rested their case on the power of man's mind, the Jacksonians rested theirs on the prompting of man's heart. However, the Jacksonian rejection of the mind was not as simple as this statement might make it seem. The reason of the university was rejected in behalf of the higher reason of nature. The attitude that underlies Jacksonian democracy can best be expressed in terms made current in America by New England transcendentalism. The conjunction of Jackson and anything connected with New England may at first seem inappropriate, but the Jacksonians not only grappled with the same problem as the transcendentalist (in different terms, perhaps) but arrived at a similar answer.

From Coleridge the transcendentalists derived the categories "Reason" and "Understanding." Understanding is a lower order of the intellect, arrived at through sensory perception and therefore improved by training in the use of the senses; Reason is intuitive, beyond empirical demonstration, and inherent in man's nature.[27] In rejecting tradition, the Jacksonians took the same ground as the transcendentalist: against "Understanding," or methodical thought, they appealed to "Reason," that is, intuition.

When in the election of 1824 the selection of the President devolved upon the House of Representatives, an article in a Western newspaper offered two reasons why Jackson should be the choice. The first reason was the simple one that he had received the most votes. The second was that he was the best qualified.

27. Although not intending the volume as an aid to the incipient transcendentalist movement, James Marsh, by editing Coleridge's *Aids to Reflection* (Burlington, Vt., 1829) made these categories available to Emerson and others. For a more thorough exposition of the distinction between the Reason and the Understanding, see Emerson to Edward Bliss Emerson, May 31, 1834, Ralph L. Rusk, ed., *The Letters of Ralph Waldo Emerson,* 6 vols. (New York, 1939), I, 412–413.

In regard to the second point [wrote the editor] we conceive General Jackson to be the only man among the candidates, to whom it will apply, and for one simple, but all-powerful reason—he alone of the three is gifted with genius—with those great powers of mind that can generalize with as much ease as a common intellect can go through detail. Endowed with the faculties to see the whole and grasp the most remote relations of vast and comprehensive designs, he is the most qualified to govern. We should blush, if we could say with truth, that he would make a good secretary of the Treasury, of the Navy, of State, or of the Post Office. We hope and we believe that he would not; we hope that he is above such works, incompetent he cannot be. But for great designs he is fashioned by nature, and therefore would he advance the general interest and glory of this republic, beyond any other man.[28]

One attribute of "genius," according to this account, is its superiority to detail, the area to which the understanding is restricted. Here again the Jacksonians anticipate the transcendental scheme which opposed Genius to Talent, just as Reason is opposed to Understanding. . . . The Jacksonians of New York City concurred: "Jackson is recommended . . . by his *capacity*. He possesses in an extraordinary degree, that native strength of mind, that practical common sense, that power and discrimination of judgement which, for all useful purposes, are more valuable than all the acquired learning of a sage."[29] . . . To express his "genius," nearly every characterization of Andrew Jackson eventually came to such words as "natural" or "native," "instinctive" or "intuitive."[30] . . . But the Jacksonians did not repudiate

28. *Illinois Gazette,* January 15, 1825.

29. *Address of the Republican General Committee of Young Men of the City and County of New York Friendly to the Election of Gen. Andrew Jackson* (New York, 1828), p. 38.

30. In addition to the above citations, compare the following: "Natural": Henry A. Wise, *Seven Decades of the Union* (Philadelphia, 1872), pp. 102–103; Felton, *Addresses,* pp. 42–43; Pliny Merrick, "Eulogy Delivered at Boston, Mass., July 9, 1845," *Monument,* p. 169; Andrew Stevenson, "Eulogy Delivered at Richmond, Va., June 28, 1845," *Monument,* p. 254.

"Native": *Address of the Republican General Committee of Young Men of the City and County of New York,* p. 15; *New-Hampshire Patriot and State Gazette,* January 14, 1828; Dallas, "Eulogy," p. 53; John Van Buren, "Eulogy Delivered at Albany, June 30, 1845," *Monument,* p. 99.

"Intuitive": George Bancroft, "Eulogy Delivered at Washington, D.C., June 27, 1845," *Monument,* pp. 37, 41, 50; A. F. Morrison, "Eulogy

academic training, personified in the Harvard Professor, simply to embrace ignorance in its stead. Pursuing the distinction between reason and understanding, they took the higher ground that the type of intelligence represented by Adams was the corruption of real intelligence.

That Mr. Adams is possessed of *learning* [wrote the Republican General Committee of New York City] we are willing to admit. We are not ignorant that he has received a college education—that he has been a professor of rhetoric. . . . He may be a philosopher, a lawyer, an elegant scholar, and a poet, too, forsooth (we know he wrote doggerel verses upon Mr. Jefferson,) and yet the nation may be little better off for all these endowments and accomplishments. That he is *learned* we are willing to admit; but his *wisdom* we take leave to question. . . . We confess our attachment to the homely doctrine; thus happily expressed by the great Englis[h] poet:—

> "That not to know of things remote
> "From use, obscure and subtle, but to know
> "That which before us lies in daily life,
> "Is the prime wisdom."

That wisdom we believe Gen. Jackson possesses in an eminent de-degree.[31] . . .

An Ohio paper stressed that Jackson did not secure his knowledge "from Voltaire, and Oriental legends," but it introduced another element by expressing confidence in the old hero because he was "not raised in the lap of luxury and wealth."[32] The corruption of wisdom by learning, of Reason by Understanding, is

---

Delivered at Indianapolis, June 28, 1845," *Monument*, p. 142; Hugh A. Garland, "Eulogy Delivered at Petersburg, Va., July 12, 1845," *Monument*, p. 206; Stevenson, "Eulogy," p. 268; Thomas L. Smith, "Eulogy Delivered at Louisville, Ky., July 3, 1845," *Monument*, p. 273.

"Instinctive": George Bancroft, "General Order [on the occasion of Andrew Jackson's death] Issued by the Acting Secretary of War and Navy," June 16, 1845, Holograph Original in the Jackson Papers (New York Public Library); *Boston Post*, July 1, 1845; Dallas, "Eulogy," p. 53; Garland, "Eulogy," p. 199.

31. *Address of the Republican General Committee of Young Men of the City and County of New York*, p. 41. Adams' poetry dogged his whole campaign. John Henry Eaton asked, "Will it be pretended that the President of this Union should be considered wanting in qualifications, because of his inability . . . in sybil strains to turn trifles into things of seeming consequence?" [Eaton], p. 9.

32. *Ohio State Journal*, November 29, 1827.

here linked to the material advance of society, the movement away
from nature. In national terms the problem could then be phrased
as the simple West versus the effete East; in a wider frame of
reference, as the United States versus Europe. For the American
mind Europe stood for tradition, training, and luxury. The repudiation of formal training was thus inextricably involved with
the repudiation of Europe, and the two attitudes lent each other
mutual support. This is part of the significance of the boast that
Andrew Jackson had not spent his life in foreign courts.[33] To
account for the fall from grace of another Westerner, the Western
press said of Henry Clay that "once he was the open and frank
servant of the people. . . . Since his return from Europe, he has
been a changed man."[34] The reason education and culture, represented by Europe, could be dismissed is that they were conceived
to be at best no more than adornments to the natural intellect.
Thus Levi Woodbury, while asserting that Jackson was a great
statesman, did not wish to claim for him "what he himself was the
last man to tolerate as deserved—any deep researches into the
writings of political economists, or that wide range of historical
reading which *sometimes* instructs, no less than it adorns. . . .
He had been endowed, by nature, with a strong intellect."[35] Even
the suggestion of qualification was repugnant to another eulogist:
"Regular and classical education has been thought by some distinguished men, to be unfavorable to great vigour and originality
of the understanding; and that, like civilization, whilst it made
society more interesting and agreeable, yet, at the same time, it
levelled the distinctions of nature. That whilst it strengthened and
assisted the feeble, it was calculated to deprive the strong of their
triumph, and beat down the hopes of the aspiring. . . . Andrew
Jackson escaped the training and dialectics of the schools."[36]
. . .

Francis Boylies of Massachusetts had made the same point

33. *Address of the Committee Appointed by a Republican Meeting in the
County of Hunterdon, Recommending Gen. Andrew Jackson, of Tennessee,
to the People of New Jersey, as President of the United States* (Trenton,
1824), p. 13.
34. [Frankfort, Ky.] *Argus, Extra,* February 13, 1828.
35. Levi Woodbury, "Eulogy Delivered at Portsmouth, New Hampshire,
July 2, 1845," *Monument,* p. 81 (my emphasis).
36. Stevenson, "Eulogy," p. 253.

when he said that [Jackson] had not the privilege of visiting *the courts of Europe at public expense* and mingling with the kings and great men of the earth and glittering in the beams of royal splendor. He grew up in the wilds of the West, but he was the noblest tree in the forest. He was not dandled into consequence by lying in the cradle of state, but inured from infancy to the storms and tempests of life, his mind was strengthened to fortitude and fashioned to wisdom."[37] The West might not have the artificial brilliance of Europe, but it possessed substance which Europe lacked. . . .

In ascribing Jackson's political wisdom to his Western origin, a eulogist at his death could say that Western statemen "imbibed together the healthy air of the forest and the pure principles of liberty, as they trod the pathless wood. In their own free hearts, they found the latent feelings which carried them straight forward in the path of building up their social institutions."[38] The speaker saw no need to make a connection between the pathless wood and the straightforward path of man's heart; it was taken for granted. With somewhat more flourish Bancroft made the same assumption.

Behold, then, the unlettered man of the West, the nursling of the wilds, the farmer of the Hermitage, little versed in books, unconnected by science with the tradition of the past, raised by the will of the people to the highest pinnacle of honour, to the central post in the civilization of republican freedom, to the station where all the nations of the earth would watch his actions—where his words would vibrate through the civilized world, and his spirit be the moving-star to guide the nations. What policy will he pursue? What wisdom will he bring with him from the forest? What rules of duty will he evolve from the oracles of his own mind?[39]

37. *Western Sun and General Advertiser,* September 20, 1828. This, of course, falls into the category of "hard primitivism," which I discussed before. . . . Compare Bancroft's statement: "And there he stood, like one of the mightiest forest trees of his own West, vigorous and colossal, sending its summit to the skies, and growing on its native soil in wild and inimitable magnificence." ("Eulogy," p. 41.)

38. Benjamin Chew Howard, "Funeral Address," *Daily Union,* July 2, 1845. Compare the similar sentiment of Henry D. Gilpin (*A Speech,* p. 8): "From the forests of the West, so late a wilderness, are returning, even to ourselves the wisest political lessons."

39. Bancroft, "Eulogy," p. 42. Bancroft made the relation between

Bancroft's choice of language here, the use of the word "oracles," suggests the support for what otherwise might seem a gratuitous assumption. The religious connotation of oracles points the way to Bancroft's belief that the prompting of man's heart was the voice of God speaking through man. Likewise, external nature was God's word writ large. The two were accepted as equivalent since God was assumed to be beneficent and not capricious. The forest was not only a surer guide to wisdom because it was pure nature, the word of God without the interlineations of man, but also because it preserved man in the condition of self-reliance since it protected him by geographical distance from the false corruptions of learning. . . .

As the nineteenth century progressed, however, a split between the two ideas was inevitable. As industrialism advanced, man's intuitive wisdom could less and less rely upon the voice of nature. But until the heart and the forest were sundered by the emergence of a new society that was not organized around nature, they worked together to support an ideology that was ostensibly democratic. Yet by repudiating the relevance of the past, the heart and the forest also supported an ideology that was violently activistic. The material development of nineteenth-century America needed a philosophy less than it needed action, but Americans satisfied both needs by developing a philosophy of action. Jackson sanctified this philosophy in his own person. . . .

Just as in Henry Wise's epigram that Jackson made law while Adams quoted it, another orator, taking the ground of the heart against the head, drew from Jackson's first seizure of Pensacola in 1814 the lesson that "statesmen see that the instincts of a heart and will devoted to the public weal, can anticipate the rule of public law."[40]

These sentiments express the desire that the law conform to deeds rather than that deeds conform to the law. It was left for a later age to question whether America could safely disregard the

---

physical nature and human mind even more explicit in treating Jackson's childhood: "On [the] remote frontier, far up on the forest-clad banks of the Catawba . . . his eye first saw the light. There his infancy sported in the ancient forests and *his mind was nursed to freedom by their influence.*" P. 33 (my emphasis).

40. Benjamin F. Butler, "Eulogy Delivered at New York City," *Monument*, p. 63.

law, whether action that was not subordinated to a philosophy that defined its ends might not call down ruin beyond repair after the event. In the more open society of the early nineteenth century the question simply never urged itself upon the people. The Age of Jackson framed a philosophy that allowed it freedom of action and elected a President who provided content for the abstractions of its creed. Andrew Jackson captured the American imagination at the Battle of New Orleans, which rightfully stands for the point in history when America's consciousness turned westward, away from Europe toward the interior. Jackson not only symbolized the negative side of this phenomenon, the rejection of the Old World, but also its positive side, the formation of a philosophy of nature (of which the new world had a virtual monopoly) with the further implication of the intuitive character of wisdom. Andrew Jackson embodied the latter two concepts for the contemporary imagination. He was presented as a child of the forest and the major incidents of his career were explained in terms of his untutored genius.

Implicit in the statements of Bancroft and Howard is the weakness of Jacksonian democratic thought. Although Bancroft and Howard rely upon a primitivistic philosophy of nature to support their belief in democracy, both are addressing themselves to the concept of progress. The end toward which the Western statesmen of Howard's address are working is "building up their social institutions." The very title of Bancroft's article is "On the Progress of Civilization," and in his funeral oration the destiny of Andrew Jackson, "the nursling of the wild," is to have his words "vibrate through the civilized world." As long as the society could rely on nature to provide economic openness and philosophical justification, a democratic ideology based on nature could survive without jarring grossly with the facts of society. But the failure of Jacksonian democratic ideology lay in its rigidity. Just as the farmer was an unstable compromise between the poles of civilization and savagery, nature could not indefinitely provide support for a democratic faith.

Bibliographical Note

The briefest biography and the one that most fully reflects recent scholarship is Robert V. Remini, *Andrew Jackson* (1966). Three older multivolume biographies have different merits. James Parton, *Life of Andrew Jackson,* 3 vols. (1861), draws heavily on the reminiscences of Jackson's associates and affords a detailed, reliable, and often absorbing account of Jackson's experiences as they appeared to an astute contemporary. John Spencer Bassett, *The Life of Andrew Jackson,* 2 vols. (1911), is a superbly judicious account by a professional historian. Marquis James, *The Life of Andrew Jackson,* 2 vols. in 1 (1938), focuses on Jackson's personality and military exploits in a vividly anecdotal style, but is weak on political interpretation.

An intimate inside view of the Jackson administration is afforded by Martin Van Buren's *Autobiography,* John C. Fitzpatrick, ed., American Historical Association, *Annual Report,* Vol. II (1918). Other of Jackson's associates recorded their experiences in Amos Kendall, *Autobiography,* William P. Stickney, ed. (1872), and Thomas Hart Benton, *Thirty Years' View,* 2 vols. (1854).

One of the most illuminating accounts of Jacksonian politics is found in Charles M. Wiltse's partisan but painstakingly researched biography *John C. Calhoun,* 3 vols. (1944–1951). Other biographies that are particularly revealing of Jackson's political role are: William N. Chambers, *Old Bullion Benton* (1956); William

E. Smith, *The Francis Preston Blair Family in Politics* (1933); and Charles Sellers, *James K. Polk,* 2 vols. (1957, 1966).

The starting point for assessing Jackson's historical role is Arthur M. Schlesinger, Jr., *The Age of Jackson* (1945), which portrays Jackson as a great leader of liberal forces in the tradition of Jefferson and Franklin Roosevelt. The counterinterpretations prompted by Schlesinger are trenchantly expressed in the following: the essay on Jackson in Richard Hofstadter's *The American Political Tradition and the Men Who Made It* (1948); Marvin Meyers, *The Jacksonian Persuasion* (1957); Lee Benson, *The Concept of Jacksonian Democracy: New York as a Test Case* (1961); Richard P. McCormick, *The Second American Party System* (1966); and Lynn L. Marshall, "The Strange Stillbirth of the Whig Party," *American Historical Review,* LXXII (January 1967), 445–468. John William Ward's *Andrew Jackson, Symbol for an Age* (1955) argues that the American people expressed their most fundamental values in the symbolic Andrew Jackson they created.

Current scholarship on the central conflict of the Jackson administration is summarized in Robert V. Remini's brief study *Andrew Jackson and the Bank War* (1967). The struggle is treated from the Bank's side in a classic of early professional scholarship, Ralph C. H. Catterall, *The Second Bank of the United States* (1902). In *Banks and Politics in America from the Revolution to the Civil War* (1957), Bray Hammond argues that ambitious entrepreneurs and the state banks furnished the impetus for the Jacksonian assault on the National Bank. The Bank's president is ably defended in Thomas P. Govan's biography *Nicholas Biddle, Nationalist and Public Banker* (1959).

Thomas P. Abernethy portrays the pre-Presidential Jackson as an opportunistic frontier aristocrat in "Andrew Jackson and the Rise of Southwestern Democracy," *American Historical Review,* XXXIII (October 1927), 64–77, and in *From Frontier to Plantation in Tennessee* (1932). An alternative view is offered in two articles by Charles Sellers, "Banking and Politics in Jackson's Tennessee, 1817–1827," *Mississippi Valley Historical Review,* XLI (June 1954), 61–84; and "Jackson Men with Feet of Clay," *American Historical Review,* LXII (April 1957), 537–551.

The Presidential campaign of 1828 is described in Robert V. Remini, the *Election of Andrew Jackson* (1963). Jackson's impact on the administration of the federal government is analyzed in Leonard D. White, *The Jacksonians: A Study in Administrative History, 1829–1861* (1954). Jackson's role in the nullification controversy is best seen in William W. Freehling's *Prelude to Civil War: The Nullification Controversy in South Carolina* (1966). Jackson is severely criticized in a series of articles by Richard R. Stenberg: "Jackson, Buchanan, and the 'Corrupt Bargain' Calumny," *Pennsylvania Magazine of History and Biography,* LVIII (January 1934), 51–85; "Jackson's 'Rhea Letter' Hoax," *Journal of Southern History,* II (November 1936), 480–496; "The Jefferson Birthday Dinner, 1830," *Journal of Southern History,* IV (August 1938), 334–345; and "President Jackson and Anthony Butler," *Southwest Review,* XXII (Summer 1937), 391–404.

Contributors

THOMAS PERKINS ABERNETHY was born in Lowndes County, Alabama, in 1890, graduated from the College of Charleston, and earned a Ph.D. degree at Harvard. After teaching at Vanderbilt, the University of Chattanooga, and the University of Alabama, he moved in 1930 to the University of Virginia, where he held the Richmond Alumni Professorship of History until his retirement in 1961. His many books on the early history of the Old Southwest include *From Frontier to Plantation in Tennessee* (1932), *Western Lands and the American Revolution* (1937), and *The Burr Conspiracy* (1954).

JOHN SPENCER BASSETT (1867–1928) was a member of the first generation of professional historians trained in the seminars of the Johns Hopkins University. He was educated at Trinity College (now Duke University) in his native North Carolina and returned there to teach and to figure in a celebrated defense of academic freedom. He wrote a number of monographs on the early history of North Carolina and contributed the volume on *The Federalist System* (1905) to the American Nation Series. Moving to Smith College, he published his *Life of Andrew Jackson* (1911), wrote a book on *The Middle Group of American Historians* (1917), and before his death finished editing the *Correspondence of Andrew Jackson* (7 vols.; 1925–1935).

GEORGE DANGERFIELD won both the Bancroft and the Pulitzer prizes for his study of *The Era of Good Feelings* (1952). Born in

228

England in 1904 and educated at Oxford, he moved to the United States in 1930 for a career as editor and writer. His other books include *Chancellor Robert R. Livingston of New York* (1960) and *The Awakening of American Nationalism, 1815–1828* (1965). He lives in Santa Barbara, California.

BRAY HAMMOND (1886–1968) grew up in Missouri, received his A.B. degree at Stanford, and taught briefly at Washington State College. Abandoning the academic world for a career in business and banking, he served from 1930 to 1950 with the Federal Reserve Board, becoming its assistant secretary. He retired to Thetford, Vermont, and pursued the studies that brought him a Pulitzer prize for his *Banks and Politics in America from the Revolution to the Civil War* (1957). A sequel that he completed before his death, *Sovereignty and an Empty Purse,* was published in 1970.

RICHARD HOFSTADTER (1916–1970) was born in Buffalo, completed his undergraduate studies at the University of Buffalo, and earned a Ph.D. at Columbia. After teaching briefly at the University of Maryland, he returned to Columbia, where he was DeWitt Clinton Professor of American History. His first book, *Social Darwinism in American Thought* (1944, rev. ed. 1955), won the Beveridge prize of the American Historical Association. A Pulitzer prize was awarded his *Age of Reform* (1955). His *Anti-Intellectualism in American Life* (1963) brought him a second Pulitzer prize, the Emerson prize of Phi Beta Kappa, and the Sidney Hillman Award. In addition to *The American Political System and the Men Who Made It* (1948), he has published books on such diverse subjects as the history of higher education and academic freedom, the origins of the American party system, *The Paranoid Style in American Politics* (1965), and *The Progressive Historians* (1968).

MARVIN MEYERS, born in 1921 in Norfolk, received an A.B. degree at Rutgers and a Ph.D. at Columbia. He has taught at the University of Chicago and is the Harry S. Truman Professor of American Civilization at Brandeis. He has been a Fellow of the American Council of Learned Societies and of the Center for

Advanced Study in the Behavioral Sciences. His interpretation of *The Jacksonian Persuasion* (1957) won him the Dunning prize of the American Historical Association.

ROBERT V. REMINI, a New Yorker, was born in 1921 and earned A.B. and Ph.D. degrees at Fordham and Columbia. He has taught at Fordham, and since 1965 has been a professor at the Chicago campus of the University of Illinois. While at work on an extensive biography of Martin Van Buren he has published books on a number of related topics: *Martin Van Buren and the Making of the Democratic Party* (1959), *The Election of Andrew Jackson* (1963), a brief biography of *Andrew Jackson* (1966), and *Andrew Jackson and the Bank War* (1968).

ARTHUR M. SCHLESINGER, JR., was born in 1917, the son of a distinguished historian, and moved with his family from Columbus to Cambridge, where he graduated from Harvard. After advanced studies as a member of the Harvard Society of Fellows and as Henry Fellow at Cambridge University, he taught at Harvard until 1961, when he became a special assistant to President Kennedy. Since 1966 he has been the Albert Schweitzer Professor of Humanities at the City University of New York. *The Age of Jackson* (1945) won him a Pulitzer prize; volumes of *The Age of Roosevelt* (3 vols.; 1957–1960) won him the Bancroft and Francis Parkman prizes; and volumes of *A Thousand Days* (I, *John F. Kennedy in the White House,* 1965; II, *The Bitter Heritage,* 1967) won him a second Pulitzer prize, the National Book Award, and the Gold Medal of the National Institute of Arts and Letters.

RICHARD R. STENBERG received M.A. and Ph.D. degrees in 1929 and 1932 at the University of Texas and taught for a time at Edinburg College. During the 1930's he made a detailed critical study of Andrew Jackson's career, publishing his findings in a series of nine articles in various journals. The most influential of these are: "Jackson, Buchanan, and the 'Corrupt Bargain' Calumny," *Pennsylvania Magazine of History and Biography* (January 1934); "Jackson's 'Rhea Letter' Hoax," *Journal of Southern History* (November 1936); and "The Jefferson Birthday Dinner,

1830," *Journal of Southern History* (August 1938). Professor Stenberg also published during the 1930's several influential articles on aspects of the Polk administration.

JOHN WILLIAM WARD, a Bostonian, was born in 1922, completed his undergraduate studies at Harvard, and earned the Ph.D. in American Studies at the University of Minnesota. He taught first at Princeton and is now a professor at Amherst. He has been a Guggenheim Fellow and a Fellow at the Center for Advanced Study in the Behavioral Sciences. His *Andrew Jackson, Symbol for an Age* appeared in 1955; he has published modern scholarly editions of Michael Chevalier's *Society, Manners and Politics in the United States* (1962) and Frederick Grimke's *The Nature and Tendency of Free Institutions* (1968); and a series of his essays has been collected under the title *Red, White, and Blue: Men, Books, and Ideas in American Culture* (1969).

CHARLES SELLERS, a North Carolinian born in 1923, received an A.B. degree at Harvard and a Ph.D. at the University of North Carolina. He taught first at the University of Maryland and Princeton, and is now a professor of history at the University of California, Berkeley. He has held fellowships from the Guggenheim Foundation and at the Center for Advanced Study in the Behavioral Sciences, and has been Harmsworth Professor of American History at Oxford. He is the editor and a co-author of *The Southerner as American* (1960), and the second volume of his projected three-volume biography of *James K. Polk* (1957, 1966) won a Bancroft prize from Columbia University.

✪

AÏDA DiPACE DONALD is a graduate of Barnard and received an M.A. from Columbia and a Ph.D. from the University of Rochester. A former member of the History Department at Columbia, Mrs. Donald has been a Fulbright Fellow at Oxford and an A.A.U.W. Fellow. She has published *John F. Kennedy and the New Frontier* and *Diary of Charles Francis Adams*.